Making the News

Making the News

Politics, the Media, and Agenda Setting

AMBER E. BOYDSTUN

THE UNIVERSITY OF CHICAGO PRESS   CHICAGO AND LONDON

Amber Boydstun is assistant professor of political science at the University of California, Davis, and coauthor of *The Decline of the Death Penalty and the Discovery of Innocence.*

The University of Chicago Press, Chicago 60637
The University of Chicago Press, Ltd., London
© 2013 by The University of Chicago
All rights reserved. Published 2013.
Printed in the United States of America
22 21 20 19 18 17 16 15 14 13   1 2 3 4 5

ISBN-13: 978-0-226-06543-4 (cloth)
ISBN-13: 978-0-226-06557-1 (paper)
ISBN-13: 978-0-226-06560-1 (e-book)
DOI: 10.7208/chicago/9780226065601.001.0001

Library of Congress Cataloging-in-Publication Data

Boydstun, Amber E., 1977–
    Making the news : politics, the media, and agenda setting / Amber E. Boydstun.
        pages. cm.
    Includes bibliographical references and index.
    ISBN 978-0-226-06543-4 (cloth : alk. paper) — ISBN 978-0-226-06557-1 (pbk. :
alk. paper) — ISBN 978-0-226-06560-1 (e-book)   1. Press and politics—United
States.   2. Journalism—United States.   I. Title.
    PN4888.P6B66 2013
    071'.3—dc23

                                                                        2013005897

♾ This paper meets the requirements of ANSI/NISO Z39.48-1992 (Permanence of Paper).

Contents

Acknowledgments

Before political science, I did a brief stint in theater. The two crafts are different in so many ways, but they share similarities, too. Both are methodical and precise. Both hinge on the ability to draw clear meaning from complexity. Both have interesting characters.

For me, the parallel to theater is sharpest when thinking about political science as an individual craft and, simultaneously, as a deeply collective endeavor. I have found that writing a book alone is very much like being alone on stage (thrilling, and a little terrifying). Yet I would not, could not, have completed this project without the many people who supported me along the way. That this book exists is due to them. That it is not better is all on me.

We so rarely have the chance to give formal thanks to those colleagues and friends who guide us and lift us up, and so I beg the reader's indulgence as I cherish the opportunity. I love the solitary aspects of political science as a craft but, truly, it is the solidarity I have found in this profession that chimes my bells. The names listed so briefly below represent countless gestures (and hours) of assistance, advice, and encouragement.

At the University of Chicago Press, John Tryneski is an editor of impeccable talent and grace. He shepherded me through the submission, acceptance, and publication processes, taking great time and care to make sure I was comfortable every step of the way. When I told him that I wanted to make substantial and time-consuming improvements to the book beyond those that the reviewers had suggested, he did not hesitate before working with me to develop a feasible time line. Also at Chicago, Rodney Powell was a master of coordination. Mark Reschke and, especially, Therese Boyd made the copyediting process seamless. Melinda

Kennedy handled the book's marketing with finesse. And before any of these fine people handled the book, the UC Davis College of Letters and Science provided publication assistance funds so that Leah Ewing Ross could wield her exceptional editing skills (her friendship, also exceptional, came without charge).

Many research assistants helped make this book a labor of love. The *New York Times* front-page dataset presented in this book was made possible by a generous grant from the National Science Foundation (No. SES-0617492) and by support from the Department of Political Science and the College of the Liberal Arts at the Pennsylvania State University. The dataset was painstakingly collected by a talented group of students at Penn State while I was a graduate student there. These students attacked the data collection effort with extraordinary attention to detail, and each deserves tremendous thanks: Arman Arvedisian, Amanda Blunt, Kaylan Dorsch, Michelle Falvey, Sarah Gosky, Jamie Guillory, Amanda Kalamar, Alysia Patterson, Kim Roth, Taylor Souter, Gabriel Uriarte, and Matt Vodzak. I am particularly indebted to Scott Huffard, who started as an undergraduate coder, quickly advanced to master coder, and then spearheaded the process of cleaning the entire database once complete; now nearing his own PhD, Scott remains a trusted research assistant on several of my projects. Tim Misiak's computer science genius introduced me to the world of automated text retrieval and analysis that, in turn, redefined the parameters of the book. When I arrived at UC Davis, Jake Delbridge tracked down evasive references. Clare Callahan investigated media explosion anecdotes. Debra Leiter valiantly updated my analysis syntax files. And I am especially grateful to Tim Jurka, whose research assistance has been instrumental in the completion of this book. Among many other magic tricks, Tim built new automated text tools to process the massive dataset of newspaper, television, and online news presented in chapter 8. He also drafted the R syntax for the simulations in chapter 7, which I had originally designed, if you can believe it, in Excel.

In writing this book I benefited from the guidance and kindness of many colleagues, and the book is vastly richer for their thoughtful and helpful comments. At UC Davis, Erik Engstrom, Ben Highton, and Bob Huckfeldt generously offered their time and advice on the project. In one of many acts of true friendship, Ethan Scheiner discerned my hummable tune when I had gone tone deaf. And after I overhauled the book at one point, Walt Stone (who had already been subjected to an unhealthy dose of my work in rough draft form) showed the patience of Job in listening to me pitch my new tune. John Scott provided counsel and encouragement way beyond the call of duty. Outside UC Davis, several additional colleagues gave selflessly of their time by reading part or all of the book and then providing invaluable feedback; my sincere thanks to Matt Baum, Lance Bennett, Daniel Diermeier, Michael Delli Carpini, Jamie Druckman, Justin Grimmer, Shanto Iyengar, and John Wilkerson (as well as very helpful anonymous reviewers). Eric Plutzer was the one to suggest that I should make sure my simulation findings held up using real-world seasonal data. I was able to do so thanks to Vladeta Ajdacic-Gross (Ajdacic-Gross et al. 2005), who shared data on suicides in Switzerland, and Frank Baumgartner, who shared data on French driving. The aforementioned dataset of newspaper, television, and online news is one I collected in conjunction with Frank Baumgartner, Mel Atkinson, Tim Jurka, John Lovett, Jon Moody, and Trey Thomas; my many thanks to Frank for funding that enterprise and to each of these colleagues for allowing me to use the data here. Marie Hojnacki pushed me, very helpfully and always kindly, to make the book more concrete. Suzie Linn is a phenomenal mentor and friend with an uncanny talent for seeing my research conundrums in new and more helpful lights; she was pivotal in the book's development and offered continued thoughts and support as it evolved. I am especially grateful to Regina Lawrence, who read the entire manuscript (twice) and offered feedback that was as encouraging as it was constructive, directing me to see not just the theoretical but also the important practical implications of my findings; I cannot thank her enough for her gracious mentorship.

The book also benefited from the insightful questions and comments I received on the project from audiences at Aarhus University; American University; Louisiana State University; Sciences Po, Bordeaux; Suffolk University; West Virginia University; and the universities of Amsterdam, Antwerp, Barcelona, California Merced, Michigan, Nebraska, Washington, and Zurich. Each of these visits was thoroughly enjoyable and helped me refine my theoretical and methodological arguments.

I worked on this book during the 2010–11 academic year, which I spent as a Marie Curie Fellow collaborating with the fantastic M^2P team at the University of Antwerp and visiting scholars at other European universities. In countless ways, the book is stronger for the academic and personal connections I made with Sylvain Brouard, Laura Chaques, Jonas Fricker, Christoffer Green-Pedersen, Emiliano Grossman, Regula Hänggli, Luk Lafosse, Jonas Lefevere, Marjolein Meijer,

Peter Mortensen, Anna Palau, Nel Ruigrok, Reto Schumacher, Rune Slothuus, Anke Tresch, Peter Van Aelst, and Wouter van Atteveldt. Particular thanks to three friends and coauthors who offered resilient support for the book and who make it a joy to collaborate: Anne Hardy, who taught me how to take time off and rescued me from Belgian bureaucracy; Rens Vliegenthart, who retaught me time series and how to ride a coaster-brake bike; and Stefaan Walgrave, who taught me how to balance productivity with good humor.

In 2010 Jay Hamilton organized an excellent conference on building digital records for computational social science at Stanford's Center for Advanced Study in the Behavioral Sciences. At that conference I had the good fortune of meeting not only Jay, who offered insight and encouragement on the book, but also Sarah Cohen, a journalist formerly of the *Washington Post* and now of the *New York Times*. Sarah offered me unfettered access to her perspective of the news-generation process, allowed me to interview her formally on two separate occasions, gave me a personal tour of the *Washington Post*'s newsroom, and pointed me in the direction of other journalists. I am indescribably grateful to Sarah and to the other reporters and editors I interviewed: Peter Baker, Art Brisbane, John Harwood, Mark Leibovich, and Alan McLean of the *Times*; and Anne Kornblut, Alan Sipress, Karen Yourish, and especially Vince Bzdek of the *Post*. Each one of these people gave me precious time for an interview but also, what is more, a reinforced appreciation of the pressures of the modern newsroom. I walked away from these interviews with a deep respect for the job these professionals do each day—amid overwhelming challenges—to give us informed, thought-provoking, and unbiased news. Sometimes they don't succeed. But the intention is clear.

My greatest academic debt of thanks is to Frank Baumgartner, my mentor, coauthor, and friend. Frank is an extraordinary intellectual advisor and, quite simply, a great guy who takes profound care of his students. I had no idea what I was getting into when I entered grad school, and I can say with confidence that were it not for Frank I would not be a political scientist today. As a graduate of St. John's College, I had solid critical thinking skills but knew nothing about political science as a discipline. Looking back, I am in awe of how much time Frank took to guide me through the scientific study of politics—not by telling me what to do but by showing me how to do it; that is, by teaching me how to fish. He never pushed me, not once, to curb my curiosity or creativity. Somehow, while never pulling punches in critiquing this book in its many stages, he unfailingly knew exactly what to say to bolster my confidence. Frank is a tremendous asset to the discipline, as both a scholar and a mentor, and it is a privilege and a pleasure to work with him.

Beyond these professional thanks, I am grateful to many additional people—too many to list here by name—who did not contribute directly to the content of the book but who offered me support that was equally valuable. I am particularly blessed to be surrounded by a community of strong, compassionate, and hilarious women. Political scientists Jan Box-Steffensmeier, Jenn Jerit, Sunshine Hillygus, and Caroline Tolbert offered excellent mentorship. Fellow UC Davis political science junior colleagues Cheryl Boudreau, Heather McKibben, and Shalini Satkunanandan offered unmitigated encouragement. The tenured women in the department, Jo Andrews, Jeannette Money, and Gabriella Montinola, offered much-appreciated advice and support. Our department is also held together by a phenomenal band of women staff who keep me organized and cheerful; thanks to them all and, especially, to their fearless leader Cindy Simmons. The ladies of the Second Sunday brunch group—Alison, Andrea, Donna, Gail, Heidi, Karen, Kari, Liz, Magali, Teresa, and Wendy—kept things in perspective (and kept me well-fed); I cherish their friendships. I-Chant Chiang, Cory Holding, Maryann Gallagher, and Dee May provided lifelines of support from afar. I am especially grateful to two women—Rebecca Glazier and Alison Ledgerwood—who are not only good friends but also my coauthors on separate projects. These women kept me grounded, fortified my sense of humor, and forgave me on countless occasions when the book invaded on time for our respective collaborations. Rebecca read several of the book's chapters in rough draft form, applying her impressive powers of persuasion to the task of convincing me to submit the manuscript in the first place; even when she had a new and adorable baby to care for, she never failed to answer the phone or drop me an e-mail to provide emotional calibration and a welcome reality check. Alison taught me a better system for to-do lists, did not laugh when I asked her to hold me accountable for my weekly book progress by sending my money to an anti-animal fund if I fell short of a goal, and accordingly kept me stocked with inspiring hedgehog photos (as if hedgehog photos come in another variety).

My family has been unfalteringly supportive, even when they could not understand why I was writing a book in the first place, much less why it was taking so long and at the expense of precious time together. I am

especially grateful that my father, Denny Boydstun, contributed his op-
timism to the cause. He arrived at the fierce conviction that the book
would be published and that everything would be all right before the
first draft was even complete, and he would not waver on this position.
He said it so often that I started to believe it, too. And, of course, he was
right.

Of four loving grandparents, the one I knew longest was my grand-
father Clarence Boydstun, who died at the age of ninety-five while this
book was under review. Having survived polio as a child but with perma-
nent paralysis in his left arm, he went on to graduate eighth grade, marry
my grandmother, and support his family by working a range of jobs that
included cutting and hauling blocks of ice from a Colorado lake, running
a dairy farm, driving supply trucks, and managing a golf course. From
such a different time and life path, he of all people might have been least
able to understand the utility of spending so many long hours at this new-
fangled computer thing. Yet somehow he understood the best; a strong
work ethic, it seems, transcends time and situation.

This book is dedicated to my mother, Faye Ashley. In a different life,
she would have thrived as a scholar. As it was, she worked tirelessly to
make it possible for me to go to college, then grad school, and now she
sustains my sanity in a job that is grueling but that I can hardly call work
because I love it so. She offered unparalleled emotional support while I
was writing and then rewriting and then rewriting the book, a brilliant
mind that kept me on my toes while discussing various chapters with her,
and much-needed humor when things got tough. She even transcribed
the several hours of my recorded interviews with journalists and, wait for
it, looked up half the DOI numbers for the bibliography. Thanks, Mom.

I have no words sufficient to thank my husband and best friend, Kyle
Joyce. He is, hands down, the most patient person I have ever known. If
the stress of my multiyear book odyssey pushed the bounds of his patience, he did not let it show. From start to finish with this book, he was
my most trusted sounding board. As an international relations scholar,
he surely knows more about media agenda setting than he bargained for
(but then, I know quite a bit about conflict expansion). He helped me
talk through ideas, helped me find more than one bug in my simulations,
single-handedly packed up our house for the year I was in Belgium, kept
my computer up and running (no small feat), kept the cats (Gaila, Sto-
chasta, and Mise Fein) fed when I forgot, and kept me supplied with tea.

While I like to think that I could be happy having made many different decisions in life—even as an out-of-work actor—unequivocally the best decision I have ever made was accepting the premises of the game tree he developed to convince me to date him. In any job, in any place, he is the one who keeps me laughing and keeps me happy.

CHAPTER ONE

Patterns in the News and Why They Matter

The media matters—to politics, to citizens, to democracy. Thus, how media attention gets distributed across issues and how it changes over time matters, too. Yet, despite its importance, we know relatively little about the forces that drive media attention and the patterns that result. At the core of this book is a deceptively simple yet powerful observation about the news: it does not ebb and flow; rather, it fixates and explodes. In turn, the explosive nature of media dynamics exacerbates the degree of skew in news coverage across policy issues, such that a few issues receive the lion's share of coverage while most issues go unnoticed. These patterns—explosiveness and skew—are endemic to the media as an institution, and they have far-reaching implications for politics and society.

Readers may call to mind ready examples of media explosions: perhaps the BP oil spill or the Chilean miners' rescue in 2010, the Anthony Weiner "sexting" scandal of 2011, or the school shooting that killed 20 children and six adults at Sandy Hook Elementary School in 2012. In some cases, media explosions seem "proportional" to events, such as the media explosions following the terrorist attacks of 9/11 and the Enron scandal in 2001. In other cases, media explosions seem to center on events that are similar to previous incidents that received very little, if any, media attention; such media explosions include the immigration dispute surrounding Elian Gonzalez in 2000, Elizabeth Smart's kidnapping in 2002, the Terri Schiavo case of 2005, and Trayvon Martin's shooting in 2012. In still other cases, a media explosion erupts when news coverage shines light on a string of events that have gone unattended for years, such as repeated child sexual abuses committed by Catholic priests, Boy

Scout leaders, or Jerry Sandusky. In all these cases, when a media explosion occupies the news there is a dearth of attention paid to other important issues: genocide, sexual trafficking, homelessness, and Alzheimer's are just a few. The phenomena of media explosions point to a media system that changes in fits and starts over time and, as a result, produces skewed degrees of attention to events and their related policy problems. Understanding the explosive and skewed nature of the news matters not only for understanding the news industry, but for understanding how media signals shape citizen and policymaker awareness of and response to policy issues.

The Case of Terri Schiavo

Let us investigate one media explosion in more detail. Theresa "Terri" Schiavo died from dehydration on March 31, 2005, days after a Florida Circuit Court judge ordered the removal of the feeding tube that had been keeping her alive for fifteen years. Those fifteen years were long ones, fraught with conflict between her husband and her parents about the appropriate nature and extent of her medical care. Their battle hinged, in large part, on the fact that Schiavo did not have a living will. United States federal legislation, state legislation (in fifty states plus the District of Columbia), and key judicial rulings all support a citizen's legal right to execute a binding living will, or advanced health care directive.[1] In essence, living wills help guide family members and doctors charged with weighing the balance between a person's life and the quality of that life.

While the presence or absence of living wills can make enormous differences in the cases of people who are suddenly incapacitated, such as Terri Schiavo, living will policy affects a much larger portion of the American population, specifically through the all-too-frequent cases of families needing to make end-of-life decisions for loved ones suffering from dementia.[2] In short, for people who want all possible life-sustaining measures employed, for those who want none employed, and for everyone in between, living will policy offers citizens powerful agency in determining their own medical treatments. And on a strictly financial note, the policy option of living wills can also save families—and taxpayers—a lot of money when those citizens who would prefer not to have extended or invasive life-sustaining measures employed use living wills to dictate their wishes ahead of time. Susan Jacoby of the *New York Times* reports that an estimated one-third of the U.S. Medicare budget is spent supporting people in the last year of life, and a third of that amount is spent on care in the final month (2012).

Yet despite the many potential benefits of existing living will policy, historically most Americans have not made use of this policy—or have even been aware of it. According to a Pew Research Center survey conducted in 1990, only 41% of Americans had heard of living wills, and only 12% reported having them. By 2005, however, much had changed. A Pew Research Center survey conducted in November 2005 found that 95% of Americans had heard of living wills, and 29% reported having them.[3]

Part of the dramatic increase in awareness and application of living will policy between 1990 and 2005 can be attributed to the Patient Self-Determination Act, passed by Congress in 1990, which requires most hospitals and long-term care facilities to provide patients with information on living wills. Yet, by most accounts, the effect of this Act of Congress paled in comparison to the impact of the single case of Terri Schiavo, which raised Americans' awareness of end-of-life medical and living will options to unprecedented levels.

One measure of the political impact of the Schiavo case was the subsequent increase in public demand for living wills. For instance, a major nonprofit group, Aging with Dignity, distributed an average of 1 million living will documents annually in the years prior to 2005. In 2005, however, the year Terri Schiavo died, this number doubled to 2 million; by 2006 the surge in requests had barely declined. Similarly, the number of visits to the U.S. Living Will Registry website, which averaged about 500 per day before the Schiavo case, rose fivefold to 2,500 per day in the year following Schiavo's death—and an astounding 50,000 visits per day during the center of the Schiavo controversy in March 2005. Furthermore, 40,000 people applied the policy option by registering living will documents with this online registry in 2006, up fourfold from 10,000 in 2005 (Stacy 2006).

These aggregate numbers reflect the behaviors of individuals across the country as citizens learned of Terri Schiavo and began to consider living will policy in their own lives. For example, in the month following Schiavo's death, researchers of an ongoing hospital study found that 92% of participants (N = 117) had heard of Schiavo. Of those who had heard of her, 61% reported that the Schiavo case specifically prompted them to clarify their own goals of long-term care, and 66% reported talking to their friends and/or families about what they would want if they were in Schiavo's position (Sudore et al. 2008).

Schiavo's case was unfortunate, but far from unique. In the United States, an estimated 15,000 people live in persistent vegetative states, and an unmeasured proportion of these cases involve family disputes about whether or not to remove the patients' feeding tubes (Hirsch 2005). Out of all the cases of heart-wrenching family disputes about whether or not to remove the feeding tube of a loved one, Terri Schiavo's case alone prompted a dramatic shift in citizens' understanding and application of existing living will policy. Why? What did the Schiavo case have that no other similar case—or the related 1990 Act of Congress—shared?

The answer is perplexingly simple: news coverage. The Terri Schiavo case got *a lot* of news coverage and, what's more, a lot of news coverage of a particular kind: a sudden surge in coverage about the Schiavo case itself *combined with* in-depth follow-up coverage examining the related policy issues at stake. In other words, Terri Schiavo was at the center of a sustained media explosion that occurred in the month leading up to her death. In that month alone (March 2005), the *New York Times* ran sixteen front-page stories about the case (up from zero front-page stories in February). That's sixteen stories in a month—an average of just over one every other day—on the *front page* of the *New York Times*.[4] The *Times* front page is prime real estate indeed, and in March 2005 the Schiavo case captured nearly 8% of its agenda space. The *Times* was not unusual. A search of thirteen major television and newspaper outlets reveals that they produced a total of 1,135 news stories on Schiavo in March 2005, up from a total of 62 in February.[5]

Why so much coverage, so suddenly, and lasting for nearly four weeks (an eternity in the news business)? Certainly, the Schiavo case was a compelling one, with many sensational attributes that lent it strong news value. Still, why *so much* coverage of this single case, when so many other similar cases had previously gone unnoticed? And why so much extended coverage in March 2005, when the Schiavo case was, in fact, not new news? Media outlets had picked up on the Schiavo case as a newsworthy storyline a year and a half before Schiavo's death, when a Florida court ordered the removal of her feeding tube (not for the first time) in October 2003. The Florida legislature responded by passing "Terri's Law," which authorized Governor Jeb Bush to reverse the court-ordered decision; Schiavo's tube was reinserted (Goodnough 2003). During this earlier period of public discussion, the U.S. media gave limited coverage to the case and surrounding events, with the aforementioned thirteen news outlets producing 188 stories in October 2003, including three front-page *New York Times* stories. By March 2005 little had changed in the underlying facts and arguments of the case. Multiple battles and court rulings had passed, including a judicial turning point in the case: the U.S. Supreme Court's refusal in January 2005 to hear a challenge to the Florida State Supreme Court's ruling striking down Terri's Law (Newman 2005). But as for the basic evidence and arguments, the case was hardly different in 2005 than it had been in 2003.

Yet, in March 2005, news coverage of the Schiavo case exploded, and with it public awareness and application of living will policy. The media explosion surrounding the Schiavo case lasted about a month. Its effects on public awareness and policy application appear to have lasted much longer.

The Story of This Book in a Nutshell

This book offers a refined way of thinking about news coverage, the institutional forces that shape it, and the media explosions that result. Over the course of the book, I present a lot of data and consider many examples, but the main story of the book is this: due to the strong role that momentum plays in the news-generation process, the media agenda is hard-wired to be highly skewed across policy issues and highly explosive in how it changes over time. These systemic patterns in the news have wide-ranging implications for understanding the limited media access that most policy problems have, as well as the manner in which citizens and policymakers receive and react to political cues in the news.

The book is premised on the significance of the media as a political institution. Media attention has been shown, empirically and repeatedly, to influence both citizen attitudes and government responses toward policy issues. But how do policy issues make the news in the first place? Because the media is a central body in the political system, understanding the forces that drive media attention is a goal central to political science as well as communication studies.

Within and across the fields of political science and communications, scholars have offered different approaches to understanding the news-generation process—that is, the process through which stories are selected and developed into the news. This book offers a unifying model of the news-generation process within three overlapping frameworks:

1. The media employs an *organizational process* in which journalists and news outlets assemble the news from each day's events based on news values as well as several other institutional incentives, such as incentives to attend to elite opinions and consumer demands.
2. The media is a *marketplace*, where competition creates additional incentives that shape the operations of news outlets, such as incentives to mimic other outlets' coverage and to distribute scarce resources efficiently (e.g., through the beat system of reporting).
3. Political agendas, including the media agenda, are *disproportionate information-processing* systems, meaning that agendas do not process real-world events in real time or in proportion to the "size" of those events; instead, agendas lurch from one hot event (and its related policy issue) to the next at the exclusion of many other important issues.

Overarching these three approaches, I stress the importance of dynamics. Momentum is key in driving the news-generation process and the patterns of skew and explosiveness that result.

At the normative root of the three interwoven approaches are questions regarding the role the media plays in the political system: specifically, the idealized notion of a watchdog press. As scholars have long noted, the news media does not—indeed, cannot—operate as an ideal watchdog, constantly surveying the landscape for potential problems. Rather, the media is a political institution and, as such, is incapable of perfect surveillance. Past studies suggest that, rather than operating as a watchdog "patrol" system, the media operates instead as an "alarm" system, attending only to those events/issues that trigger the social or political equivalent of an alarm (usually by nature of the size and type of event at hand). Zaller (2003) explains that, in its best form, this alarm model would mean that journalists and news outlets should not even try to monitor politics and society for all important information to convey to the public. Not only is doing so infeasible, he says, but also the public does not require such detailed information on so many issues. Instead, "as with a real burglar alarm, the idea is to call attention to matters requiring urgent attention, and to do so in excited and noisy tones" (122). Thus, the reigning alarm model of news generation implies that the media's institutional incentives simply do not—perhaps should not—support patrol-style surveillance journalism. This book, however, challenges the alarm model as a complete account of the news-generation process.

Of additional normative importance, past work suggests that an alarm system of news generation produces a strong prevalence of "soft" news (more sensational and entertainment-driven; see Patterson 2000), as opposed to "hard" news (more substantive). Zaller suggests that the increased pace of alarm-based coverage in the modern media marketplace is largely responsible for the increased prevalence of soft news that scholars have observed, noting potential benefits of this result, such as enhanced citizen engagement with political issues via soft news as a more engaging vehicle (2003; see also Baum 2002, 2003; Baum and Groeling 2008; for conflicting evidence see Prior 2003). Bennett confirms that the alarm model is a largely accurate depiction of the current media system, but he also identifies several normative problems that the alarm model raises. Bennett notes that despite the strong incentives to operate strictly in alarm mode, many journalists and news outlets continue to exhibit some adherence to the "full news" standard of good journalism, producing a healthy amount of hard news as a result (2003). In this book, I touch only theoretically and briefly on the important distinction between hard and soft news.[6] Nevertheless, the soft-news implications of the model presented in this book are important to bear in mind throughout.

Building on this past research, I argue that while news outlets certainly do not operate strictly as patrol watchdogs, neither do they operate strictly under an alarm system of news generation. Rather, we can best understand the news-generation process using a hybrid of these two models, what I call the alarm/patrol hybrid model. This model explains how and why news outlets lurch attention (selectively) to alarms that are sounded in key policy or geographic "neighborhoods," namely by dispatching journalists and other resources to report on those alarms. But once these scarce resources are deployed, under the right conditions news outlets can then be driven—by news values and other institutional incentives—to stay locked on the hot news item. The dispatched journalists thus shift quickly into patrol mode, scanning the surrounding policy/geographic neighborhoods for additional stories, often pursuing these stories through more in-depth, investigative reporting. It is this *conjunction* that sometimes occurs between the alarm and patrol modes of journalism that turns what would have been a brief alarm-driven spike in attention (a "momentary media explosion") into a more robust, and often more politically meaningful, "sustained media explosion." ("Timed media explosions," a third category, are born of patrol-driven coverage surrounding an anticipated event like an election or the Olympics.)

This book, then, is about how event-driven issues become news in general and, in particular, how and why media explosions occur. News coverage in the United States may often seem erratic, driven by unpredictable events. Events drive the news, without question. But so do institutional incentives, which we can conceptualize (and measure) in the form of key variables. For example, variables such as how much attention policymakers are giving to an issue, how concerned citizens are about it, and how the issue is defined (or framed) should all affect how much subsequent media attention the issue receives.

The alarm/patrol hybrid model explains how these and other variables do not operate in isolation at each point in time—or in isolation from one another. Momentum matters. The incentive-based newsroom decisions that occur each day are largely self-propelling. Under some conditions, when the media's incentives pull it toward a new hot event/issue (driving the media into "alarm" mode), this momentum produces cascades of change. Under other conditions, when the media's incentives compel it to stay locked on the event/issue at hand (driving the media into "patrol" mode), this momentum produces periods of fixation. The result of these momentum-linked variables is a hybrid process of news generation that fluctuates between alarm-style frenetic reporting and patrol-style in-depth journalism. And sometimes news generation of the same event/issue transitions quickly from one mode to the other, when shifting conditions rocket the media from alarm mode directly into patrol mode (or vice versa). This alarm/hybrid process is responsible for sustained media explosions like the one surrounding Terri Schiavo.

Beyond describing the variables that drive the news under an overarching system of dynamics, the alarm/patrol hybrid model predicts two stark patterns of media coverage that are *necessarily* produced by this new-generation process: news that is highly skewed in its distribution across policy issues, and news that changes explosively over time.[7] These patterns of skew and explosiveness are of heavy political consequence, both good and bad. For example, consider one key benefit of this news-generation process: the strength and velocity of sustained media explosions—uniquely the product of the alarm/patrol hybrid model—are often responsible for bringing important policy issues (such as living wills and other end-of-life decisions) to the focused attention of citizens and policymakers. In a media system geared predominantly for brief explosions (alarm-only model) or predominantly for small or gradual changes in coverage (patrol-only model), media attention might not surpass the invisible salience threshold required to make an impact on citizens or policymakers. In this way, the alarm/patrol hybrid model describes a media system that can bring valuable awareness to issues that might otherwise be ignored. Additionally, patterned explosiveness means that even the most powerful political elites (e.g., politicians and lobbyists) cannot control the news for long. Yet, by contrast, consider that media explosions (momentary, sustained, and timed) take up much of the oxygen in the media agenda, focusing attention on just a few issues. Consequently, the media agenda has very little room left over for other important policy problems. The resulting patterned skew in the agenda means that most policy issues, most of the time, have restricted access to public attention via the news. Moreover, the explosive nature of media coverage (present in an alarm model of news generation but much starker in the alarm/patrol hybrid model) makes it extremely difficult for citizens and policymakers alike to process and respond to policy issues in the news in any long-term, meaningful way.

With these political implications on the line, it is important that we understand the forces that shape the news. This book unpacks these forces. The endeavor is twofold. First, it is important to understand the individual forces, or variables, that influence the news-generation process. Second, we need to understand how these variables combine to produce systemic patterns of skew and explosiveness in the news.

In this endeavor, it is crucial to understand the futility of parsing out every variable influencing the news-generation process; it simply isn't possible to predict the news on any given day. Yet, just as genetic adaptations—individually unpredictable—comprise a larger process of evolution that exhibits clear patterns that can be understood in the aggregate, or at the population level, so too do the unpredictable day-to-day decisions of the newsroom aggregate to a much larger system with distinct patterns of operation and change.

The Importance of Attention

Why should we care about media attention? Because attention is one of the most powerful resources in the political system. While less concrete than other political resources—like money, troops, or votes—atten-

tion has the power to move people. Indeed, it has the power to move nations. As the case of Terri Schiavo illustrates, attention can mean the
difference between ignorance and action, between silence and solution.
In Congress, attention is what distinguishes the policy problems that are
addressed from those that remain in disrepair. In the courts, attention
is what distinguishes the judicial precedents that are deliberated from
those that are left unquestioned. And in the institutional context studied
here—the U.S. news media—attention is what distinguishes the events
and related policy issues that become matters of media (and public) discussion from those that go unnoticed.

Leaving aside feature stories about sports, weather, culture, and human interest, many political news stories, even in the *New York Times*,
do not explicitly link events to policy. Many stories take the form of
soft news as mentioned above (e.g., Baum 2003; Bennett 2003; Patterson 2000) or focus on the game-playing aspects of politics, such as election coverage centered more on the "horse race" between the candidates
than on the issues themselves (Domke, Fibison, Shah, Smith, and Watts
1997; Iyengar, Norpoth, and Hanh 2004; Lawrence 2000a; Plasser 2005).
Nevertheless, in this book the focus is on attention to "issues" by virtue of attention to the events that directly or indirectly implicate those
issues. The guiding assumption here is that most (though certainly not
all) non–feature news stories in the national news, both hard and soft,
carry implicit policy cues. This assumption is a simplified approach adopted for the purposes of theoretical and empirical traction in this book.
Nonetheless, past research supports the assumption, showing that hard
news stories framed as matters of political conflict, and soft news stories, too, prompt people to consider the implicit policy ramifications of
these stories—in many conditions even shaping their views on policy issues (Baum 2002; Price, Tewksbury, and Powers 1997; Prior 2003). Work
also suggests that emotional cues, which are often found in horse-race
stories devoid of hard policy substance, can heighten citizen engagement
(Brader 2006; Gross 2008).

Mindful of the important distinction between explicit policy news and
soft news or horse-race coverage, I examine media attention to issues
by treating each news story as relating, either explicitly or implicitly, to
a primary "issue." Methodologically, I equate issues with the subtopics
encompassed in the Policy Agendas coding scheme, including "policy"
issues like unemployment and immigration as well as feature, or "nonpolicy," issues like sports and weather. Thus, in the *New York Times*

front-page agenda dataset presented here, a news story about political candidates' competing views on immigration is coded as a story about the issue of immigration, even if framed as a horse race. An election story that is, truly, just about the horse race is coded under Elections.

An additional assumption guiding this book's empirical work is that each policy issue primed by a given news story is underpinned by at least one policy *problem*. Policy problems can be understood and defined in many ways. But in one way or another, we tend to care about policy issues because of the policy problems, however defined, that are captured within those issues and addressed (or not addressed) by governmental policy (Baumgartner and Jones 2009). The issue of immigration, for instance, contains a range of component policy problems, such as how to balance the legal demands for citizenship with the moral demands for providing health care to all people, including undocumented immigrants.

To be sure, not all policy problems that get attention in the political system are solved by politics. But we know one thing for sure: the problems that *do* get solved are the ones that receive attention on one or more political agendas. And for those problems in particular that move from being ignored to being in the news, media attention generally increases their chances of being addressed politically. Thus, the agenda-setting (or agenda-building) process, by which some issues gain attention but most do not, is of vast consequence.[8]

Media attention—and political attention more broadly—is so important in part because it is so scarce. On any given day, the world is faced with thousands of political problems that demand solutions. Poverty, prescription drug coverage, corporate corruption, war . . . all these issues warrant attention. Yet while these and most other important problems continually rise and fall in severity, we ignore most of them most of the time—neither the human brain nor the political, public, or media agendas have the capacity to keep track of thousands of emerging social and political issues. Consider that each year the U.S. Supreme Court decides about eighty cases, Congress and the president work to sign approximately 260 bills into law, the average American spends about five hours—total—thinking about politics, and the *New York Times* publishes 365 front pages, each one holding about eight stories.[9]

This book focuses on the *New York Times* front page as a pivotal gatekeeper of the public agenda. As detailed in chapter 4, the *Times* is largely representative of other national news outlets across the country and by some accounts helps to lead national news coverage. Each day the issues captured on the front page send signals to politicians and citizens alike about which problems are important and which are not. Again, media attention can shape public opinion, governmental attention, and public policy (Dearing and Rogers 1996; Iyengar and Kinder 1987; McCombs 2004). Thus, like the other agendas in the political system (e.g., the president's agenda, the congressional agenda, the public agenda of citizen concerns), "the" media agenda—comprised by myriad diverse U.S. news outlets—plays a major role in shaping the political system as a whole. Without media attention, policy needs generally have slim chances of garnering public endorsement, financial support, or legislative action (Cobb and Elder 1983).

In many cases, these different agendas have mutual influence over one another (Edwards and Wood 1999; Peake and Eshbaugh-Soha 2008; Soroka 2002). For instance, public concern about a policy issue will often prompt media attention to that issue, while at the same time media attention often drives public concern. In the case of *Times'* front-page coverage, this book shows that policymaker attention to and public concern about policy issues help drive media attention to those issues (see chapters 5 and 6), but also that media attention influences policymaker attention and public concern in turn (see chapter 9). Within the political system of mutually reinforcing agendas, the media agenda is no more important than any other. Yet the media is of particular significance in that, in addition to influencing other agendas directly, it also serves as the primary vehicle of information between these other agendas, conveying policymakers' messages to citizens, for example, and vice versa.

Because of its ability to influence politics and society, media attention is worth studying as a powerful political resource. It is a scarce resource, too, as I discuss in the following section. The limited size of the media agenda exacerbates the tendency for most policy issues not to make it into the news most of the time, just as they do not make it onto other political agendas; instead, the majority of issues are attended to on smaller agendas within specialized policy communities (Carmines and Stimson 1989; Downs 1972; Jones and Baumgartner 2005).

The issues that *do* achieve agenda status, including in the media, determine the parameters of political debate. Schattschneider (1960) laid the theoretical groundwork for studies of attention distribution through the concept of conflict displacement: the redistribution of political attention or resources from the status quo to a new division of debate. Consider the space of a given agenda. In essence, attention distribution is the process of slicing this agenda along changing division lines, distributing and redistributing the resource of attention across a small handful of issues selected from the larger issue population.

It is here that we see how a study of attention distribution is really a study of influence (Gaventa 1980; Riker 1986). If politics is about "who gets what, when, and how" (Lasswell 1936), then which issues get media attention (and when, and how) is really a question of political power. In distributing attention one way or another, power is wielded by limiting the scope of the political agenda "to public consideration of only those issues which are comparatively innocuous" to members of a given group (Bachrach and Baratz 1962). As Nobel laureate Herbert Simon said, "What information consumes is rather obvious: it consumes the attention of its recipients. Hence a wealth of information creates a poverty of attention, and a need to allocate that attention efficiently among the overabundance of information sources that might consume it" (as quoted by Varian 1995).

It is important to note that the *amount* of news coverage an issue receives is only one aspect of media influence. The *type* of news coverage matters, too. For example, the level of informational content offered by a news source can directly influence citizens' feelings of social capital, even driving political and civic engagement (e.g., Delli Carpini 2004; Norris 1996, 2011; Xenos and Moy 2007). Perhaps most notably, a rich literature shows that citizens often react differently to issues in the news depending on how the issue is defined, or framed.[10] What forces drive how an issue is framed? As Lawrence (2000b) demonstrates in the case of police brutality, and as Hänggli (2013) demonstrates in the case of Swiss politics, the way events are defined as "issues" in the first place and then framed in particular ways depends on a variety of journalistic, institutional, and social forces and how these forces interact with the specific nature of the events at hand. Thus, while coverage of events is often shaped by factors such as which actors are involved in an event, the actors who become involved can also be influenced by the salience of the event (via news coverage). In other words, there can be considerable interplay—that is, endogeneity—between the nature of an event and the nature of the news coverage it receives. Generally speaking, though, the many forces that shape how an event is defined tend to restrict access to the media agenda, focusing the news on mainstream issues and views.

As a result, marginalized perspectives tend only to have rare and limited moments of agenda access and, thus, few and infrequent windows of policy opportunity (Kingdon 1995; Rochefort and Cobb 1994; Schattschneider 1960; Schneider and Ingram 1993).

Given the scope of this book, which examines news coverage across topics and over time, I do not examine distinctions of media attention *type* (e.g., degree of informational content, different types of frames). I do identify a variable, *diversity of discussion*, which at the issue level captures the diversity of the frames used in news coverage of that issue. As the diversity of media framing about an issue increases, so too does the overall level of media attention to that issue (and vice versa). But much more research is needed; our understanding of the media's role in politics and society rests largely on our understanding of framing.

In short, media attention is important. Really important. Yet compared to this documented importance, we know much less about the mechanisms by which media attention gets distributed. How is media attention spread among issues? How does the media agenda change over time? And above all else, what are the factors driving the news-generation process—that is, the process by which real-world information and ideas are sifted and then evolve into the daily news?

The Scarcity of Attention

Reflecting on the case of Terri Schiavo, we might like to think that a policy issue as important as medical directives would gain attention on its own merits—that if the Schiavo case had not prompted public and political awareness, the next similar case would have done so. But attention, especially media attention, doesn't work like that. Which policy areas gain media attention, and when, is determined not only by the inherent worth or severity of a policy area, but also by a number of other factors in the complex news-generation process.

By any measure, the policy issue of medical directives is important. But consider that each of the front-page *New York Times* articles devoted to the Terri Schiavo case in March 2005 (recall that this single storyline consumed nearly 8% of the front-page agenda that month) was an article spot *not* given to competing events and their related policy issues. Here is a sampling of other policy-related events that also occurred in March 2005 that received a scant amount of front-page coverage or, in most cases, no coverage at all:[11]

> Government investigations continued of alleged detainee abuses and more than 30 alleged detainee homicides by American soldiers in multiple detention centers in Iraq, Afghanistan, and other nations (11 stories).
>
> President Bush advocated his plan to institute private social security accounts (4 stories).
>
> On the Red Lake Reservation in Minnesota, sixteen-year-old Jeffrey Weise shot and killed nine people (including seven at his high school) and then committed suicide (3 stories).
>
> In Santa Barbara County, a court case unfolded against Michael Jackson, on trial for seducing and molesting a young boy (3 stories).
>
> Forty U.S. servicemen and -women were killed in various incidents in Afghanistan and Iraq, raising the total number of U.S. troops killed in these conflicts to 1,698 (2 stories).
>
> The U.S. Supreme Court ruled that the application of the death penalty for juveniles under age eighteen is unconstitutional (1 story).
>
> In the Dominican Republic, 133 inmates were killed in a prison fire (1 story).
>
> More than 200 people died in floods in Afghanistan (0 stories).
>
> In Angola, the death toll from the recent outbreak of the Ebola-like Marburg virus reached 127 (0 stories).
>
> Pentagon officials admitted to holding "ghost detainees"—enemy combatants detained without any record—at Abu Ghraib, including several women and juveniles as young as age eleven (0 stories).
>
> In Pakistan, five of the men accused of gang-raping a woman on the orders of the local tribal council (in retaliation for an alleged romantic relationship the woman's thirteen-year-old brother had with a woman from another clan) were acquitted (0 stories).
>
> U.S. chess champion and fugitive Bobby Fischer was granted Icelandic citizenship (0 stories).
>
> The United Nations released a report concluding that malnutrition rates in Iraqi children had nearly doubled since U.S. troops entered the country (0 stories).
>
> Fifteen South Darfur officials were arrested, constituting the first arrests on charges of ongoing war crimes in the region (0 stories).
>
> Ukrainian officials revealed that eighteen nuclear-capable missiles had been smuggled into Iran and China by Ukrainian arms dealers between

1999 and 2001; the current location of the missiles is still unknown (0 stories).

The U.S. Senate rejected two proposals (one sponsored by a Democrat, the other by a Republican) to raise the minimum wage (0 stories).

The point here is not that the issue of medical directives does not warrant attention, but rather that the news-generation process is in many ways a news-*selection* process through which a small number of events/issues are selected for attention while a much, much larger number are ignored. Given the scarcity of media agenda space relative to the daily onslaught of new information, journalists must act as gatekeepers, filtering information into each day's news (Gandy 1982; Lewin 1947, 1951; Shoemaker and Vos 2008, 2009; White 1950).

Considering agenda setting as a zero-sum game in this way—where every news story given to one issue is one less story available for all other issues—is a simplification of a complicated process, but the approach is theoretically and operationally appropriate (Zhu 1992). As the alarm/patrol hybrid model explains, attention scarcity does not itself produce aggregate skew in media attention across issues (see chapter 7). In theory, scarce attention can be distributed evenly (or normally) across issues by rotating those issues through the agenda. But in practice, limited agenda space makes a more even distribution very difficult, thereby exacerbating the skew (and explosiveness) produced in the news.

It is within this zero-sum perspective that momentum helps explain the ebb and flow of the seemingly paradoxical U.S. media system—a system capable of maintaining public interest in the complex "Obamacare" health care debate for months on end in 2009 and 2010, while often ignoring important policy issues to devote stories instead to items like the "balloon boy" hoax of 2009 (McDonald 2009). Consider, for example, the October 2011 release of a report confirming earlier findings of global warming, which had been the subject of heated criticism during the 2009 "Climategate" discussion. Jon Stewart's *Daily Show* tracked media coverage following the release of this report, with Stewart saying: "Climategate was a huge news story. I bet debunking Climategate is gonna be huger."[12] Yet cable news paid a total of twenty-four seconds to the report, while giving considerable airtime (instead) to the re-release of McDonald's McRib sandwich. At face value, decisions like these—about what is news and what isn't—often don't make a lot of sense. But we can understand them better by examining the bigger picture of how institutional forces operate via a system of momentum to shape the news. These forces include institutional incentives to track policymaker activity (e.g., Obamacare); news values that put a premium on conflict and scandal (e.g., Climategate), but not on scientific reports per se; and media marketplace incentives to mimic coverage of current hot items (e.g., balloon boy, McRib).

An Overview of the Alarm/Patrol Hybrid Model

The alarm/patrol hybrid model describes how the news-generation process is shaped by events as well as institutional incentives, which together push the media to engage alternately in alarm *and* patrol modes of reporting. These fluctuating modes yield systemic skew and explosiveness in the news. Specifically, I categorize the forces that drive the news into eight key variables, including events and a range of institutional incentives (e.g., policymaker attention, public concern). Overarching these variables is the all-consuming phenomenon of dynamics—specifically, momentum. I describe these variables in chapter 2 and outline the alarm/patrol hybrid model in chapter 3.

In (overly) broad terms, we can think of news coverage of an event/issue as falling into one of four categories: alarm mode, with the media rushing to cover a breaking event; patrol mode, with the media surveying the policy or geographical neighborhood surrounding an event; periods when neither mode is fully engaged (for many low-level or one-off news items); or alarm/patrol mode, when an initial alarm mode transitions directly into patrol mode (or vice versa). Usually, a given news outlet operates in alarm mode for some storylines while simultaneously operating in patrol mode for others. It is an oversimplification to categorize the news-generation process in this way. Yet this categorization finds theoretical purchase for our understanding of the news-generation process, allowing us to see how the alternation between aggregate modes of reporting produces aggregate patterns of skew and explosiveness.

Each of the four main modes in the alarm/patrol hybrid model produces a different pattern of media attention. However, this book focuses on those cases when conditions align so that the two main modes operate in quick succession (i.e., the alarm/patrol mode). In a generic version of this process, news outlets respond (selectively, based on news values and other institutional incentives) to an alarm triggered in politics or so-

ciety (by events or other new information). But after dispatching journalistic resources to attend to the selected alarms, the media's incentives
drive it into patrol mode. Often, the result is a sustained media explosion
of particular political significance.

The eight variables described in this book shape news coverage generally, and also help determine these varying modes of news generation. For instance, news outlets have incentives to attend to those issues
to which the president and Congress (and other policymakers) attend.
These incentives drive the media to track with policymaker attention
generally, and help fuel media explosions in particular. When policymakers are locked in a heated policy debate, for instance, the media will
often respond to this "alarm." As news outlets start to fixate on the policy debate, policymakers may seek to capitalize on the attention by offering additional press conferences, interviews, and informational subsidies, in turn eliciting more media attention still. By contrast, when the
media is in patrol mode, continued elite access serves to keep it there, inhibiting a shift in attention away from the issue at hand.

Momentum propels individual news outlets and the media as a whole
to lurch between modes of news generation, alternating between periods of dramatic agenda overhaul and periods of fixation. When in alarm
mode, media attention dispatches abruptly to the policy/geographic
neighborhood of concern. But once resources are focused on that neighborhood, the resulting patrol mode produces a (brief) period of equilibrium during which the news stays locked on that area. Media attention
thus moves in explosive fits and starts, fluctuating between rapt attention
and rapid change. In other words, media attention is explosive.

Fueled by this explosiveness, the fluctuating alarm and patrol modes
combine to produce high degrees of skew in attention across issues, such
that a few issues get a dominant amount of attention—indeed, arguably a disproportionate amount of attention—while most issues receive
barely any. Under the alarm/patrol hybrid model, both the alarm and patrol modes contribute to systemic skew. Alarm mode contributes to this
skew because news values play a strong role in selecting which alarms to
respond to. In patrol mode, journalists must seek out additional angles
for ongoing stories and are also more likely to notice—and pay attention
to—issues directly in front of them (again, with regard to policy or geographic proximity). Thus, we might think of patrol mode as enhancing
the representation of issues in the news, thereby minimizing the skew.
However, because these patrol resources are often dispatched in the first

place to a specific policy/geographic neighborhood, patrol mode tends to unearth a wider diversity of issues only *within* that neighborhood, meaning the neighborhood's issues get "over"-represented in the news.

For example, presidential elections serve as (anticipated) alarms, and news outlets accordingly shift into patrol mode by dispatching resources and attention to the primary race(s) as soon as each election year begins, producing a timed media explosion. Thus, in general, election coverage is highly skewed around the key issues of the election—and of course the horse-race coverage of the election itself. But then, within each election period, news outlets can also go into additional alarm modes in response to key developments in the campaigns, such as a scandal (e.g., Kerry's Swift Boat incident in 2004) or a candidate's focus on a controversial policy perspective (e.g., Republican Congressman Todd Akin's comment about "legitimate rape" in 2012). This alarm coverage can then transition into more narrowed patrol coverage of the surrounding policy (or scandal) neighborhoods. Once on patrol mode in these very specific neighborhoods (e.g., reproductive rights), journalists can uncover a range of important items, producing a diverse distribution of attention across considerations within that neighborhood—but only at the expense of other neighborhoods.

Empirical Evidence

The alarm/patrol hybrid model predicts aggregate patterns of skew and explosiveness that can be verified empirically. This general model maps onto specific variables representing the forces that drive different modes of news generation. Together, variables like policymaker attention, the degree of public concern, and the level of congestion on the media agenda allow us to estimate conceptually (and model statistically!) how much news coverage a given issue is likely to receive in a specific time period. Moreover, these variables drive the give-and-take between alarm and patrol modes of news generation, producing aggregate patterns of skew and explosiveness. Thus, the alarm/patrol hybrid model yields three core hypotheses.

> Hypothesis 1: The amount of attention a policy topic receives at a given point
> in time is influenced by six key variables: *events*, *prior attention*, *policy-*
> *maker attention*, *public concern*, *diversity of discussion*, and *agenda con-*

gestion. Two other variables also matter, but I do not test their effects: *institutional setup* and *context*.

Hypothesis 2: News coverage is highly skewed across policy areas.

Hypothesis 3: The media agenda changes explosively over time—that is, it moves in "fits and starts" between very low levels of incremental change and short-lived, but very strong, bursts of change.

Several different sources were used to test these expectations. Chief among these is an original dataset comprised of all *New York Times* front-page stories—every single one—between 1996 and 2006 (over 31,000 stories in all). Each story in this dataset is coded according to the primary issue being discussed (e.g., prescription drugs, immigration, war, sports, weather) using the Policy Agendas Project Topics coding scheme (Baumgartner and Jones 2006). As such, this dataset offers an unprecedented opportunity to examine a major media agenda in its entirety. Using statistical analyses as well as a multitude of descriptive examples, we can understand and predict aggregate patterns of media attention.

An analysis of the *Times* front-page dataset offers strong support for the hypotheses outlined above. Simple graphs presented in chapter 4 provide a clear view of what the front-page agenda looks like and also shows the first suggestive evidence that, in the big picture, the front-page agenda is patterned by skew and explosiveness. While a few issues receive the vast majority of coverage, most receive hardly any attention. And looking over time, the front-page agenda does in fact tend to change hardly at all or all at once.

The idea that we can explain much of the variance in front-page news as a function of key variables (hypothesis 1) is tested in two chapters. Chapter 5 presents a statistical model predicting monthly front-page attention from 1996 to 2006 across all major policy topics, such as health care, education, and foreign trade. Using pooled cross-sectional time series analysis, this model is estimated in three forms: (1) across all policy topics; (2) across domestic policy topics only; and (3) across foreign policy topics only. Each model predicts the total number of front-page *Times* stories each policy topic receives each month as a function of five explanatory variables that are measurable in the case of all policy topics over time (excluding events from the list of variables in hypothesis 1): *prior attention*, *policymaker attention*, *public concern*, *diversity of discussion*, and *agenda congestion*. The results of these models are presented in graph form to depict intuitively how these results translate into real front-page stories. All three models support my theory. Interestingly, the effects in the case of front-page coverage of international topics are two to three times the size of the effects in the case of domestic topics.

Chapter 6 demonstrates the ability to explain variance in news coverage in the specific contexts of two important policy issues: the U.S.-led military conflicts in Afghanistan and Iraq (a.k.a. the "war on terror") and capital punishment. This war and the death penalty represent very different kinds of policy debates. Yet the alarm/patrol hybrid model helps explain the rise and fall of both issues in the news over time. Two statistical models—one for the war, one for the death penalty—explain the amount of news coverage the given issue receives at each time point as a function of the same five explanatory variables used in chapter 5, while also accounting for a sixth and very important variable: *events*. For the war, I use a dataset collected with Rebecca Glazier comprised of more than 3,000 randomly sampled *New York Times* and *Wall Street Journal* stories about the war, 2001–2006. For the death penalty, I use a dataset collected with Frank Baumgartner and Suzanna Linn (De Boef) comprised of all full-paper *Times* stories on capital punishment, 1960–2006 (nearly 4,000 stories in all). Time series analysis reveals strong support for both models, further supporting hypothesis 1. Among other findings, the results highlight the effect that *diversity of discussion* about an issue—measured as the diversity of the frames used in the news—has on the attention the issue receives. *How* an issue gets talked about directly affects *how much* it gets talked about.

Chapter 7 demonstrates skew (hypothesis 2) and explosiveness (hypothesis 3) in the news. The skew we see in the news is due in part to the issues' varying degrees of political and social importance. But skew of this degree—much stronger, for example, than that found in many other institutional agendas—is also the result of the give-and-take between the dual forces that structure the alarm/patrol hybrid model: negative feedback (which mutes change) and, especially, positive feedback (which fuels change). Positive feedback is a *necessary* condition for agenda skew of the degree we see in the news. This fact is demonstrated in a basic formal model representing the news-selection process. Running this model through computer simulations produces three alternate scenarios of reality—one in which events alone drive the news; one in which the news is driven by events and negative feedback forces (e.g., capturing an uneven distribution of perceived issue importance); and one in which the news is driven by events, negative feedback, and also positive feedback forces (e.g., capturing journalist and policymaker incentives to give more attention to issues already in the news). Comparing the results from each scenario against the skewed attention actually found in front-page news reveals not just that positive feedback produces skew, but that the type of skew we observe can *only* be produced by positive feedback. Positive feedback, in other words, is one linchpin of the news-generation process.

The generalizability of skew and explosiveness across media types can be tested using an original, enormous dataset of news coverage across newspaper, television, and online news outlets (nearly two million stories total). Findings in chapter 8 show that other media types likewise show strong patterns of skew (hypothesis 2) and explosive change (hypothesis 3). Moreover, online news exhibits even stronger skew and explosiveness than do newspapers—exactly as we should expect, given the heightened marketplace competition and scarcer resources of online news outlets and how the interactive consumer selection of online news exacerbates these patterns.

The analytic approach taken throughout this book—and the systemic patterns in news coverage that I find—in no way minimizes the challenge or importance of the newsroom or, for that matter, the role of events. Events certainly matter in shaping the news. So do the judgment calls that journalists and editors make each hour of the day; most people could not do these jobs well. The art of news judgment—evaluating how newsworthy a story is—is a rare skill, as is crafting each story, usually under deadline pressures and with minimal staff and financial resources. Yet institutional forces matter, too. The integrated perspective offered in this book suggests a deeper understanding of how microlevel decisions can produce (unintended) emergent patterns of political and social significance.

Implications

The alarm/patrol hybrid model of news generation has important implications for academia, the political system, citizens, and policymakers. For academia, this book shows how the different theoretical frameworks of understanding news generation are each needed, but are not additively sufficient. The alarm/patrol hybrid model represents a more complete understanding of the media and how it works that is more than the sum of the past literature parts.

For the political system as a whole, the alarm/patrol hybrid model holds both positive and negative implications. On the bright side, this model reinvigorates our notion of the media functioning, at least sometimes, as a surveillance mechanism. This notion in turn reinforces some of our normative notions of the role of the press in a democracy. The idea—of the media serving as a watchdog mechanism acting on behalf of society's best interests has largely been cast aside as romantic myth. Woodward and Bernstein–style journalism (that broke the Watergate scandal in 1972) is, it seems, a quintessential but also endangered ideal. Yet this book shows how, in fact, the media frequently goes into surveillance (i.e., patrol) mode surrounding those hot news items on which news outlets have incentives to fixate. Paradoxically, however, such periods of surveillance exacerbate skew and explosiveness in the news by "over"-representing policy issues in the policy/geographic neighborhoods to which the media dispatches patrols. Thus, for every issue brought to light through media surveillance of specific areas, many more policy problems continue unnoticed outside the reach of these fleeting surveillance spotlights. Still, some issues *are* brought to light, including policy problems that might go unnoticed but for the fact that they are in the right neighborhood at the right time. And for these issues unearthed through alarm/patrol coverage, the resulting sustained media explosion can draw a critical mass of attention beyond that which would be produced if the news-generation process operated exclusively as a patrol-only or an alarm-only system.

For citizens, one troubling implication is the type of information "diet" this system of news generation produces. The systemically skewed nature of news coverage—often out of whack with the underlying severity of problems—suggests that citizens see a much narrower, more myopic view of the world's policy problems than exists in reality. Similarly, the explosive nature of news coverage means that citizens are cued to consider these policy problems at a frenzied rate, lurching attention to new hot issues usually before being able to consider the "old" ones in any depth. These patterns that shape the information citizens receive from the news are endemic to the media as an institution, yet they have become increasingly stark in the context of the twenty-four-hour news cycle provided by online news sources (see chapter 8 for a discussion of the shifting media landscape and what it means for newspapers in particular). Citizens can counteract these disproportionate signals by proactively consuming news from diverse sources, including traditional newspapers in particular, but such consumption patterns do not come easy for people with busy lives; it is simply easier to get the news via quick online news flashes rather than paper or online versions of in-depth news stories (Johnson 2012).

For policymakers, the systemically disproportionate nature of news coverage holds stark implications for efforts to respond to policy problems in meaningful ways. The skewed nature of the news means that media (and thus largely public) attention is likely to pass over many deserving but low-news-value policy issues that policymakers may want to address. And systemic media explosiveness means that those hot issues in the news—that policymakers are often compelled to address—are likely to have been kicked off the agenda before a full and conscientious policy response can be developed, much less implemented. Although we know that the president, members of Congress, and other policymakers give sustained attention to many policy issues whether or not the issues are in the news, the fact that media attention is systemically disproportionate means that any proportionate response the government makes to policy problems occurs against the grain of media attention. That said, the same forces that limit policymakers' abilities to be deliberate and conscientious in their work also limit their abilities to manipulate the media. Studies have shown that presidents and other elites can wield considerable power over the media for key periods of time, such as following the September 11, 2001, attacks and lasting through the beginning of U.S. military operations in Iraq in 2003 (Bennett, Lawrence, and Livingston 2007). Yet the inherently explosive nature of the media agenda acts as an antidote against efforts to control the news indefinitely. Because media explosions are endemic to the news, and because these explosions often coincide with key shifts in how an issue is defined and understood, most elites who attempt to govern the news will eventually see it spin out of control. As *New York Times* reporter Sarah Cohen notes, "If you wanted to push an agenda through this process, it'd be pretty damn hard."[13]

CHAPTER TWO

The Forces That Drive the News

Media attention matters, this much we know. News coverage frequently shapes which issues people think about, how they think about them, and often what actions government takes (Baumgartner and Jones 2009; Iyengar and Kinder 1987; McCombs, Shaw, and Weaver 1997). Yet we know very little about how issues become news in the first place. Since the news affects us—all of us—the process by which it is produced deserves our attention.

This chapter examines the factors that drive the news-generation process and, in turn, the content and dynamics of the news itself. The process of making the news is messy and complex, with many moving parts. Although we cannot account for the multitude of factors that determine the news on any given day, we can point to systemic forces that affect how news outlets and the people who run them behave. Past approaches have contributed a great deal to our understanding of the individual forces (i.e., variables) that shape the news. I integrate these past approaches through an overarching discussion about momentum, developing what I term the alarm/patrol hybrid model of news generation. This model (see the next chapter) explains how the variables discussed here combine through momentum to produce aggregate patterns of skew and explosiveness in the news.

Like other institutions, the media is shaped by specific incentives that derive from its formal rules and informal norms of operation. Against this institutional backdrop, three (overlapping) scholarly frameworks can help us understand the news-generation process. First, the "organizational process" approach focuses on how journalists and editors respond to professional incentives by using specific mechanisms, such as news judgment and elite indexing, in order to sort through each day's inflow of events and generate that day's news. This organizational process approach encompasses a wide range of variables: from how different types of events have different news values, to news outlets' incentives to stay attuned to the public's concerns, to the importance of issue-framing in making the news. This approach, detailed below, thus provides a useful and intuitive understanding of the news-generation process from the journalistic perspective. Second, the "marketplace" approach explains how competition-based incentives dramatically shape newsroom operations and, thus, the stories that make the news. In particular, these marketplace incentives drive news outlets to distribute their scarce resources in such a way, and to mimic the behavior of other news outlets in such a way, that media coverage is strongly driven by path dependency. To these perspectives, I add a third approach from the policy agendas literature: the framework of "disproportionate information processing," which describes how scarce agenda space and self-reinforcing mechanisms of negative feedback and positive feedback lead institutions to process information disproportionately, "under"- and "over"-reacting to events and other information.

Throughout this chapter, I connect these overlapping approaches through a unifying discussion of dynamics. Particularly within the marketplace and disproportionate information processing approaches, we see the stark ways in which momentum shapes the news-generation process. Past work has provided a good foundation for understanding the interplay between the three perspectives.[1] My contribution is to flesh out this interplay and put it in motion, pulling forward the significance of momentum. The result is a sharper understanding of the news-generation process. The chapter ends with the first of three explicit hypotheses to be tested in this book. We can explain much of the variance in the news as a function of the key variables discussed in this chapter. The effects of these variables (collectively, hypothesis 1) will be tested in chapters 5 and 6.

I rely on two types of sources for the discussion presented in this chapter. First, the theoretical story of the news-generation process is based on the three main scholarly approaches described above. Second, these theoretical arguments are grounded through excerpts from personal interviews with ten journalists—five at the *New York Times* and five at the *Washington Post*—offering insight into how these theories map on to practice. While social scientists and journalists perceive the news-generation process from very different perspectives and use very different terms, these dual perspectives align to a surprising (and compelling) degree. The chapter thus illustrates how general phenomena that scholars have identified as being important at the institutional level play out in the day-to-day workings of the newsroom.[2] At the same time, microlevel operations of the newsroom are, as *Times* reporter Mark Leibovich says, "very much an organic process."[3] Both perspectives contribute to understanding the news-generation process as, in former *Times* executive editor Bill Keller's words, "part art, part science, with a little bit of serendipity" (2006).

The Media as an Institution

All of the discussion in this book is based on the premise of the media as an institution. In his pivotal book, *Governing with the News*, Tim Cook reminds us that institutions are constituted by systematic "rules and procedures" that endure and evolve over time and extend across the sphere in question (1998, 71). Since the media conducts its work based on systematic rules and procedures that have endured and evolved over time and that span across news outlets, the diverse array of news outlets that comprise "the" media constitute an institution (Cook 1998).

Media scholars do not always agree on exactly what role the media institution serves in the political system, and, certainly, the role varies according to the political system. In the case of the United States, Douglass Cater—the first scholar to advocate formally for considering the media as an institution—describes the media's institutional role as an integral part of the checks-and-balances system. For better or for worse, Cater says, the reporter "helps to shape the course of government. . . . At his worst, operating with arbitrary and faulty standards, he can be an agent of disorder and confusion. At his best, he can exert a creative influence on Washington Politics" (1959, 7). Bartholomew Sparrow counters that the media "are not a 'fourth branch' in the sense of being part of the government itself . . . instead, it may be that the news media constitute a 'fourth corner' in the 'iron triangle' model of the policy process" (Sparrow 1998, 133).[4] Whatever the geometric shape, the literature is clear on this point: the media *is* an institution (Cater 1959; Cook 1998; Sparrow 2006; Zaller 1998).

Any study of the news-generation process must therefore be grounded in an understanding of the media's institutional characteristics. Specifically, we can conceptualize the news-generation process as being shaped by key institutional variables that derive from our understanding of the media's organizational process, marketplace competition, and disproportionate information processing. I hone in on eight variables—or, rather, eight categories of variables—that shape newsroom decisions and, thus, the likely amount of news coverage that a given issue will receive at a given point in time.

Eight Variables that Drive Issue Coverage in the News

1. *Institutional setup*: The rules and norms that govern the given media system.
2. *Events*: The characteristics of current real-world events relevant to the issue.
3. *Policymaker attention*: How much attention policymakers (e.g., politicians, lobbyists) are giving the issue.
4. *Public concern*: How concerned the public is about the issue.
5. *Diversity of discussion*: How concentrated or diffuse media discussion of the issue is across the component dimensions of that issue.
6. *Agenda congestion*: How consumed the media agenda as a whole is with "mega storylines" and, thus, how accessible it is to other issues.
7. *Context*—political, economic, and social: For example, how soon the next national election is, whether the country is at war, the state of the economy, the state of political movements and social mores.
8. *Prior attention*: How much attention the given issue has received lately.

In one way or another, each of these variables can be thought of as a manifestation of institutional incentives. For example, professional and marketplace incentives drive the media to focus in on mega storylines like the Enron financial collapse or Hurricane Katrina. These incentives thus make *agenda congestion* a variable that helps explain news coverage to a given issue.

We can think of these variables as operating simultaneously, on a day-to-day basis, on two levels. At the newsroom, or "micro" level, these pressures shape the news judgments of editors and journalists. At the system, or "macro" level, these *same* pressures affect how the media system as a whole functions. The parallel micro/macro perspectives are, of course, strongly intertwined. For example, the institutional incentive to cover the workings of the White House (captured by the more encompassing *policymaker attention* variable) shapes journalists' day-to-day decisions about which stories to pursue and run. This same incentive influences newsroom decisions about how to distribute news beats.

The macro/micro distinction drawn here is thus not about temporal aggregation, but rather about distinguishing between, on the one hand, the structure of the media as an institution (i.e., formal and informal incentives and constraints) and, on the other hand, the individual agency of journalists and editors who operate within this larger system of incentives and constraints. The daily "output" of the news looks sporadic at both levels: individual newsroom decisions as well as the news produced by the media as a whole. The systemic forces that operate at both levels are what combine to produce aggregate temporal patterns in the news.

Institutional Setup

The first variable to consider is the *institutional setup* of a media system—that is, the media's institutional rules (formal powers and constraints) and norms (informal powers and constraints). From the White House to the Federal Reserve to the local department of motor vehicles (DMV), institutions vary considerably in their institutional setups, and this variance plays out in the behaviors each exhibits (e.g., Shepsle 1979; Shepsle and Weingast 1981, 1987). The media is no exception; the formal powers (i.e., binding rules and laws) and informal powers (i.e., norms) it has to do certain things and the constraints that restrict it from doing other things combine to govern its operations (Cook 1998). Specifically, these powers and constraints form many of the incentives, or "rules of the game," that shape how journalists, editors, and news outlets behave. As Hallin and Mancini have shown, variance in institutional setup across time and even across different types of media within a single system can lead to very different news-generation processes (2004).[5]

The modern U.S. mainstream media, for its part, is characterized by broad formal and informal powers, relatively few formal constraints, but a complex array of informal constraints. For example, the First Amendment and Freedom of Information Act endow the media with formal powers of free speech and access to key governmental information. The media is also formally constrained by such forces as libel laws and Federal Communications Commission (FCC) regulations on decency, and of course by its lack of any of the formal powers to initiate, interpret, or execute policy change possessed by the traditional three branches of government. As *Washington Post* reporter Anne Kornblut puts it, "We don't have subpoena power. . . . We don't actually run the government. . . . We just get to talk and ask questions."[6] Other institutional factors that shape the U.S. media are informal, but with incentives and consequences that are nonetheless real, such as the need to maintain readership/viewership. Every aspect of the media's institutional setup has some degree of influence over the news-generation process: from constitutional provisions, to chain-of-command etiquette between reporters and editors, to the physical configuration of desks in the newsroom.

This last item is a good illustration of how even small aspects of institutional setup can matter. Traditionally, newsrooms are arranged with reporters stationed at desks in a large, open-area newsroom, with editors housed in offices with glass walls. Consider that if journalists and editors worked in individual offices with a closed-door culture, we might see fewer investigative stories based on journalist collaborations; fewer interrelated stories in each day's news; and perhaps less journalist "productivity" altogether in the form of new story initiatives driven by both collaboration and competition. Indeed, Woodward and Bernstein explicitly reference observing each other work (in the open floor plan of the *Post* newsroom) as the beginning of their collaboration on Watergate (1994). Or think of the potential osmosis effects at work in the modern newsroom, where reporters, graphic artists, and website managers work just desks away from each other. Even a seemingly innocuous rearrangement of a newsroom, shifting the international desks farther to the newsroom's periphery, for example, can affect the social and coffee-migratory patterns of journalists. These small daily routines can influence which items catch journalists' attention and, ultimately, which issues make the news.[7]

At a larger level, consider the effects that a newsroom's editorial leadership and professional norms can have on the news-generation process (Iyengar and McGrady 2007). Most major news outlets have undergone the transformations and vagaries of different leadership epochs and generational shifts over time (Diamond 1993). For example, the executive editorial shift at the *Washington Post* from Leonard Downie Jr. to Marcus Brauchli in 2008 influenced the *Post*'s trajectory and, in turn, the likelihood of an issue making it into the news on a given day, contingent on events. *Washington Post* news editor Vince Bzdek describes one change in particular that he "can pinpoint to the arrival of our new editor." Brauchli, he says, has "really pushed writers to write in a different

way, write page one stories that are more analytical and forward looking." Brauchli introduced the buzzword of "predictive analysis," meaning an emphasis not just on what has happened with an issue already,
"but on where this issue is going." The result of Brauchli's entrance was
a shift in front-page *Post* stories to involve "a lot more blending of analysis and reporting."[8] We can imagine that this shift may have translated
into subtle shifts in the content of the front page, with a higher prevalence of stories geared toward economic and political forecasting. Such
a shift holds potential implications for the effects of news coverage on
news consumers, given the differential effects that thematic-framed stories (focused on broader patterns) and episodic-framed stories (focused
on individual incidents) can have on citizens (Gross 2008; Iyengar 1991).

In short, the media's institutional setup is a complex variable (or category of variables) that is difficult to measure systematically. I do not
tackle this variable in the empirical analyses (chapters 5 and 6), leaving
this task for future work. Nevertheless, elements of institutional setup,
both big and small, are critical to our general understanding of the news-
generation process (Iyengar and McGrady 2007).

The Organizational Process Approach

It is within this institutional context that journalists must sift through
the relentless flood of each day's events and information to generate each
day's news. The "organizational process" approach within communication studies describes the forces that shape how journalists and editors
conduct this process (Gans 2004; Molotch and Lester 1974). The organizational process approach begins with the simple but powerful fact
of attention scarcity. Attention scarcity produces journalistic gatekeeping, or "the process by which countless messages are reduced to the few
we are offered" in the daily news (Gandy 1982; Lewin 1947, 1951; Shoemaker and Vos 2008, 2009; White 1950).[9] Journalists and editors handle
their gatekeeping responsibilities by relying on professionally ingrained
instincts (Berkowitz 1990). These instincts comprise "news judgment,"
which is the "faculty of determining what is a story, what's an interesting
story, what's new and different and what's been said before."[10] In general,
an event—and the story that might capture it—has a high news value, or
newsworthiness, if it maps onto the media's incentives (many of which
will be described in more detail below). For example, stories have higher

news values if they involve events that are interesting and relevant to readers/viewers, since news outlets have professional incentives to serve their audiences and marketplace incentives to maintain this consumership. Likewise, because news outlets have strong incentives to cover the perspectives of policymakers and other elites, events and related news stories about presidential or congressional activity will tend to have high news values (Galtung and Ruge 1965).

In many cases, the news judgment to follow a story—or a "storyline," a string of stories surrounding an evolving news item—is an obvious one. For example, in the month of May 2004, exactly one-quarter of the *New York Times*' front-page agenda (56 of 224 articles) focused on the allegations of detainee abuse by U.S. soldiers at Abu Ghraib. Likewise, exactly one-quarter of the front-page agenda of June 26 and June 27, 2009 (3 of 12 articles) were about Michael Jackson's death on June 25. The sensational nature of these storylines made questions about running these stories all but moot.

Most of the time, though, news judgment is more nuanced. As much craft as skill, news judgment is difficult to define (even for those who have it) and harder still to measure. In a fuller version of the quotation used above, Keller (2006) describes the process this way: "There is no rigid formula to the selection of stories and photographs for the front page. We—an argumentative group of editors—try every day to assemble a selection of articles that are important and interesting, but many variables influence the outcome. . . . It's part science, part art, with a little serendipity."

When asked to break news judgment into its key components, however, journalists and editors can identify core variables that map strongly onto previous academic findings about the news-generation process: namely, the eight variables discussed throughout this chapter. Six of these eight variables derive from the organizational process perspective. While no list of variables could forecast the news, these variables represent clear pathways for favoring certain story characteristics (and their underlying policy issues) under certain conditions. They also speak to the role of momentum. I embed these variables in four sections of discussion that follow: What's the story (*events*)? What other attention is it getting (*policymaker attention* and *public concern*)? What are the angles of the story (*diversity of discussion*)? And what else is going on (*agenda congestion* and *context*)? Some of these variables will be reiterated when we turn to considering the media from a perspective of marketplace competition and then, again, when we account for disproportionate information processing.

What's the Story? Events

The most immediate force affecting the newsworthiness of a story is the nature of the real-world *events* at hand.[11] Because all news stories contain event information, all news is event-driven news in some form. And with the increasing role of technology in journalism, real-time events are playing an increasing role in driving the news (Livingston and Bennett 2003). Studies consistently show the strong role that events play in shaping the media agenda (Dearing and Rogers 1996; Kingdon 1993, 1995; McCombs 2004). Major events, especially sudden and harmful "focusing" events, can send news outlets into a frenzy, sometimes upending the political landscape in the process (Birkland 1998; Livingston 1997). The way in which events drive the news depends, of course, on the type of event. But beneath every news story, big and small, is an event of some kind. "Society's problems," Lawrence writes, "are often identified and defined against a backdrop of single, concrete events" (2001, 92). Asked what a statesman fears the most, Harold MacMillan (Britain's prime minister, 1957–63) is reported to have said "events, dear boy, events" (Rhodes 2007; Spencer 2002).

EVENTS AS A NECESSARY BUT INSUFFICIENT CONDITION FOR NEWS COVERAGE.   The news is far from a perfect mirror of reality (Grusin and Utt 2005; Parenti 1986; Patterson 1994). Simple counterfactuals demonstrate this point. Consider the problem of homicides compared to media attention of homicides. If the media simply reflects real-world events, the number of stories printed about murders should correlate highly with the number of murders that occur. As more homicide events occur, more news stories about homicides should be printed. As homicides decrease, reports of homicides should fade from the media agenda. But such correlation is not always (or even usually) the case, as we can see by comparing the homicide rate in a city with the amount of news coverage of homicides in that city's newspaper. For example, in Portland (Oregon) and Seattle, the yearly correlation between murders and number of newspaper stories on murders is strong (0.73 and 0.60, respectively), but in St. Louis, San Diego, and San Francisco, the correlations are negative (−0.29, −0.22, and −0.23, respectively).[12] We can repeat this exercise with any measurable real-world events—high school dropout rates, rates of illegal immigration, endangered species, carbon emissions, and so on. In most cases, we are likely to find the same result: a generally low correlation between the frequency of events (as one way of measuring the severity of a policy problem) and the amount of news coverage reporting on those events.

Thus, while events can have a profound effect on news coverage, most events most of the time receive news coverage out of proportion with their "objective importance," either receiving less or more coverage than might be warranted, relative to larger trends. In thinking of examples of disproportionately high news coverage, we might include the dispute over the young Cuban boy Elian Gonzalez in 2000, the kidnapping of Elizabeth Smart in 2002, and the arrest of Senator Larry Craig for alleged lewd conduct in a men's bathroom in 2007. Each of these events was important, but received more attention than similar events in different circumstances or involving a different type of actor would likely receive. At the other end of this spectrum are events that receive a scarcity of attention in comparison with their significance, by any quantifiable standards. Examples include instances of human trafficking in China (one story on the *Times* front page between 1996 and 2006); female genital mutilation in Africa and the Middle East (zero front-page stories); humanitarian violations in the Sudan (twenty-one front-page stories); and domestic abuse cases in the United States (one front-page story). In fact, of the 31,034 stories appearing on the *Times* front page between 1996 and 2006, barely 1% (348) focused on human rights concerns around the globe. While every news story reflects a real-world event, events are not enough to warrant news. Scarce agenda space means that an event is a *necessary* but *insufficient* criterion for news coverage, especially on the front page.

THE VARYING NEWSWORTHINESS OF EVENTS.   Thus, in addition to the "objective" severity of an event, other characteristics of the event often matter just as much, if not more so, in determining the likelihood that it will make the news. The determination of event newsworthiness is a complicated formula, well beyond the scope of this study. Still, the nuances of this concept are important to keep in mind. A wide range of studies, including seminal descriptions by Galtung and Ruge (1965), Gans (2004), and Iyengar and McGrady (2007), point to several event characteristics that may affect newsworthiness. These often-overlapping characteristics are described below.

The type of event. Events can be categorized in many ways. For example, we can distinguish between routine events that are anticipated, such as elections (Molotch and Lester 1974); triggering events that draw attention to an existing problem such as an increase in attacks on U.S. troops in Iraq, or a scandal such as sexual abuse by Catholic priests (Cobb and Elder 1983; Molotch and Lester 1974; Wien and Elmelund-Præstekær 2009); serendipitous events that are unintended, yet are politically fortuitous occurrences (Molotch and Lester 1974); and key events that "create" a problem that did not previously exist such as a terrorist attack, an accident such as an oil spill, or a natural disaster such as a tsunami (Molotch and Lester 1974; Vasterman 2005). Research points especially to the high news value of a particular type of key event, what Kingdon calls a focusing event (1995). Focusing events are sudden, uncommon, harmful, geographically concentrated, and "known to policy makers and the public simultaneously" (Birkland 1998, 54). As such, focusing events have a special tendency to draw media attention.

When events receive media attention, the policy issues they implicate gain attention, too. This attention can open windows of opportunity for shifts in public and governmental response to the issues (Birkland 1997; Dearing and Rogers 1996; Gamson and Modigliani 1989; Kingdon 1995). Note, however, that the effects media attention wield on governmental policy response strongly depend on how the issue is framed in a given policy venue (Baumgartner and Jones 2009; Birkland and Lawrence 2009; Lawrence 2001). While I do not parse out the varying influences that different types of events (and different ways of framing them) have on the news-generation process, these relationships warrant future research. Indeed, studies on how variation in types of events and frames prompt different media dynamics holds particular promise for advancing our understanding of the mutually reinforcing cycle linking events, news coverage, news consumption, and political effects (Baum and Groeling 2008; Baumgartner, De Boef, and Boydstun 2008; Entman 2003; Lawrence and Birkland 2004).

The policy area related to the event. The newsworthiness of an event is innately tied to the underlying policy area it brings to light (e.g., Galtung and Ruge 1965).[13] Events related to issues of national defense, for example, will likely be perceived, subjectively, as more important or interesting than events related to transportation or environmental issues. For example, Soroka (2002) points to how the news-generation process should vary across three broad types of issues: prominent (e.g., inflation, unemployment), sensational (e.g., AIDS, crime), and governmental (e.g., national debt, taxes).[14] Additionally, valence issues (issues with only one legitimate side of debate, such as child abuse or drug abuse) can prompt especially sudden surges in news coverage, although often yielding fewer concrete policy shifts (Baumgartner and Jones 2009; Nelson 1984). Here, too, the role of issue type in the news-generation process warrants considerable future research.

The level of sensationalism. Related to (but not always in line with) the inherent interest that different policy areas hold, events themselves vary in their levels of intrigue or sensationalism. In his landmark book on the news-generation process in TV and magazine media, Herbert J. Gans downplays the role of sensationalism in the news-generation process. He agrees that major news outlets attempt to enlarge their audiences by "resorting to 'sensationalism' and 'yellow journalism,'" but "only when the economic indicators fall drastically" (2004, 84). Yet while this claim may have been true of the media Gans studied in the 1960s and 1970s, it is certainly less true today. We see the importance of sensationalism in the growing prevalence of soft news (Baum 2002; Bennett 2003; Zaller 2003). Sensationalism is often at the root of "media hypes" giving disproportionate amounts of attention to politicians and members of the Hollywood A-list embroiled in sex scandals, drug abuse charges, or general corruption (Elmelund-Præstekær and Wien 2008; Vasterman 2005). Be it the Bill Clinton and Monica Lewinsky affair, the mysterious death of Anna Nicole Smith and ensuing custody battle, Eliot Spitzer's involvement in an interstate prostitution ring, or "Weiner-gate," some storylines just have that magic buzz. Significantly, this buzz derives not only from human preference for sensational news items, but also from institutional incentives this preference instills. "As in the case of horse race news," Iyengar and McGrady write, stories about "sex and scandal meet both the economic and the professional aspirations of journalists" (2007, 73).

The level of conflict. Speaking of horse-race news, the level of conflict (real or portrayed) in a news item influences how much news coverage it will receive (Iyengar and McGrady 2007). For example, in their study of the page placement of stories about social movements, Rafail, Walker, Tripp, and McCarthy (2008) find that the level of violence displayed in a social movement event—such as whether the event results in physical altercations, property damage, or arrests—significantly affects where in the paper a story about the event is placed. The more violent the event, the closer to the front page the article appears.[15]

The clarity or complexity of the issue concepts at play. The newsworthiness of an event also likely depends on how "easy" or "hard" it is to understand the issue evoked by the event (Alvarez and Brehm 2002). For example, child abuse and other valence issues can be emotionally complex and difficult to understand. Issues like the death penalty or abortion, by contrast, are seen (rightly or wrongly) as more straightforward. Thus, events surrounding these "easy" issues may be more likely to appear in the news (Baumgartner and Jones 2009).

The actors involved. The people involved in an event matter as well. Gans's study (2004) suggests that the vast majority of news stories focus on people with political power and status ("knowns"), whereas only a slim proportion of stories focus on "unknowns." And stories about "knowns" that also involve some kind of scandal are particularly ripe for media attention (Galtung and Ruge 1965; Molotch and Lester 1974). Additionally, the same type of event can often receive different levels (and types) of media attention depending on the race of the people affected. For example, Armstrong, Carpenter, and Hojnacki (2006) show that the media pays significantly less attention to diseases that disproportionately afflict black individuals compared to white individuals. As another example, Valerie Smith discusses how the 1989 "Central Park Jogger" rape received news coverage that dwarfed the other twenty-seven cases of first-degree rape or attempted rape reported in New York that same week, including several cases of rape victims who were women of color that received no media attention at all (1990). These findings of disproportionate racialized news coverage result from a host of complex societal variables, including the tendency of white readers and viewers to gravitate toward stories about white victims. News outlets have financial incentives to produce stories that resonate with this inclination (Min and Feaster 2010).

The population affected. The number of people affected by an event helps to determine how much coverage the event receives. Events that receive strong news coverage are often focusing events that affect a large population, while similar events with less dramatic outcomes tend to receive less coverage.[16] Who is affected matters, too. Downs suggests, for example, that the sudden concern for a latent policy problem that plays

out in the issue-attention cycle is most likely to occur when the population affected is both sympathetic and in the minority (1972). Within
our comfort zone, vulnerable and sympathetic populations in general attract heightened attention (Schneider and Ingram 1993), such as children
killed in mass shootings (e.g., Columbine High School in 1999, the youth
camp members killed on Norway's Utoya Island in 2011, Sandy Hook Elementary School in 2012). When events fall outside the comfort zone of
social norms, however, even vulnerable and sympathetic populations are
less likely to get attention, as tends to be the case with human trafficking, female genital mutilations, or domestic violence; the near-absence of
attention in these cases may also be due to the valenced nature of the issues (Baumgartner and Jones 2009; Schneider and Ingram 1993). And,
just as the main actors involved in a story will tend to receive different
amounts of attention based on race, so too do the demographic attributes of the broader affected population shape media attention (Smith
1990).

The proximity to readers/viewers. Proximity matters, too. Events that
occur outside the United States, for example, are generally less likely to
receive U.S. media coverage—and will likely stay on the agenda for a
much shorter time—than domestic events. While most of this discrepancy in coverage is due simply to the higher accessibility of domestic
news items (Iyengar and McGrady 2007), some part is due also to the
greater significance we all tend to put on events in our own "backyards."
We can bring the importance of proximity into sharper focus by comparing the attention given to three natural disasters in different parts of the
world—the Indian Ocean tsunami in 2004, Hurricane Katrina in 2005,
and the Haiti earthquake in 2010. Approximately 1,600 people from
Louisiana lost their lives in the 2005 hurricane Katrina (Sharkey 2007).
The 2004 tsunami killed an estimated 350,000 people (219 times as many
as Katrina) (Athukorala and Resosudarmo 2005), and the Haiti earthquake killed an estimated 230,000 people (144 times as many as Katrina)
(Bilham 2010). Figure 2.1 shows the number of news stories each of these
three events received in sixteen major U.S. news sources over the forty-
five days following each natural disaster. Recognizing that many factors
distinguished these cases from one another, figure 2.1 shows that while
the Indian Ocean tsunami and Haiti earthquake had death tolls greater
than that of Katrina by factors of hundreds, Katrina news coverage was
significantly higher. Few would say that Katrina did not warrant each
and every news story published about the storm, its aftermath, and its

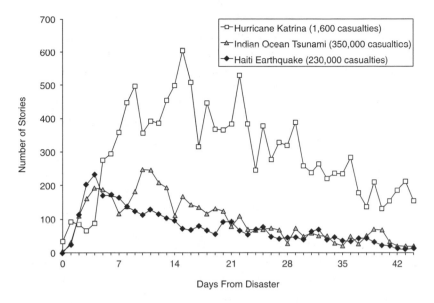

FIGURE 2.1. Different natural disasters, different levels of coverage
Note: This figure shows the number of news stories for each natural disaster for the 45 days following that disaster across 16 major news outlets.
Sources: LexisNexis keyword searches across the *Boston Herald, Chicago Sun-Times, Denver Post, Houston Chronicle, New York Times, Philadelphia Inquirer, San Diego Union-Tribune, San Francisco Chronicle, Wall Street Journal [abstracts], Washington Post,* and six television news outlets (ABC, CBS, CNN, Fox, MSNBC, NBC).

long-term effects—indeed, we might say that not nearly enough attention was paid. Yet the decided contrast between the coverage of these three disasters demonstrates case in point how proximity (both geographical and social) affects perceived newsworthiness.

What Other Attention Is It Getting? Policymaker Attention and Public Concern

While the inherent characteristics of an event matter, the news judgment process is also affected by who else is paying attention to the event and its implied policy issue. We can conceptualize (and measure) this other attention as the amount of *policymaker attention* and the degree of *public concern*. Take the example of people living in a vegetative state. Events surrounding these people and their families' decisions happen every day. We can think of the inherent characteristics of this issue as endowing it with a baseline likelihood of receiving news coverage, which is generally quite low. For issues like this, with low subjective newsworthiness, it often takes a shift in another variable—like the issue gaining traction on the public's radar or, as happened in Terri Schiavo's case, the radar of policymakers—in order for it to make the news.

As suggested by both the policy agendas literature and work stemming from Bennett's indexing theory (1990), the level of *policymaker attention* surrounding an issue tends to affect the amount of coverage the issue will receive. A "policymaker" is any person with an active role in the policy process—be it making policy (e.g., the president, members of Congress, and related staff), influencing policy (e.g., lobbyists), interpreting policy (e.g., judges), or administering policy (e.g., bureaucrats). Institutional incentives lead journalists to base their stories heavily on information they obtain from policymaker sources (Bennett 1990; Gandy 1982; Iyengar and McGrady 2007). These incentives can prompt the media to follow official sources to the detriment of press independence (Bennett, Lawrence, and Livingston 2006, 2007; Livingston and Bennett 2003; Reese 1991)—although other research points to evidence of journalistic discretion wielded within an interdependent system connecting elites, the press, and the public (Althaus 2003; Entman 2003; Reese 1991). More broadly, studies demonstrate how governmental agendas can affect the media agenda (e.g., Berkowitz 1992; Edwards and Wood 1999; Flemming and Wood 1999; Peake and Eshbaugh-Soha 2008). When the president proposes a constitutional amendment banning same-sex marriage, when members of Congress speak out against illegal immigration, or when the Supreme Court accepts a death penalty case, these policy issues have a greater likelihood of becoming news. Policymakers, for their parts, have strong incentives to try to shape the news-generation process, although such control is hard won and easily lost. Of course, the causal arrows run in both directions. Often media attention to a policy problem can pressure policymakers to address that problem; generally speaking, policymakers and news outlets move in tandem as part of mutually reinforcing (i.e., positive feedback) attention cascades (e.g., Edwards and Wood 1999; Entman 2003; Eshbaugh-Soha and Peake 2004; Vliegenthart and Walgrave 2010). But focusing here on the news as a dependent variable, policymaker attention is an important explanatory variable.

Similarly, we can identify *public concern* as bearing influence on the news. Here, too, causality runs in both directions, often in mutually reinforcing ways, with news coverage shaping public awareness of issues under many conditions. In 1963 Cohen wrote: "The press is significantly more than a purveyor of information and opinion. It may not be successful much of the time in telling people what to think, but it is stunningly successful in telling its readers what to think about." This quintessential statement would prove an apt summary of decades of media agenda-setting and priming studies to follow.[17] But, again, in thinking of news coverage as a dependent variable, we can gain theoretical and empirical traction by considering public concern as an explanatory variable.

The public's influence over the media stems primarily from the media's professional and marketplace incentives to provide stories of interest to its consumers. The influence readers have on the content of each day's paper is really "a timing issue," according to Bzdek, a matter of identifying "issues that we think are going to resonate and that seem to be the most important at the moment."[18] Editorial decisions about the content of the newspaper are based on a notion of what will inform the public as well as what will sell papers. Between these twin incentives, public concern sets the stage for which stories are most newsworthy today. As Gans writes, "competition is endemic to the profession" (2004). News sources that do not pay heed to public perception of which issues are most important risk losing readership and advertising dollars to competitors (Hoskins, McFayden, and Finn 2004).

What Are the Angles of the Story? Diversity of Discussion

The newsworthiness of an event also varies according to which—and how many—angles, or dimensions, can be used in defining its underlying policy issue. The effect of issue-definition on news coverage can be conceptualized and operationalized in many forms. Here, I focus on the specific notion that the amount of coverage an issue receives is positively influenced by the diversity of attention previously surrounding that issue. As a measured variable, *diversity of discussion* is relatively new to the political communication literature (Boydstun, Bevan, and Thomas 2013). But the concept dates at least back to Schattschneider, who described how increasing the "scope" of a debate—often achieved by redefining the line of conflict in the debate—draws people in, expanding attention to the debate overall (1960). An expanding debate is an exciting debate. As the diversity of discussion widens, attention increases.

Similarly, Downs (1972) points in particular to the role of framing in propelling the issue-attention cycle. The redefinition of an issue can help keep an issue on the agenda for longer. The sustained media explo-sions predicted by the alarm/patrol hybrid model are directly in line with Downs's description of how cyclical surges in attention can be amplified and extended through framing.[19]

We can think of this relationship at the level of issues (e.g., prescrip-tion drug coverage, water pollution) as the diversity across each issue's component "frames," and also at the level of broader topics (e.g., health care, the environment) as the diversity across each topic's component is-sues. These two levels involve very different mechanisms, regarding both policymaking and political communication. But the property of multi-"dimensionality" applies at both levels (multiple frames, multiple is-sues), as does the draw of diversity. At both levels, the basic idea is nu-anced but intuitive: the more angles of an issue/topic are at play in its debate, the more interesting the issue/topic becomes and the more atten-tion it attracts.[20] Simultaneously, the more attention the issue/topic re-ceives, the more "room" there is for its discussion to diversify, meaning that the *diversity* of attention and the overall *level* of attention given to an issue/topic tend to go hand-in-hand.

At the issue level, we can think of the diversity of discussion as the diversity of frames used to define a single issue. A frame—a term com-mon to both journalists and academics—is "a central organizing idea or story line that provides meaning to an unfolding strip of events" (Gam-son and Modigliani 1987). A frame portrays an issue along a certain di-mension, or from a certain angle, at the necessary exclusion—in same moment, anyway—of alternative perspectives (Chong and Druckman 2007b; Nelson and Oxley 1999). Media framing is a complicated phe-nomenon, as evidenced by a wealth of academic studies (Chong and Druckman 2007b), and one that must be understood as a multistage pro-cess encompassing not just news outlets, but also policymakers and cit-izens (Hänggli 2013).[21] Unquestionably, though, framing has a role to play in the news-generation process.

As an example of the important role framing plays in news judgment, the *Washington Post* has an enterprise editor "whose whole job is this: to read the stories and think about the framing . . . [and] how we can bring broader narratives to those stories." This enterprise editor "sits there and he looks at the stories and says 'Well, we could reframe this this way. We could push the story in this direction.' And he often rewrites along those lines." Specifically, news outlets have incentives to divert agenda atten-tion to those issues that can be framed from multiple perspectives—that is, those issues on which the diversity of discussion is wide. New and different frames are "especially relevant when you're trying to set yourself off from other media," says Bzdek.[22]

The effect of framing diversity on the overall level of media attention has played out dramatically in the case of capital punishment in the United States (Baumgartner, De Boef, and Boydstun 2008). For decades, media coverage defined the death penalty along status quo dimensions of morality ("thou shall not kill" vs. "eye for an eye") and constitutionality ("cruel and unusual punishment" vs. "justice is served"), with overall levels of attention varying with events, but remaining mostly in low-level equilibrium. In the mid-1990s, media discussion of the death penalty expanded to include the "new" dimension of fairness. The notion of innocence was especially prevalent ("wrongful execution" vs. "acceptable price to pay"), but the shift to fairness frames broke the debate open to a range of angles. As chapter 6 shows, this increase in diversity of discussion helped propel a surge in media coverage to capital punishment.

We can think of the diversity of discussion influencing levels of news coverage at the topic level, too. Similar (though not identical) to how individual issues comprise multiple frames, broader topics comprise multiple issues, which we can think of here as dimensions of a sort. Take the environment. This topic can be talked about with regard to air pollution, water pollution, toxic chemical regulation, endangered species protection, land conservation, waste disposal, recycling, global warming, and so on. But not all of these angles, or dimensions, are always in play. Sometimes the media's discussion of the environment is diverse, spanning several different relevant issues. At other times, the scope of the discussion is narrower, focusing, for example, on water pollution alone. When discussion is narrow, media attention will tend to move in response to signals in those issues alone. But when attention begins to diversify, often as a result of events that span multiple policy issues, the shift will be self-propelling, drawing more attention to the topic overall than could be explained by the sum of the individual issue events. In the case of topics as well as issues, I expect the diversity of discussion in past media coverage to have a positive influence on the overall level of current coverage.

What Else Is Going On? Agenda Congestion and Context

The likelihood of any given news item making it onto the agenda is affected by forces beyond the characteristics of the item itself. Of particular note are the degree of *agenda congestion* and the surrounding political, economic, and social *context*.

The term *agenda congestion* refers to how clogged or open the agenda is to new items. The problem of attention scarcity means that issues must "compete" for space on the agenda, with the intensity of competition directly affecting the chances of a given issue gaining access to the front page. The exact same event may get different amounts of front-page coverage depending on whether it occurs during periods of low congestion (when even "small" issues like agricultural subsidies or wind energy have a shot at the front page) or high congestion (when even major events get pushed behind page A1). Most commonly, we can think of congestion as the result of a mega storyline unfolding in the news. In the immediate aftermath of Hurricane Katrina, for example, the front page was highly congested with stories about the crisis, reducing an already tight agenda even further. In this way, when determining how much front-page attention will be paid to an event like a social protest, a Supreme Court decision, or a football game, the question is not whether the event is "big" enough to make the front page; the question is whether the event is big enough to pass the particular threshold set by that day's level of agenda congestion.

Finally, newsworthiness is underpinned by the ever-changing *context* of the economic, political, and social landscapes. As Klaus Bruhn Jensen writes, "the news depiction of social reality has been decisively shaped by economic, political and organisational forces at various levels of the social structure" (1986). We should expect the same event, occurring in different political environments, to receive slightly different amounts and types of attention, contingent on the economic, social, and political elements at work.

Gans identifies several communication theories that help explain how the news-generation process is shaped by "forces outside the news organization" (2004). Economic determinists believe that the national economy is key in shaping the news. Ideological determinists argue that the media tailors the news to the political ideologies of the elites currently in power. Cultural determinists make a broader argument, claiming that journalists select stories that reinforce the current values of the national culture. These arguments, while hard to test, all make sense.

For example, compare the *Times'* front-page coverage of Afghan and Iraqi civilian deaths in the U.S.-led war on terror beginning in 2001 with the *Times'* front-page coverage of the Soviet War in Afghanistan between 1979 and 1988. The Soviet-Afghan War was fought between Soviet forces supporting the Marxist People's Democratic Party of Afghanistan and the Mujahedeen resistance, which found international support from a number of nations, including the United States, Saudi Arabia, and Pakistan. By the end of the war, estimates put the number of Afghan civilian casualties between 1 and 2 million, with approximately 15,000 Soviet troop casualties. During the nine-year Soviet-Afghan War, 38 front-page *Times* stories reported on Afghan civilian deaths. Compare that number to front-page attention to the more recent U.S. military conflicts in Iraq and Afghanistan. Between the U.S. occupation of Afghanistan in 2001 and the end of 2007, depending on the source, somewhere between 100,000 and 500,000 Afghan and Iraqi civilians combined were killed in the conflict, with approximately 4,500 U.S. troop casualties. During this six-year time period, 447 front-page *Times* stories reported on Afghan or Iraqi civilian deaths.[23] In short, somewhere between twice and ten times as many civilians were killed in the Soviet-Afghan war as compared to the war on terror during the time periods studied, yet these deaths received less than one-tenth the amount of front-page coverage given to civilian deaths during the war on terror.

From one view, the discrepancy between the 38 and 447 front-page stories on civilian deaths in these two wars is largely explained by the news value of proximity discussed above: Americans (and U.S. newspapers) pay more attention to events in which Americans are involved. The journalistic tradition of beat reporting from the earlier discussion of *institutional setup* matters again here too, as do the concepts of *policymaker attention*, *public concern*, and *agenda congestion*. When the United States is at war, a heightened awareness of all things defense-related permeates the national consciousness, a significant number of correspondents are assigned to those events as they unfold, and the presence of the war as oft-mega-storyline tends to push other issues off the agenda. But we can think of the more general concept of context as its own important category of variables, in many cases overlapping these individual factors. In many ways, it is the context of the war that drives these other variables, pushing the media to make room for stories about battlefield events, international negotiations, proud homecomings, and grieving families.

Consider examples of how other context variables—like the level of racial tensions, the state of the national economy, the time until the next presidential election—cast the rest of the political system in a particular light, and in doing so affect the media's agenda. When racial tensions run high, we may be more likely to see race-related issues in the news. During the heat of a presidential election, media attention gravitates toward the horse race and whatever issues the horses happen to be talking about: defense, education, tax cuts, whatever. Periods of recession will be marked by surges in front-page attention to jobs, housing prices, and other economic issues, just as periods of economic prosperity will be reflected in a front page that focuses on noneconomic issues.

The Media Marketplace Approach

Overlaying the organizational process perspective is research considering the media as a competitive marketplace. Hamilton offers a comprehensive explanation of why and how we can think of the U.S. media as a marketplace, operating as a function of the economic demands of news organizations as businesses (2004). Related to this marketplace perspective, studies of the news-generation process have also pointed to the importance of the economic subsidies unique to each media system (Cook 1998) and of information as a key market commodity (Baum and Potter 2008). Today's U.S. media marketplace is highly concentrated (i.e., a few conglomerates own most of the news outlets) and highly competitive—and becoming more so over time (Bagdikian 2004; Franklin and Murphy 1991; Livingston and Bennett 2003; McCombs, Shaw, and Weaver 1997; Schudson 2002).

While journalistic ideals may often lead news outlets and their shareholders to feel as though they are operating under a "not-for-profit" business model, news outlets simply cannot function as "for-loss" outfits. A news outlet's financial obligations have several implications for the news-generation process. Not all of these implications are at odds with the ideals of good journalism. Often, the stories that help sell papers really are stories that citizens *should* know about. And in order to be successful financially, a news outlet must maintain a strong journalistic reputation, as a loss in integrity will swiftly lead to a loss in profits. Still, other implications of the media marketplace are more difficult to reconcile with the notion of unmitigated journalism, such as the tendency mentioned above for the media to pay more attention to white crime victims than nonwhite crime victims. The normative debates over the alarm versus patrol models of news generation and soft news that I discuss in the next chapter speak directly to this tension (Bennett 2003; Sparrow 1998; Zaller 2003).

Normative debates aside, a news organization's financial structure directly shapes the day-to-day operations of its newsroom. For better or for worse, news outlets need to attract and retain readers/viewers and advertisers. This need translates into a particular system of incentives that, in turn, produces particular media behaviors (Beaudoin and Thorson 2002; Hamilton 2004; McManus 1995).

In line with these economic constraints, successful news outlets are those that maximize the value of their information as commodities. A news outlet's goal is not just to inform the public, but also to attract and retain consumers by being the best supplier of information with the greatest newsworthy value. In this vein, a news outlet's success depends in large part on its ability to offer information consumers cannot get from competing organizations; news outlets have a keen incentive to scoop and not to be scooped.[24]

Whether we think of the U.S. media marketplace from the perspective of economic demands or information commodities, the result is the same: heavy competition. News outlets respond to this competition in many ways, but two elements are especially relevant to our discussion: resource distribution and mimicking behavior. Both elements point to the final variable in our list of eight—*prior attention*—which is discussed first below.

Prior Attention

The single variable of prior attention captures the many incentives for news outlets to adhere to path dependency in selecting each day's news—incentives that manifest in part through the media's patterns of resource distribution and mimicking. The single-best predictor of today's news should be yesterday's news. This fact is less true on the front page of a newspaper or in the headline features of television news, since these smaller agendas are forced to move more quickly through issues in order to stay fresh. Yet even here, prior attention is a strong determinant—again, probably the strongest determinant—of current attention.

In general, news outlets have a baseline distribution of attention across policy areas, and this baseline distribution is reinforced by institutionalized patterns of how resources are divided. Thus, the issues featured in the news yesterday (or last week or last month) are the most likely candidates to appear there today, while those that were ignored before are likely to be ignored again, in large part because patterns of resource distribution serve to earmark space on the news outlet's agenda for some issues over others. Moreover, as described in the next chapter, when the media goes into alarm mode surrounding an event, the dispatching of scarce resources and the marketplace incentives for mimicking mean that news coverage of the event the first day leads to even more coverage of it the next day. Likewise, when news outlets go into patrol mode, with reporters scanning the given policy neighborhood for additional information and angles, coverage of the issue continues to beget more coverage. Only during those brief moments when the media lurches between alarm mode and patrol mode (or vice versa) should prior attention not serve as a strong predictor of current attention. In short, the media, like any institution, is largely the product of its dynamics. In the case of the media in particular, momentum is key.

Resource Distribution

One way of understanding why *prior attention* plays such a strong role in determining each day's news is to consider how media resources are distributed. Marketplace competition drives news outlets to be strategic about how they spend their scarce resources (Hamilton 2004). *Washington Post* deputy business editor Alan Sipress puts it this way: much of the news-generation process "really is about resources: room in the paper, reporters to do the jobs, reporters who have different strengths."[25] Successful news organizations—including, especially, surviving broadsheet newspaper outlets—are those that tailor their operations to the resources they have.

News outlets compensate for scarce resources in part by relying on a well-established network of information sharing (Bennett, Lawrence, and Livingston 2007; Graber 2007; Skewes 2007). In particular, reporters sometimes rely on concise press releases and even boilerplate stories—what Oscar Gandy (1982) calls "information subsidies"—that politicians and activists offer (Cook 1998). By providing policy-related information, these subsidies allow reporters a way to reduce their costs associated with seeking and obtaining information on their own, as long as the reports are reliable and unbiased (Kollman 1998). Political actors are happy to provide this service because it increases the chances that their issues—and perspectives on those issues—will get covered in the

news. Thus, the information they provide serves to subsidize the additional attention that the political actors receive for their chosen issues
(Gandy 1982).

Another way that news outlets compensate for scarce resources is
through the aforementioned norm of assigning reporters to beats that
narrow the range of their attention to their particular topics. Some beats
are strongly institutionalized; most major news outlets, for example, have
a White House correspondent who submits daily stories from the White
House no matter what else is happening in the world. Other beats arise
ad hoc in the wake of events or shifts in editorial philosophy or simply
newsroom staff availability.

In some cases, beats heighten the influence that elite voices—and
policymaker activity more generally—have on the issues that make it
into the news (and how they are framed), due to journalistic norms and/
or the proximity of the beat to elite perspectives (Birkland 1997; Livingston 1997; Schudson 1997, 2002). For example, in the case of media
coverage of police brutality accusations Lawrence notes that "the norm
of media professionalism as inculcated on the beat creates news that is
careful always to tell the police side of the story" (2000b, 56).

Most relevant to the current discussion is how the beat system acts as
a key force of momentum in the news generation process, leading prior
attention to drive current attention. Reporters who are entrenched—
cognitively, and sometimes geographically—in a particular event or policy area will continue to focus on that topic until instructed to shift focus.
Meanwhile, other policy issues, no matter how important, are simply less
accessible relative to the events and issues surrounding the beat issue
(Iyengar and McGrady 2007). Reporters stationed abroad or embedded
with U.S. troops, for instance, really have no choice but to continue writing stories about the situation on the ground where they are located, even
if the situation happens to be a slow news day, and even if other important storylines are unfolding elsewhere with no one to cover them. Beat
reporters stationed in the local newsroom can more easily shift gears, but
still the costs of developing expertise on a particular beat mean that stories between beats can fall through the cracks. For example, when *Washington Post* staff writer Howard Schneider shifted away from his normal
beat of covering financial regulation, leaving this job vacant for several
months, it simply meant that "no one was reporting on these issues," says
Sipress. "Readers following the paper during these months would think
these issues weren't important for that time period."[26]

Beats aside, news outlets are incentivized to continue following on-going storylines by the notion that readers/viewers will be more likely to return to that news outlet if they are hooked by stories that are part of a larger unfolding storyline, not unlike episodes of a soap opera. And whether or not a storyline falls into a journalist's beat, once a journalist has poured time and energy into covering a story news outlets can max-imize resources by having that journalist churn out as many stories as possible on the related storyline.

In general, then, journalists and news outlets are incentivized to stick with the same issues today that they were covering yesterday. As de-scribed in the next chapter, these incentives help explain why, even when the main information of a major event has already been transmitted to the public in alarm form, the media often shifts into patrol mode, where it can stay entrenched for days or weeks on end (which, in media years, is an eternity).

Mimicking Behavior

We can further understand the role of *prior attention* in driving current attention by considering how news outlets interact with their competi-tors in the media marketplace. National news outlets respond to market-place competition by striving to be the first to cover a major news item—and, just as important, jumping on a hot item quickly even if other news outlets have reported it first. Says former *Washington Post* (now *New York Times*) reporter Sarah Cohen, if a competing newspaper "runs a story you were about to run," a newspaper will sometimes kill the story and "completely ignore it as if it didn't happen." But if the story is large enough, "you need to run it again but you have to take it from a differ-ent perspective."[27]

It is much better to be the news outlet that scoops the competition, resulting in institutional payoffs as well as invaluable bragging rights in a competitive environment that is usually professional, even friendly. Cohen says: "It used to be that if the *Times* had to say 'According to the *Washington Post*' on their front page they'd send over a case of champagne."[28]

Still today, as a professional courtesy each evening the *New York Times* and *Washington Post* send each other layout drafts for their next day's front pages. The tradition was initiated in the early 1990s by re-spective then–executive editors Joseph Lelyveld and Leonard Downie Jr.

The businesses of the two papers were already linked by their joint ownership of the *International Herald Tribune* (from 1967 to 2003). Plus, "it seemed logical," Downie said, "because for years we would always try to get a copy of each other's papers as soon as they came out. It made sense to both of us to make it simpler for everybody" (Strupp 2005). (Relations have not always been so cordial. During a period of particularly fierce competition between the *New York Times* and the *Herald Tribune* in the 1960s, for example, the managing editor of the *Times* routinely waited until he viewed the early edition of the *Tribune* and then strategically adjusted the content of the front page right before going to press [McCombs, Einsidel, and Weaver 1991]).

Likewise, the news outlets in Gans's classic study looked habitually to the *New York Times* for direction on what to cover (2004). Cook tells of how one broadcast network correspondent told him that Capitol Hill correspondents begin the process of figuring out what news items to cover each day "by looking at the *Washington Post*, the *New York Times*, the *Wall Street Journal*, the *Washington Times*, *USA Today*" (1998, 79). Thus, the marketplace incentives for news outlets to not be left out in the cold of a big news item lead outlets to track their competitors closely. Iyengar and McGrady explain how this copycat journalism is a function not only of marketplace incentives, but also of professional pecking order norms (2007).

In the aggregate, this competition-driven imitation between individual news outlets can lead to large-scale mimicking behavior, whereby news outlets will swarm to hot news items they see covered elsewhere (Boczkowski 2009; Graber 1971; Leskovec, Backstrom, and Klienberg 2009; Schudson 2003). As *New York Times* reporter Peter Baker puts it: "Reporters are like eight-year-old boys playing soccer. We're all going to run after the ball."[29] This frenzied mimicking usually constitutes an alarm mode of news generation.

But then, once news outlets have descended on a major story, the same marketplace incentives drive them to cover it diligently, often into the ground (Hoskins, McFayden, and Finn 2004; Kovach and Rosenstiel 2007). This is the patrol period of the alarm/patrol hybrid model. In the best-case scenario, this patrol period can provide citizens a variety of perspectives on the same breaking news item. At the same time, the same incentives that drive mimicking behavior mean that news outlets can get locked in a stalemate of sorts during these patrol periods, with no one wanting to be the first one *not* to run a front-page story about the issue. Examples include the contested 2000 U.S. presidential election, the September 11th attacks, and Hurricane Katrina. Cohen recalls this dilemma being particularly strong following 9/11: "We felt like there was nothing new to say, but you can't stop saying it's the most important thing."[30] Additionally, mimicking can turn into "pack journalism" (coined by Crouse 1972), where news outlets get so caught up in following a storyline that they fail to think and act independently (McCombs, Einsidel, and Weaver 1991)—a dramatic form of the general indexing principle, as demonstrated by Bennett, Lawrence, and Livingston in the cases of the war on terror and Hurricane Katrina (2007).

The Disproportionate Information Processing Approach

A more textured understanding of the role that dynamics play in the news-generation process can be found in the policy agendas literature (e.g., Baumgartner and Jones 2009; Jones and Baumgartner 2005). This literature is grounded in the concept of attention scarcity, which maps onto the notion of gatekeeping, discussed above. When an institution has an agenda of finite size (as they all do) and forces of positive and negative feedback (more on these concepts below), the institution will necessarily process information disproportionately. Policy agendas scholars have documented evidence of this phenomena in the United States and in other countries across a range of institutional contexts, such as legislative policymaking, executive speeches, budgetary spending, and also news coverage (e.g., Baumgartner, Breunig, et al. 2009; Baumgartner and Jones 2009; Repetto 2006; Workman, Jones, and Jochim 2009).

We can conceptualize disproportionate information processing in the case of the media most easily by imagining how news outlets handle the boatload of event information they receive each day. How is it that these outlets select a handful of news stories from each day's onslaught of real-world happenings?

Let's start with a null hypothesis, however implausible, positing that news outlets process information in an even, methodical, proportional fashion. Under this idea, when a new piece of information unfolds, individual journalists and news outlets as a whole would act to prioritize that piece of information in relation to all the other pieces of information on the table at the time, and the media's agenda would be updated accordingly. When high school dropout rates begin to rise, for example, the problem would start to show up in the news. When the problem begins to recede, so, too, would media attention to the issue, clearing room on the agenda for a more important problem.

Over time, this null hypothesis of proportional processing would predict an agenda that would change gradually through a churning process of issue replacement. As new event-driven problems arise and old problems are dealt with, the new would gradually replace the old. Some issues would inevitably receive more agenda space than others because the underlying problems simply demand more attention. Yet, over an extended period of time, most issues would get at least some play on the agenda. Overall, the agenda would not be distributed evenly across issues, but neither would it be dramatically skewed—we would instead expect to see something like a normal distribution.

If we were to calculate the amount of *change* in the agenda at each point in time and graph a histogram distribution of these change values, this null hypothesis would predict a roughly normal distribution here, too. We have good reason to believe that events are, generally speaking, normally distributed over time in terms of their change; dramatic worsenings of a situation, for example, alternate with improvements of that same situation, but most of the time events are moderate in nature (Jones and Baumgartner 2005).

In short, the proportional processing hypothesis offers two key predictions: First, news stories would be allocated across issues in proportion with the perceived relative importance of those issues, meaning the agenda would be moderately, but not dramatically, skewed. Second, *changes* in the agenda would occur proportionally over time, with a predominance of moderate change and very few sudden, big changes.

This story of proportionality breaks down, however, when we consider the vast discrepancy between the amount of information the media must process and its processing capacity. As a human-run institution, the media simply cannot handle all this information, and certainly not in a way that prioritizes incoming information in terms of objective (or even perceived) severity. Journalists as people, and news outlets as institutions, do their best to keep up. But with so much information coming in and such a shortage of agenda space, news outlets end up following a much different behavioral pattern than the null hypothesis would predict.

In the face of a constant stream of new information that far exceeds

available attention, human beings and institutions alike end up processing information in a boundedly rational manner (Jones 2001; Kahneman
2003; Padgett 1980; Simon 1957). Unable to keep pace with information
as it comes in, the people who staff each news outlet do the best they
can with what they have. Journalists, editors, and thus the media as a
whole can only keep so many stories on the radar at once. The result is
that the news tends to fixate on a small number of issues at a time, getting "stuck" in equilibrium as it gravitates around this small set of issues. Meanwhile, though, information continues to unfold in other areas of life. When mounting information in one of these areas becomes
too great to ignore—usually in the form of dramatic and evocative events
(key, triggering, or focusing)—the media does not shift attention to this
new information gradually, but rather lurches over to it, overhauling the
agenda in the process. Together, this pattern of fits and starts represents
"punctuated equilibrium" dynamics (Baumgartner and Jones 2009).
These dynamics characterize the larger theory of disproportionate information processing that Jones and Baumgartner (2005) use to explain
patterns of change in politics in general, and which can be applied to media attention in particular.

The theory of disproportionate information processing pivots on the
twin concepts of negative and positive feedback, which are central to
our understanding of skew and explosiveness in the news. *Negative feedback* is the process by which changes in a system are "corrected" by an
opposing pull back toward an equilibrium. Think about a digital ther-
mostat set at a baseline temperature. Each time the temperature in the
room starts to get too cold, the heat comes on to warm things up. When
the room heats up to a level above the programmed temperature, the air
conditioning kicks in to cool things down. *Positive feedback* is just the
opposite process. Changes in the system are not corrected but instead
reinforced, leading the system to spiral, explosively, away from equilibrium; think of fashion trends, population booms, and viral spreads of
disease or information, where in each case change begets even more
change at an exponential rate.

In the context of an institutional agenda, negative feedback serves
to stabilize the agenda around an equilibrium, such that the allocation
of attention across issues remains relatively fixed. Many of the institutional constraints that shape the agenda are forces of negative feedback,
as discussed in the context of the media marketplace above. When ex-

ternal changes start to pull the agenda's attention in a new direction, these constraints work against those changes to reinforce the status quo. The agenda never stays perfectly still, of course, but under the force of negative feedback, the system never veers too far from its (current) self-correcting point of equilibrium.

As an example of how negative feedback works, consider the organizational and marketplace incentives that drive news outlets to maintain readership/viewership by competing with rival sources to cover—and to continue to cover—the hot topics of the day. If a news outlet like the *Times* started to pay *less* attention to the current hot issue (such as a terrorist attack, a school shooting, or an election), shifting this agenda space instead to an important yet neglected issue (like agricultural subsidies or tribal-sponsored retaliatory rapes in Pakistan), some portion of its audience would respond by switching to a different news source in order to get its fix of the hot issue coverage. The *Times*, in turn, would respond to this loss of readership by reversing strategies and covering the hot issue once again—this is negative feedback. In reality, this kind of give-and-take rarely occurs, because editors and journalists are acutely aware of the constraints of their business; they do not need to try the agriculture subsidies experiment to know that readers would rather read about the hot issue *du jour*. Thus, it is the anticipation of audience demands that serves as a negative feedback mechanism in the case of the media, helping to keep the news fixated, in a very path dependent way, on the current hot issues until "new" issues explode.

By contrast, positive feedback mechanisms reinforce changes that begin to take hold on an agenda, leading to sudden and dramatic agenda upheaval, displacing the current allocation of attention with an entirely new one—often centered on a hot issue that helped spark the overhaul. Consider again the incentives that news outlets have to compete for coverage of the current hot issues. Once a hot issue is identified, these incentives serve as negative feedback mechanisms, producing the path dependent behaviors that stabilize the agenda around an equilibrium. But right at the moment a hot news item breaks, these same incentives serve as positive feedback mechanisms, driving news outlets (and policymakers, too) to run—not walk—to shift attention to that news item. In this way, positive and negative feedback forces are always playing tug-of-war in the media system.

In generalized terms then, positive feedback drives periods of alarm mode in the news-generation process, while negative feedback drives periods of patrol mode. The alarm/patrol hybrid model explains the give-and-take between these modes.

Predictions

The process of news generation is staggeringly complex; it involves many moving and interacting parts, and many unknowns. Trying to predict the selection of stories for tomorrow's front page is like trying to predict which genetic mutations will shape the next generation of flamingos. But when we pull back to look at the media over time, patterns emerge.

These patterns can be explained when we understand the primary components of the system. On any given day, we cannot predict exactly whether a policymaker's efforts to influence media attention for an issue will pay off, whether journalists will heed public concern or ignore it, or whether an expanding diversity of the debate will fade out or lead to a cascade of attention. But we can understand these and other key variables that drive media attention and, just as importantly, the dynamic movement of the system that produces patterns in the aggregate.

The following expectations derive from the discussion above. The eight variables discussed here are, again, really categories of variables from which many different hypotheses can be drawn. *Prior attention* is listed first here, although it was the last one discussed in this chapter, because it is the core variable of interest in testing the hypothesized role of momentum and, as such, will be listed first in the models presented in chapters 5 and 6.

Hypothesis 1 (collectively): Each of the following variables will have a significant influence on news coverage.

> *Prior attention*: The more news coverage given to issue i at time $t-1$, the more news coverage issue i will get at time t.
>
> *Institutional setup* (not tested in this book): Hypotheses vary according to proxy measures.
>
> *Events*: The more event activity in issue i at time $t-1$, the more news coverage issue i will get at time t.
>
> *Policymaker attention*: The more policymaker attention given to issue i at time $t-1$, the more news coverage issue i will get at time t.

Public concern: The more public concern given to issue i at time $t-1$, the more news coverage issue i will get at time t.

Diversity of discussion: The more diversity of discussion used in news coverage of issue i at time $t-1$, the more news coverage issue i will get at time t.

Agenda congestion: The more agenda congestion at time t, the less news coverage issue i will get at time t.

Context (not tested in this book): Hypotheses vary according to proxy measures.

CHAPTER THREE

The Alarm/Patrol Hybrid Model of News Generation

L et's think about Watergate. This quintessential instance of journalism at its finest began not with reporters patrolling the political streets for signs of wrongdoing. It began with an alarm—literally. The nighttime break-in at the Democratic headquarters at the Watergate Hotel in Washington, DC, in June 1972 triggered in turn a figurative news alarm that the *Washington Post* (and other news outlets) picked up on. Bob Woodward (at the time a city beat reporter) and Carl Bernstein (on the Virginia political beat) were assigned to look into the break-in and report what they found (Bernstein and Woodward 1994).

But, as we know, they didn't stop there. Picking up on the scent of scandal, Woodward and Bernstein acted in line with the model detailed in this chapter, shifting from alarm mode into patrol mode. The fact that they did so was, arguably, a major reason that the nation learned about the full scope of the political wrongdoing at hand. Although obvious in retrospect, the entire Watergate scandal could easily have been missed. Had the *Post* and other DC news outlets not followed up on the largely routine police report of the break-in, or had Woodward and Bernstein reported the initial facts and then moved on to the next potential alarm, the nation might well have learned much less (Bernstein and Woodward 1994; *Time* 1974). Or, had the *Post* been operating in the context of today's increasingly resource-strapped newsrooms, the distribution of beat assignments might simply have been stretched too thin to allow time for follow-up on what appeared on the surface to be a relatively minor incident. Many incidents, of course, occur outside the boundaries of standard beat reporting.

In other words, Woodward and Bernstein unveiled a major political story not because they were patrolling the political scene, but because they responded to a relatively minor alarm and *then* went into patrol mode. And other news outlets followed. Competing news outlets might have seen the *Washington Post*'s coverage, decided the *Post* was taking care of alerting the public to the scandal alarm item, and turned their resources and attention to other important alarms. But instead, news outlets swarmed to the news item, as they tend to do, propelled by positive feedback in the form of institutional incentives described in chapter 2, such as the incentive to mimic other news outlets (Boczkowski 2009; Graber 1971; Iyengar and McGrady 2007; Schudson 2003). The resulting patrol coverage uncovered the basic facts of the scandal and much more.

In today's twenty-four-hour news cycle, as in 1972, much of journalism continues to hinge on journalists responding to alarms, but also following up on them in patrol mode, producing sustained media explosions with profound political and social implications.

This Chapter

The previous chapter outlined three approaches to understanding the forces that drive the news: organizational process, marketplace, and disproportionate information processing. A more robust understanding of the news-generation process comes not from combining these approaches in additive fashion, but from considering how they interact dynamically. In the alarm/patrol hybrid model presented here, the key variables discussed in chapter 2 combine to shape the news via self-reinforcing and mutually reinforcing dynamics. Through this momentum, the variables identified drive the media to alternate between sudden bursts of change and periods of entrenched stability. The fluctuation between these two dynamic forms constitutes explosiveness. Those issues covered during periods of agenda overhaul or fixation receive large amounts of coverage, at the neglect of many others. In this way, explosiveness heightens the degree of skew in media attention across issues. Out of the apparent cacophony of daily news, aggregate patterns of skew and explosiveness emerge.

Under the alarm/patrol hybrid model, we can think of these lurching dynamics as the give-and-take between two modes of news generation: alarm mode and patrol mode. In alarm mode, the media rushes to cover breaking news. In patrol mode, the media digs in, surveying the geographical or policy "neighborhood" surrounding the event/issue at hand. These modes can be singularly present (alarm-only or patrol-only mode) or present in quick succession (alarm/patrol mode), and often neither mode is fully engaged in coverage of an issue. Thus, the alarm and patrol modes yield a 2×2 categorization (see table 3.1 to follow). The distinction between these modes is highly theoretical; in practice, things are not nearly so clean. Within each newsroom, journalists and editors rarely make conscious decisions to be in one mode or the other. Nor would they likely accept the premise behind categorizing modes of news generation in the first place; their focus is on working within a complicated set of incentives to produce the best news possible each day. But as a rubric for understanding aggregate media dynamics, the oversimplified distinction between alarm and patrol modes of news generation is useful. This model's high-level purpose is to push us to think about the role that dynamics play in shaping media attention and, thus, the effects of media attention.

This chapter begins with a discussion of the normative underpinnings of a patrol model of journalism, followed by an outline of the alarm model, which has been proposed by past studies as a more accurate depiction of the U.S. media in practice. Building from this discussion, I detail the alarm/patrol hybrid model and explain how the key variables from chapter 2 link with this overarching model, before focusing in on the particular alarm/patrol mode of news-generation and offering examples of how it plays out in practice. Finally, I detail the systemic patterns in the news that result from the alarm/patrol hybrid model. The model predicts dramatic skew across policy issues (hypothesis 2) and explosive change over time (hypothesis 3). I test hypotheses 2 and 3 in chapters 7 and 8.

The Patrol Model

At stake in our understanding of the news-generation process is our understanding of the role of the free press in a democracy. In the United States, the notion of a watchdog press pervades culture and academia despite its clear infeasibility. This watchdog archetype suggests a patrol model of news generation, where journalists and news outlets scan the metaphorical streets of society and politics in order to convey any threats to citizens and policymakers.

News coverage of the Watergate scandal in 1972 typifies this patrol-model archetype. Woodward and Bernstein's in-depth investigating helped to uncover one of the greatest political scandals in U.S. history, contributing to the notion of journalists as "alert, courageous newsmen standing as sentries against the abuse of power" (*Time* 1974). Today, although Americans' trust in the U.S. media is on the decline (McCombs, Holbert, Kiousis, and Wanta 2011), the notion of a watchdog media remains pervasive in Hollywood portrayals of the news industry (Ehrlich 2004) and in scholarly portrayals as well. Past scholarship describes how the media does not operate perfectly as a surveillance patrol, helping to explain when and why this patrol model breaks down (Bennett 2003; Zaller 2003). Still, the notion that the media is geared to perform as a surveillance body—indeed, in a social evolutionary sense—remains a normative staple of communication studies (Shoemaker 1996). As Schudson says, "many studies of media coverage of politics smuggle in the assumption that the news media should serve society by informing the general population in ways that arm them for vigilant citizenship" (2002, 263).

To what extent does the media actually operate in patrol mode, scanning the landscape for potential threats to transmit in each day's news? Not at all, according to much scholarship. Having long ago dismissed the notion of news coverage as a mirror of real life (Lippmann 1922), political communication scholars have worked to untangle the many pressures that restrict the media's incentives—and ability—to operate as a surveillance body on constant lookout. Among political communication scholars, there is general consensus that the patrol model of news generation is simply not feasible given news outlets' institutional incentives and resource constraints (Bennett 2003; Graber 2003b; Patterson 2003; Zaller 2003).

The Alarm Model

Instead of a patrol model of news generation, this scholarship has considered instead an alarm model (Bennett 2003; Zaller 2003), paralleling earlier research by McCubbins and Schwartz (1984) in the area of congressional oversight. McCubbins and Schwartz explain how, rather than maintaining constant surveillance over administrative compliance with its legislative goals, Congress instead waits until an alarm is sounded—through a variety of alarm-pulling mechanisms—and then responds to that alarm. In the case of congressional oversight, McCubbins and Schwartz argue that an alarm-driven response system is more rational and efficient than a patrol system. In fact, they call the alarm model "an optimal enforcement strategy, given opportunity costs, available technology, and human cognitive limits" (1984, 165).

Whether an alarm system is normatively optimal in the case of news coverage is another matter, and one of healthy debate. Zaller argues that an alarm model of news coverage allows citizens to stay efficiently informed; by relying on the media to alert us only to major problems, we citizens can focus more of our attention on other, more important activities in our own lives (Zaller 2003; see also Popkin 1991; Schudson 1998). By contrast, Bennett argues that while a patrol model may be infeasible, an alarm model of news coverage is normatively flawed because of the potential for false alarms (dramatic coverage alerting citizens to problems that are inconsequential or nonexistent) and for the false absence of alarms (little or no coverage of important problems) (Bennett 2003; see also Patterson 1994, 2000).

One particular criticism scholars level at alarm-style media coverage is that it promotes soft news coverage, with little or no policy substance and questionable benefit to society (Bennett 2003; Patterson 1994, 2000; Prior 2003). Other scholars argue that soft news can, in fact, serve to inform citizens about underlying policy issues, potentially reaching sections of the public that hard news does not; Baum and Jamison call this the "Oprah effect" (2006; see also Baum 2002, 2003). But whatever the value of soft news, an alarm model of news coverage would suggest a higher degree of soft news than would a patrol model. At the root of many complaints about horse-race coverage and suspicions of media ideological biases are citizens' normative hopes, if not expectations, of a patrol-style media. (Again, the evidence presented in this book does not distinguish between hard news and soft news, nor does it address media bias, but the theory presented here holds implications for these concepts, warranting future studies.)

Another normative criticism of alarm-based news coverage comes from the policy agendas literature. Studies demonstrating disproportionate government responsiveness to real-world issues leave open the idea that a patrol-based media could mitigate such disproportionate government responsiveness by supplying policymakers with a more diverse array of surveillance-produced information (Baumgartner, Breunig, et al. 2009; Jones 2001; Jones and Baumgartner 2005; Jones, Larsen-Price, and Wilkerson 2009). In short, scholars continue to entertain and debate the normative notion of the U.S. press as an aspiring, if imperfect, surveillance body, working to inform policymakers and citizens about the issues they "should" know about.

What scholars do appear to agree on is that observed news coverage tends to match an alarm model better than it matches a patrol model (Bennett 2003; Graber 2003b; Patterson 2003; Zaller 2003). As applied to the news-generation process, an alarm model holds that news outlets and journalists do not patrol metaphorical neighborhoods. Rather, the media "wait" (while occupied with other stories) until alarms are sounded—for example, through events or whistleblower information—and then respond (selectively) to those alarms. The alarm model does not suggest that all alarms receive attention, as the volume of alarms exceeds journalistic resources and agenda space. Indeed, the selection process by which some alarms are attended to and others ignored is at the root of Bennett's normative concerns about the alarm-response system. Modern news coverage, Bennett notes, consists of "the continual sounding of burglar alarms on any number of issues—often just because they are shocking" (2003, 131). Thus, normative concerns notwithstanding, the alarm model is seen as an accurate depiction of the news-generation process. As Bennett says, Zaller's description of the alarm model, while not up to the patrol-like "full news" standard that we should demand from the press, "turns out to be a nearly perfect account of what the news is already doing" (131).

The Alarm/Patrol Hybrid Model

But does the alarm model alone capture the news-generation process? I argue that it does not. The media does not operate strictly as a patrol system, but neither does it operate strictly as an alarm system. Rather, the media represents a particular *hybrid* of these two general models. The alarm/patrol hybrid model accounts for the apparent paradoxes between the two perspectives. Importantly, the alarm/patrol hybrid model is not a model of how the media *should* operate, but a model of how it *does* operate—and more specifically, how it operates in the aggregate.

Under this model, modes of news generation can be conceptualized (in oversimplified terms) as falling into one of four categories:

1. Sometimes the media operates in alarm mode only, producing a brief burst of coverage around an event/issue—what I call a momentary media explosion.
2. Sometimes the media operates in patrol mode only, producing an extended period of attention to an event/issue; this attention manifests either as low-level sustained coverage or high-level sustained coverage—including beat reporting and what I call a timed media explosion.
3. Sometimes neither mode is fully engaged, producing low (or no) levels of coverage to the event/issue.
4. Sometimes the media operates in alarm/patrol mode (usually alarm mode followed quickly by patrol mode, though the shift can be blurry), producing a surge in coverage that is then continued for a period—what I call a sustained media explosion.

Which mode of news generation the media adopts is driven by the key variables identified in chapter 2, under the overarching influence of momentum. Thus, which mode of media coverage an event prompts depends on a host of factors, not the least of which is the nature of the event itself.

Table 3.1 captures these four modes of news generation. For each mode, we should expect various combinations of the variable conditions identified to lead—in theory—to the media adopting that mode of coverage. Table 3.1 also lists the type of news coverage that tends to characterize each mode, as well as example news items. The table is far from comprehensive. And, certainly, exceptions exist to the typical variable conditions that correlate with each mode. Still, the table helps illustrate how the conceptual alarm/patrol hybrid model maps on to news coverage in practice. Because news generation can occur in different modes, news coverage comes in many forms, including brief but dramatic, buzz-like coverage (alarm mode); central beat or investigative journalism storylines (patrol mode); peripheral beat storylines or the "man bites dog" style one-shot human interest story (neither alarm nor patrol mode); and dramatic, buzz-like coverage that captures the nation's attention but then also digs into the underlying issues and themes at hand (alarm/patrol mode).

The alarm/patrol hybrid model of news generation thus suggests a lurching pattern of news coverage, from one surge of attention to the

TABLE 3.1 **A typology of news-generation modes**

	Alarm Mode	Nonalarm Mode
Patrol Mode	*Example Variables at Work*	*Example Variables at Work*
	Focusing/key/triggering events Sensational/"easy" policy issue (or in rare cases no explicit policy issue) Many key actors involved High policymaker attention High public concern Many frames available; accessible thematic framework Low media agenda congestion	Beat items or routine/seasonal events Unsensational/"hard" policy issue (or no explicit policy issue) Many key actors involved High policymaker attention High public concern Many frames available; accessible thematic framework Low media agenda congestion
	Resulting Type of News Coverage	*Resulting Type of News Coverage*
	Sudden surge of coverage followed by continued high-level coverage (i.e., a sustained media explosion)	Low-level sustained coverage *or* high- level sustained coverage (i.e., beat stories or a timed media explosion)
	Example News Items	*Example News Items*
	9/11 Baseball doping scandal Hurricane Katrina 2000 election re-count Clarence Thomas's Supreme Court nomination Catholic priest abuse scandal Treyvon Martin's shooting	Ongoing military actions overseas Olympics General weather patterns General election convention Stephen Breyer's Supreme Court nomination Pope's visit New York City's war on crime
Non-Patrol Mode	*Example Variables at Work*	*Example Variables at Work*
	Focusing/key/triggering events Sensational/"easy" policy issue (or no explicit policy issue) Few key actors involved Low policymaker attention Low public concern Few frames available; accessible episodic framework High media agenda congestion	Any nonfocusing/key/triggering event Unsensational/"hard" policy issue (or no explicit policy issue) Few key actors involved Low policymaker attention Low public concern Few frames available; accessible episodic framework High media agenda congestion
	Resulting Type of News Coverage	*Resulting Type of News Coverage*
	Sudden surge of coverage followed by low-level (or no) coverage (i.e., a momentary media explosion)	Low-level coverage for brief period (no media explosion)
	Example News Items	*Example News Items*
	Haiti earthquake Michael Jackson's death	Human interest stories Most crimes

next—a broader form of the classic issue-attention cycle proposed by Downs (1972). Usually, a news outlet will be engaged in at least one media explosion (momentary, timed, or sustained) at any given time. Beneath and between these cyclical explosions are inter-event periods of relative calm—in some policy issue areas, at least—when a news outlet will continue to attend to the bread-and-butter issues of its beat reporting system; Birkland calls these quiet periods (1998, 61–62).

This hybrid news-generation process is more complicated—and more normatively relevant—than either the alarm or patrol models alone would suggest. For example, because being in patrol mode takes significant time and resources, the alarm/patrol hybrid model suggests that the media is not able to respond to as many alarms as it might if following a strict alarm model. At the same time, news outlets tend to only patrol those neighborhoods covered by beats or triggered by alarms, falling short of the normative ideal of the patrol model.

How Key Variables Fold Into the Alarm/Patrol Hybrid Model

The eight key variables discussed in chapter 2 together help explain how much attention an issue will receive in a given time period. Linked by an understanding of dynamics, these variables also suggest systemic lurching between alarm responses, entrenched patrol periods, and the stretches of relative calm in between. In all modes of news generation, the single variable of *prior attention* captures the constant drive of momentum in the process, spurred by competing positive and negative feedback forces.

Specifically, these eight variables capture core mechanisms of positive and negative feedback. For example, we can understand the importance of *policymaker attention* to issues as having a direct effect on news coverage: in general, the more attention policymakers give an issue, the more news coverage that issue should receive. But we can also understand policymaker attention as fueling the news-generation process more broadly, serving at times as a negative feedback mechanism and at other times as a positive feedback mechanism, and thereby helping to produce aggregate patterns of skew and explosiveness in the news. Consider that, in many cases, policy beliefs and special interest obligations lead policymakers to focus, in an entrenched, path-dependent way, on the same core issues over time (Baumgartner, Berry, et al. 2009; Browne

1990; Heclo 1978; Mahoney 2008), serving as a negative feedback mechanism to reinforce the status quo equilibrium of (skewed) attention distribution in the news. Yet, although policymakers tend to operate within the niches of their particular issue networks, they rarely have all of their eggs in one basket. When events or circumstances offer opportunities to draw focus to one of their issues in particular, policymakers (who process information disproportionately, too) have incentives not to maintain the status quo of the spread of their attention across their issues in a "don't need to worry about that one anymore" manner. Rather, understanding the power of inertia, policymakers are incentivized to redistribute their resources to pay *more* attention to the issue in question, riding the coattails of the system-wide wave in attention that can develop into a cascade (Wolfsfeld and Sheafer 2006). These instances of lurching shifts in policymaker attention act as positive feedback forces within this larger mutually reinforcing process, exacerbating the explosive nature of changes on the media agenda.

Let us say, for instance, that Congress is locked in a heated policy debate and the media lurches attention to this alarm. As the media starts to fixate on the policy debate, members of Congress may seek to capitalize on the attention bandwagon by offering additional press conferences, interviews, and informational subsidies, eliciting in turn yet more media attention—this is positive feedback in action. But once the media is in patrol mode, continued elite access serves instead as a negative feedback mechanism, inhibiting a shift in attention away from the policy debate and to the next issue. And, between media explosions, elite influence serves as a negative feedback mechanism by reinforcing a (varying) baseline equilibrium distribution of attention during those periods of relative calm. Yearly congressional attention to budgetary issues, for example, tends to capture a portion of media attention in routine fashion, thereby inhibiting—but obviously not preventing—the media from diverting attention to new alarms.

Similarly, we can think of *public concern* not only as shaping which issues become news, but more broadly as exacerbating the aggregate media patterns of skew and explosiveness. Like news outlets and policymakers, citizens process information disproportionately, commonly becoming absorbed (or disinterested) in the current equilibrium of news items. During these periods, public concern operates as a negative feedback mechanism, reinforcing the media's continued coverage of issues, reinforcing the equilibrium. But when a "new" hot item arises—whether initiated by events, the media, policymakers, or the public itself—citizens often lurch their attention, too, again often as part of a mutually reinforcing, system-wide attention cascade. It is perhaps in these cases that public concern has the strongest influence on the news, acting as a positive feedback mechanism and urging news outlets to race against market competition to cover the issues they know will resonate with consumers in an optimal state of attentiveness.

As a final example, consider the *diversity of discussion*. The entrenchment of an issue/topic discussion along status quo angles acts as a negative feedback mechanism, reinforcing the equilibrium-level of media attention (or lack thereof). With no new angles to investigate, news coverage tends to stay the same. But when discussion expands to include more dimensions, the newly activated angles make the issue/topic relevant to a wider range of policymakers and citizens, and simply more interesting in general. In these cases, diversity of discussion operates as a positive feedback mechanism—again, often as part of a system-wide mutually reinforcing attention cascade—reinforcing the lurch of news coverage to the issue.

Thus, as captured by these variables, the news-generation process hinges on both positive and negative feedback. Each time the media lurches into alarm mode, this lurching represents the same positive feedback process that underlies punctuations in other policy agendas contexts, albeit through different institutional mechanisms (e.g., the marketplace incentives not to miss out on a hot news item). When the media shifts into patrol mode, institutional incentives to stick to the hot news item serve as negative feedback mechanisms that result in a period of relative fixation, or equilibrium.

The Alarm/Patrol Mode

Of the four modes of news generation the alarm/patrol hybrid model describes (illustrated in table 3.1 above), the namesake alarm/patrol mode holds particular significance. We can think of this hybrid mode unfolding as follows: The nature of an event and institutional incentives combine—via momentum—to send the media into alarm mode. But then this same host of momentum-fueled incentives drive the media into patrol mode in the metaphorical surrounding neighborhoods, be they substantive (e.g., related to health care or economic policy) or geographical (e.g., New Orleans or Iraq). The media is rarely propelled into this alarm/patrol mode by policy problems per se. Usually the media responds to events that, in turn, relate to underlying policy issues. But recall that even purely event-driven news coverage can open a brief window of opportunity for social and policy change related to the policy problem involved (Baumgartner and Jones 2009; Birkland and Lawrence 2009; Kingdon 1995; Lawrence and Birkland 2004).

Sometimes individual news outlets shift from alarm mode to patrol mode surrounding a news item of particular interest to journalists or readers. For example, the Catholic priest abuse scandal discussed below was initially uncovered not by a change in events but by investigations conducted by a single news outlet, the *Boston Globe*. More often, we observe multiple news outlets moving together in herd formation. Usually, this simultaneous swarming occurs in response to incentives that lurch the media into alarm mode in response to a major event *or* that shift the media into patrol mode surrounding a central neighborhood of interest. In both cases, the behavior plays out the same way: the media appears to respond to alarms not only as signals of threats to which to alert society, but also as signals of key neighborhoods worth patrolling. When any given news outlet follows this alarm/patrol mode of coverage, the result is a dramatic and sudden surge in attention by that news outlet, called a media storm (Boydstun, Hardy, and Walgrave 2013). When multiple news outlets follow this same pattern surrounding the event/policy issue(s), we might instead call it a media swarm. Both concepts are encompassed in the notion of a sustained media explosion.

Examples of the Alarm/Patrol Hybrid Mode in Action

Again, the media does not always behave in alarm/patrol mode; sometimes it operates in alarm-only mode, sometimes patrol-only mode, and sometimes in neither mode, as table 3.1 illustrates. But when the key variables outlined in this book align to prompt a combined alarm/patrol mode of news generation, the results can be dramatic. And while few news items prompt this hybrid mode of news coverage, the resulting news coverage is so vast that these news items in fact constitute a vastly disproportionate amount of all news stories (Boydstun, Hardy, and Walgrave 2013). What's more, they capture political attention in a way that other news items simply do not (Boydstun, Vliegenthart, Walgrave, and

Hardy 2013). Examples abound, a few of which will be discussed here: the Catholic priest abuse scandal in 2002, the case of Terri Schiavo in 2005, Hurricane Katrina in 2005, the Jerry Sandusky scandal in 2011, and the shooting of African American teenager Trayvon Martin in 2012. These examples help illustrate the alarm/patrol hybrid model, and they also help explain the resulting patterns of skew and explosiveness in the news. These patterns have stark implications for politics and society. As the examples below show, sustained media explosions can create windows of opportunity for social and policy change (Kingdon 1995). When the media operates in alarm/patrol mode, the resulting sustained media explosions can pass a critical threshold of attention. Beyond this invisible threshold, news coverage can have a heightened effect on public and political attention. Issues pulled into the media limelight in the context of a sustained media explosion are very hard to ignore.

At the same time, these examples hint at how very difficult it is for deserving policy problems to gain attention in the first place.

Catholic Priest Abuse Scandal

When the story of systemic child sexual abuse by Catholic priests broke in 2002, it received a swell of alarm-mode attention across news outlets both because of the nature of the event (a scandal) and also the actors involved (priests). Simultaneous with this alarm coverage, however, was a strong undercurrent of patrol-mode coverage, grounded on the five-month-long *Boston Globe* investigation that broke the story in the first place. The resulting torrent of alarm/patrol coverage was powerful enough, it seems, to shift perceived social stigmas about the abuse victims. Of all alleged abuse incidents that occurred between 1950 and 2002, less than one-half of 1% occurred in 2002 (the year that the story broke). Yet nearly *one-third* of victims from that fifty-three-year span came forward in 2002 alone. While it is impossible to say for sure, we can imagine that, were news coverage to operate in patrol-mode only, coverage would likely have been much more moderate, and probably below the invisible threshold that was required for many victims to feel safe in coming forward. But were news coverage to operate in alarm mode only, via dramatic but surface-level bursts of attention, coverage would likely have been much shorter lived, stopping short of the depth and breadth of perspective needed to coax these important shifts in stigma. (For more on the Catholic priest abuse scandal see chapter 7.)

Terri Schiavo

Arguably, it was the involvement of the Florida legislature and Governor Jeb Bush that first promoted the Schiavo case in 2003 from an important but less-than-newsworthy family dispute (which had been boiling for more than a decade) to front-page news. But the news item was largely contained within the state of Florida. Moreover, there was stiff competition for media attention in 2003, especially given the initiation of Operation Iraqi Freedom in March of that year. By 2005, however, the U.S. Congress and several other political elites were proactively involved in the Schiavo debate. This involvement included heated public and media attention to—and framing of—the case (Bellafante 2005). March 2005 was also a relatively slow news month; one month later, the Schiavo case may have been drowned out by the breaking scandal of detainee abuse by U.S. soldiers at Abu Ghraib.

Together, these and other factors propelled the media to lurch into alarm mode and then quickly transition into patrol mode in March 2005. News outlets camped out, metaphorically speaking, by fixating journalists on the Schiavo storyline as it unfolded, conveying each nuance of the case to the public. More important, journalists patrolled the surrounding policy neighborhood, submitting multiple reports—both in-depth journalism stories and human-interest soft news stories—about the history and intricacies of living will policy and, of course, the family drama surrounding Schiavo. The surge of media attention drew more engagement by political elites, which in turn further incentivized the media to stay in patrol mode. By the time of Schiavo's death, her case had embroiled pro-life religious groups, disability rights advocates, members of Congress, at least one state governor, the pope, and the creators of the popular TV animated show *South Park* (the "Best Friends Forever" South Park episode paralleling the Schiavo case, first aired on March 30, 2005, won an Emmy Award that same year). The involvement of these political and social actors in response to the media coverage acted as mechanisms of positive feedback, further fueling the explosion.

The sustained media explosion surrounding the Schiavo case was, it seems, enough to lodge living will policy on the public's radar in a way that no previous case (or coverage of the Schiavo case in 2003) had done. It stands to reason that the more than twofold increase in the number of Americans who had heard of living will policy and had applied this policy in their own lives between 1990 and 2005 was prompted not by the fact that a sensational case like this one received attention, but by the fact that it got *so much* attention in a short but sustained period of time.

Hurricane Katrina

While many variables were at play in pushing the media into alarm/patrol mode surrounding Hurricane Katrina, the main force driving this hybrid coverage was the event itself; Katrina constituted a focusing event, marked by its suddenness and also the extreme harm it inflicted (Birkland 1997). The event was dramatic, as was the immediate alarm-based coverage that surrounded it. But, arguably, it was the patrol-based coverage that quickly followed that prompted heightened national attention to a wide range of systemic issues that ran deeper even than the disaster itself. In the surveillance coverage that followed Katrina, journalists on patrol in the geographic area of Louisiana helped shed light on several pre-existing policy problems, including racial disparities in the distribution of social services, the fallibilities of the federal emergency response, and housing regulations. Forman and Lewis, for example, examine "the collective surprise that resulted when, in the light of the national media spotlight, Americans came to discover that the consequences of natural disaster are not equally shared, and that, lo and behold, large numbers of Black people are not doing so well" (2006, 181). As Britain's *Guardian* newspaper put it, "Hurricane Katrina not only destroyed New Orleans, but also laid bare the ugly truth about America's racial divide" (King 2005). Of course, Katrina illustrates how the "sustained" aspect of sustained media explosions is a highly relative term. Even in the case of major sustained media explosions like Katrina or the war on terror, media attention tends to shift away from the revealed policy problems well before those problems are addressed.

Jerry Sandusky

On November 4, 2011, Jerry Sandusky, former assistant coach of the Penn State football team under Joe Paterno, was indicted by a grand jury of forty counts of child sexual abuse; he was criminally charged with these counts the following day. Among Sandusky's alleged crimes were accusations that he had sexually abused multiple young boys in the shower area of the Lasch Building (home of the football program) on the Penn State campus (Viera 2011).

The story was picked up by news outlets across the country immediately following the grand jury's ruling. The media went into quick alarm mode, transmitting information about Sandusky's alleged crimes in a flurry of coverage. And then, even as the main facts of the case were still being unpacked, the media shifted into patrol mode, with journalists digging into the surrounding policy and social implications. The result was a sustained swell of stories framed around the incident-level evidence in the Sandusky case as it unfolded (or what Iyengar [1991] calls episodic evidence), but also wide-ranging reports on related considerations. For example, these stories brought to public consideration the social shame and healing that accompany child sexual abuse scandals (De Souza 2011); the shifting dominance of sports as a religion-like presence in university life (Pappano 2012); the dangers of enforcement systems entrenched within college campuses and other insular cultures (Bernstein 2011); and the role the media plays in the public's emotional reaction to scandals (Timpane 2012). News coverage, in other words, focused also on the larger, thematic picture of the problems at hand (Iyengar 1991).

The media swarm surrounding the Sandusky scandal had a near-immediate impact on the university's official position on the case. Penn State officials had known about the allegations against Sandusky for many years (Freeh 2012). But on November 6, 2011, two days after the grand jury's ruling, the university took its first formal action against Sandusky, barring him from campus (ESPN 2011). Presumably, the university's response was motivated in large part by the grand jury's ruling, but the explosion of media attention probably helped spur them to action (Zinser 2011).

University officials were not the only individuals who knew of the allegations against Sandusky well ahead of the scandal breaking in November 2011. Local news outlets reported the allegations much earlier, too. News coverage of the grand jury investigation dates back at least to March 2011, including a Pulitzer Prize–winning series by the *Harrisburg Patriot-News* (Ganim 2011) and print and radio coverage by Mark Madden, a prominent Pittsburgh talk show host (Madden 2011). But Penn State officials did not revoke Sandusky's campus access following the early, but limited, media exposure; they waited seven more months, until the grand jury ruling and the onslaught of media attention. It is impossible to know, of course, how those seven months might have mattered; for example, whether Sandusky used campus facilities for purposes of abuse during that time. But it is not difficult to imagine that if the media had latched onto the news item in March 2011 the way it did in November 2011, university officials might have responded sooner.

What distinguishes the initial low-level coverage of Sandusky in March 2011 from the media swarm that erupted in November 2011 is not only the *level* of news coverage, but also the type; namely, the initial coverage transmitted information about the alarm without shifting into patrol mode. Why? Many reasons—not the least of which is the significant distinction that lies between allegations and criminal charges. But momentum was also a factor. The initial coverage by a few news outlets was not enough to spark a cascade of attention. Once backed by additional information, however, coverage in November 2011 spread across the media as a whole, driven by incentive-based momentum. The alarm/patrol hybrid model helps explain why the media exploded around the Sandusky scandal in November 2011, but did not do so seven months earlier.

Trayvon Martin

On February 26, 2012, in a gated Florida community, George Zimmerman (Hispanic) shot and killed seventeen-year-old Trayvon Martin (African American). Martin, unarmed, was returning to his father's home after buying iced tea and Skittles from a nearby convenience store. Zimmerman thought Martin looked suspicious, called the police, and confronted Martin. Zimmerman had a license to carry a concealed weapon and, during the confrontation that ensued, he shot and killed Martin (Alvarez 2012). The media went quickly into alarm mode, rushing to sort out the facts of the case from the 911 calls and neighbors' accounts of the incident. But then, settling into patrol mode, the media began to dig into Florida's "Stand Your Ground" law, which supports a citizen's right to use force when encountering an imminent threat without being obliged to retreat. For example, when Florida's Stand Your Ground law was passed in 2005, the *New York Times* ran two articles on it. Martin's death in 2012 prompted ninety-three *Times* articles on the law. The sustained media explosion surrounding Martin's death drew citizen and policymaker attention. According to the Pew Research Center, in April 2012 George Zimmerman's incarceration and court case garnered 32% of public news interest (Pew 2012). Under the bombardment of media pressure, Florida state senator Chris Smith assembled a state task force to revise the seven-year-old legislation (Fineout 2012). The sustained media explosion affected lobbying groups as well: the National Rifle Association abandoned its efforts to pass a version of the Stand Your Ground law in Alaska (Crawford 2012); and supporters of the American Legislative Exchange Council conservative policy group withdrew contributions that were estimated to total hundreds of thousands of dollars, prompting the group to shift its policy focus as a result (Lichtblau 2012).

Skew and Explosiveness

The results of the tug-of-war between positive feedback (producing alarm mode) and negative feedback (producing patrol mode) are skew and explosiveness. These patterns are the necessary products of the dynamics driving the news-generation process. While the scarcity of agenda space often serves to exacerbate skew and explosiveness, it is neither a necessary or sufficient condition to produce these patterns. The simulation results in chapter 7 demonstrate this point: even given an artificial agenda space of just three stories per day and an embedded skew in the perceived importance of different issues, still it is only in the presence of both negative and positive feedback mechanisms that the agenda produces high levels of skew.

These patterns of skew and explosiveness hold important political implications (described in more detail in chapter 9). On the one hand, the hybrid alarm/patrol mode of reporting can produce sustained media explosions, embodying a larger and longer-lasting volume of media attention than either the alarm or patrol model alone would yield. As the examples above illustrate, these sustained media explosions can draw much-needed attention to underattended policy issues. In many cases, these sustained media explosions leave a meaningful mark on politics and society. Additionally, systemic explosiveness in the news means that the media is resistant to elite control. Yet, at the same time, this news-generation process makes it tremendously difficult for most policy problems to make it into the news. For each Watergate and Sandusky, many other policy problems lurk unnoticed between the media's limited and fleeting patrols. Also, these patterns suggest that the signals citizens receive from the news about the world portray real-world problems as being vastly less diverse than they in fact are, and as dissipating much more quickly than they in fact do. The news-generation process thus hinders the abilities of citizens—and policymakers—to process and respond thoughtfully and thoroughly to items in the news.

We might wonder whether one mode in particular—the alarm mode or the patrol mode—is directly responsible for the resulting patterns of skew and explosiveness in the news. Let's consider that question. A hypothetical (if impractical) patrol-only model, in which news outlets survey all policy issues and then distribute stories across issues based on perceived severity, would produce a media agenda that is skewed in direct proportion with whatever skew might exist in this distribution of perceived severity. Since events, for example, tend to be normally distributed in severity, we can imagine some degree of media skew produced by the patrol model, but nothing like we see in reality (Jones and Baumgartner 2005). Also in this hypothetical scenario of a patrol-only model, we would expect to see largely incremental change in the media agenda over time as news outlets updated each issue's coverage daily (or minute-by-minute) based on unfolding information.

Thus, we might hold the alarm function of media coverage accountable for most, if not all, of the dramatic skew and explosiveness we see in the news. And indeed, the alarm function contributes to skew by fueling the agenda with alarm news items that are more likely drawn from a narrow type of high-news-value issues. The alarm function also contributes to the explosiveness of the agenda by producing instances of dramatic change.

However, the patrol function also serves to exacerbate both skew and explosiveness because, in this context of media coverage, patrol reporting is often a function of the initial alarm reporting. That is, in the alarm/patrol mode of reporting, the patrol mode is usually centered on the policy or geographic neighborhood initially targeted by the alarm mode. Thus, the fixated attention that the patrol mode produces overrepresents those neighborhoods in the news, relative to the degree of representation they would receive under either the patrol-only or the alarm-only models of news generation. The patrol mode also exacerbates the explosiveness of the media agenda, since the patrol mode is what produces the friction-induced equilibria of coverage that is one-half of the explosiveness equation (explosiveness = equilibrium stability + punctuated change).

Thus, roughly speaking, we can think of the media's alarm mode as operating (mostly) through positive feedback mechanisms, whereas the patrol mode operates (mostly) through negative feedback mechanisms. We might also think of positive feedback as the key ingredient to produce skew and explosiveness, but in fact the two tend to operate as dual products of friction (see chapter 7). Positive feedback serves to concentrate the agenda on a few key issues for a brief period, but negative feed-back can keep attention fixed there, together producing a skewed agenda. It is the switching back and forth between negative and feedback processes that constitutes explosiveness, which, in turn, produces skew.

Predictions

In addition to the collective hypothesis 1 listed in the previous chapter, the alarm/patrol hybrid model suggests two additional hypotheses:

> Hypothesis 2: News coverage will exhibit dramatic skew in the distribution of attention across policy issues; most issues will get scarce amounts of attention, while a few will receive the vast bulk of attention.
>
> Hypothesis 3: News coverage will exhibit dramatic explosiveness in how it changes over time; rather than changing gradually, the agenda will lurch from periods of relative stability (patrol periods and periods of relative calm between major events) to moments of large change (alarm periods).

CHAPTER FOUR

Content and Change on the *New York Times* Front Page

The front page of the *New York Times* is approximately twenty-two inches tall and twelve inches wide: just big enough to wrap a fish. Big enough, too, for about eight stories—half that many on days when a major storyline dominates the page, and half again as many on slow days. Like the front pages, home pages, or leading story segments of other major news outlets, this single sheet of newsprint constitutes a powerful political agenda. In the case of the *Times* especially, the stories printed here help drive the rest of the U.S. media agenda. For people who read the *Times* and for people who don't, these front-page stories influence which issues we (citizens) think about and how we think about them. If food safety is on the front page, we tend to worry more about food safety. If it's not, we generally don't. Although we know rationally that the news is not a perfect mirror of reality—that just because the media isn't talking about food safety doesn't mean food safety isn't a concern—our brains are usually too busy juggling all the issues that *are* front-page news to think much about those that are not. More to the point, we are too busy juggling our daily lives. In many ways, the media is to most citizens what congressional investigative hearings are to the U.S. government. Whatever the process by which news coverage is generated (alarm, patrol, the alarm/patrol hybrid model I propose, or otherwise), citizens tend not to think about policy issues unless these issues are defined (via events) as policy *problems* in the news. Education, domestic abuse, tax policy . . . even genocide: no matter what the objective importance of these issues, they shift to the back burners of our minds—

and, often, the government's agenda—when they fall out of the news or even just off the front page.

Combining the influence of the *Times* front page with its small size, each of the eight or so daily front-page story slots represents a pretty penny of social and political purchasing power. Again, the structuring assumption behind the analyses in this book are that most front-page nonfeature stories prime citizens and policymakers to think about the policy issues implied by the events in those stories. But even stories that have no policy bearing exude influence simply by occupying space on the agenda. Vacuous stories about political campaign horse races, feature stories about the Red Sox or the British royal family, and even the softest news stories about the balloon boy hoax or the annual return of the McRib—each of these stories appears at the expense of all other stories that could have been run in its place. Thus, how front-page attention is distributed across issues has tremendous political import.

So how *is* front-page attention distributed? This chapter provides an answer based on all front-page *New York Times* articles from 1996 through 2006. The *Times* is a reasonably good representative—some studies suggest even a leading force—of U.S. national news coverage. As such, this single broadsheet offers a window into which topics of debate were most salient in the United States on any day during these eleven years and, more generally, into patterns in the news.

To investigate these patterns, we need to consider the precise nature of the attention scarcity at work on the front page. Attention scarcity by itself is not responsible for the patterns of skew and explosiveness (as I show in chapter 7), but attention scarcity adds weight to the institutional incentives under which news outlets operate. We also need to look at how front-page news is spread across issues and at how it changes over time, since variance exists in both cases. Accordingly, this chapter is structured around three questions: (1) Just how big is the front-page agenda? (2) How is front-page attention distributed across issues? (3) How does front-page attention change over time?

Here are the nutshell answers: (1) Really small, and getting smaller over time. (2) In a highly skewed manner, even more so than in the case of many other political agendas. (3) Explosively: the agenda tends to hover around a (shifting) baseline distribution of attention that is broken frequently by brief but dramatic bursts of attention; again, even more so than in the case of other agendas.

Many of the findings we will see in this chapter will be unsurprising. The front page contains more stories about war, for example, than about agriculture subsidies—no shock there. Yet the aggregate patterns of skew and explosiveness should give us considerable pause. We will see, for instance, a concrete measurement of exactly *how much* agenda space the top topics receive at the expense of other topics (or how little, depending on our perspective). And although some events like the Clinton/Lewinsky scandal or Hurricane Katrina send the media into alarm/patrol mode, producing the sustained media explosions illustrated by several examples in the previous chapter, many other explosions are the brief punctuations we would expect from the media being in alarm-mode only (i.e., "momentary explosions"). Additionally, patrol-based coverage, usually in the form of journalists and resources dispatched to cover a scheduled major event like the Olympics or an upcoming election, can produce a high volume of coverage that, under the right time lens, likewise appear as punctuations in the agenda (i.e., "timed explosions"). But, because this is the media, even a "sustained" media explosion is short-lived by the standards of any other political institution. Momentary explosions last for a few days, while sustained explosions last for maybe a month or two. Although major events like the 9/11 terrorist attacks can change the baseline equilibrium of how attention is distributed, the front-page agenda is simply too small to sustain a saturation of coverage for longer than a few months, even for the sustained media explosion surrounding 9/11 and the subsequent war on terror.

By exploring the rise and fall of issues on the *Times* front page over this eleven-year period, we can get a good sense of what this restricted agenda looks like and how it changes over time. Throughout this investigation, it is important to remember the two core types of variance at stake: variance in attention by issue, and variance over time. In fact, we can look empirically at whether variance in issue or variance in time is more responsible for determining how much front-page attention an issue receives. In other words, what matters more for whether an issue makes it to the front page: being the right issue or being at the right time? Statistical analyses run at the monthly level (other time units naturally produce different results) show that, for major topics, 66% of the "prediction" in how much front-page coverage a topic receives is driven by which topic it is, while 34% is driven by time. For subtopic issues, however, only 38% of the variance attention can be explained by subtopic, while time accounts for 62%.[1] So then, both the issue and the tim-

ing matter in determining how much front-page attention an issue receives; both play a role in producing patterns in the news. Most of the
analyses presented in chapters 5 and 6 focus on explaining over-time
variance; even in the cross-sectional models in chapter 5, I do not control for variance in issue "type" beyond distinguishing between domestic
and international topics. But the descriptive findings in the current chapter help keep us grounded in the importance of issue variance.

Beyond examining how the agenda is distributed across topics and
how specific topics and issues rise and fall over time, this chapter will
also present stark aggregate patterns of skew and explosive change, the
mechanics of which chapter 7 will help unpack. The theoretical discussion from chapter 2 begins to take hold here, as we start to see how not
only events but also variables like public concern and agenda congestion
help shape which issues become news—relationships that chapters 5 and
6 will test more explicitly. But first, let us tour the front page.

The *New York Times* Front-Page Agenda Dataset

The dataset compiled for this book contains all front-page stories in the
New York Times from January 1, 1996 through December 31, 2006: a total of 31,034 stories.[2] Rather than sample articles from the *Times* as a
whole, I limit my analysis to the front page because the eight or so stories
appearing on this page each day occupy the topmost echelon of societal
awareness—the core of attention. To be sure, dealing only with stories
appearing on one page of this very thick newspaper limits the immediate generalizability of this study to just that—the front page. Yet using
only the front page offers the enormous benefit of a fine-grained yet full-
census (i.e., nonsampled) dataset. In this way, the front page is an especially attractive subject of study, as it allows examination of an agenda in
its entirety.

Still, the choice to use only the front page is based not on sampling
considerations but rather on the particular *kind* of observations located
on this agenda. The goal of this book is to understand how events get
processed and generated into the daily news and, thus, signaled to the
political system at large; that is, how it is that some problems penetrate
political consciousness while most others go unnoticed. The front page is
the most appropriate medium for this endeavor. It stands to reason that,
for those people who read the news, front-page stories are the ones they

read first and, generally, the ones to which they pay the most attention. For those people who get their news primarily from television or websites (or who don't actively seek the news at all), the *Times* front page is still a good representation of the information they receive. To the extent that the *Times* tracks with (and drives) the agendas of other media outlets as discussed below, these front-page articles are the most likely to overlap other sources and, thus, the most indicative single measure of national media coverage.

The front-page agenda differs from the full *New York Times* in several ways, and it is important to understand these differences at the outset of this investigation—differences that likely apply to the front-page versus in-fold news of most newspapers, as well as to the headline (and often last-to-be-aired) versus interior segments of television news casts, and the home page versus outer link stories of news websites. Space is even more limited, and thus issue "competition" is even higher on the front page and its equivalents. As a result, the front page has much more stringent barriers to entry for issues and, thus, a much higher salience threshold than the full agenda.

The effect of this high salience threshold is greater friction on the front-page agenda, leading to greater skew in attention given to issues on the front page and greater explosiveness over time (Baumgartner and Jones 2009). As I will demonstrate, the topics that gain space on the front page fall into two main categories: those that receive sparse attention—a few stories a year at most—and those that receive an enormous amount—dozens and dozens of stories. The full paper also has great variance in the amount of attention paid to different policy topics, but the skew of attention there is not quite as stark. This difference means that the front page, even more than the paper as a whole, deals more in "mega storylines"—issues that consume the vast bulk of attention, as much as 65% of the agenda in a given month. The *issue* underpinning a mega storyline at one point in time will not necessarily be one in the next time period; for example, stories about Hurricane Katrina consumed 48% of the front-page stories in September 2005, but at no other point between 1996 and 2006 does a weather or natural disaster event take up more than 7% of the agenda. Other issues—like the U.S. conflicts in Afghanistan and Iraq—function as mega storylines for long stretches of time. Whatever the type, the front page is very often dominated by mega storylines of one kind or another, forcing all other problems to the margins.

Moreover, the front page and full paper differ in the specific type of issue most likely to receive the bulk of attention. While at the top of the front-page agenda are "high politics" issues—such as war, diplomacy, and elections—the full-paper agenda is more concerned with "nonpolitics" issues—such as business news, sports, arts, and entertainment. "Low politics" issues—such as agriculture, energy, and transportation—only rarely receive attention from either agenda (Wolfe, Boydstun, and Baumgartner 2009).

Beyond the substance of the policies showcased on each agenda, the front page also has a greater tendency than the full paper to showcase bad news over good news, with important consequences for public perception of policy issues (Soroka 2006). The routine human interest article or sports report keeps the front page from reading like an unrelenting doomsday account, but nearly all the policy issues on the front page are there because of policy *problems* transmitted by problematic events. The tendency to report bad news over good is true of most news sources, including the full text of the *Times*, but it comes to bear even more on the front page with its high salience threshold. When policies are working, they rarely make the news; they almost never make the front page. When important policies fail, or show threat of failure, however, they are much more likely to gain top billing as front-page stories. And when the policy is especially important and the failure especially large, it is common to see a mega storyline emerge and, thus, attention to all other issues decline. In any case, whether good news or bad, front-page news cues citizens about which problems to consider, among all the problems in the world.

The *Times* and the Larger U.S. Media Market

I focus on the *New York Times* for two reasons. First, the *Times* serves—and continues to serve, even in today's digital media context—as a key political agenda. As former Obama press secretary Robert Gibbs says, the *Times* "has the ability to drive the news" (Auletta 2010). Whatever the reasons, the *Times* simply has an unparalleled degree of social and political influence (Smith 1992).

This degree of influence would make a study of the *Times* interesting in its own right as the national paper of record even if the coverage of this lone newspaper bore no relation to that of other news outlets. But, and the second reason I focus on the *Times*, it does. The *Times* is by no means a perfect proxy for U.S. news coverage, but as representative and even leading indicators go, it's pretty good. Several studies suggest that the *Times* is generally representative of U.S. national newspaper coverage and, in many instances, national television coverage as well.[3] For example, a comparison of the *Times* with other major national newspapers in the case of the death penalty suggests that both the levels of attention and the issue-definitions, or frames, employed in the *Times* are consistent with other major newspapers (Baumgartner, De Boef, and Boydstun 2008). Some research suggests that the *Times* even has a leading influence on the agendas of other newspapers (national and local) and of television; that is, that it has strong internews-outlet agenda-setting power (Golan 2006; Reese and Danielian 1989).

That said, each news outlet is a unique animal. As Graber notes: "Political news coverage by the *New York Times*, which is read carefully by political elites worldwide, cannot be equated with news coverage by the *Detroit News*, which takes a far more populist, tabloid approach" (2003a, 140–41). I said earlier that the media is to most citizens as congressional investigative hearings are to the U.S. government. The "everyman" does not likely rely on the *New York Times* specifically for cues on which events/issues to follow (though many elites do). Still, given the studies cited above showing that the *Times* is a strong proxy for national news, we can treat it as a strong proxy for the cues sent to citizens more generally about which issues to think about (and which they can ignore).

Precisely how the day-to-day stories of the *Times* map onto coverage by other news outlets is not at issue here. The main story of this book is about the *aggregate patterns* of skew and explosiveness that the alarm/patrol hybrid model predicts. Thus, what is at issue here is whether the *Times'* aggregate patterns are generalizable to the U.S. media more broadly. To demonstrate this generalizability, chapter 8 contains the results of a large-scale study comparing levels of attention to forty-five policy issues across national newspapers, television news programs, and online news sources. By examining these patterns, we can see that the *Times* is indeed strongly representative of other national newspapers and, to a large extent, television and online news as well. At the same time, key differences exist between print, television, and online news. Yet rather than mitigating the relevance of this *New York Times* study to modern media, these differences show that the patterns of skew and explosiveness in the *Times* are even *more* applicable in the context of television and online news. As we would expect, these more modern media sources operate at a much quicker pace than do traditional broadsheets. The marketplace incentives described in chapters 2 and 3 are even more strongly in play in the case of television and online news outlets, and online news outlets (currently) tend to operate under stricter resource budgets. Plus, despite the vast theoretical expanse of the Web, in many ways both television and online news outlets operate with smaller agenda spaces than do newspapers. The accelerated pace, heightened marketplace pressures, and narrowed agenda space of modern media exacerbate the disproportional nature of how these news outlets process information. The result is that television and online news outlets exhibit the same patterns of skew and disproportionate change found in the *Times*, but in even sharper relief. From these findings, we can conclude that skew and explosiveness are generalizable media phenomena.

Content Analysis

Grounded in this understanding of the *New York Times* front page as different but largely representative of the U.S. national news media, I move now to describing the process of collecting the *New York Times* front-page agenda dataset. Each *Times* front-page story was coded, based on manually reading the headline and the first three paragraphs, by topic and subtopic according to Baumgartner and Jones' Policy Agendas Codebook.[4] Coders underwent extensive training before coding stories to add to the dataset.[5] All indicators show that the intercoder reliability of the dataset is strong.[6]

By employing the Policy Agendas Project codes, the *Times* front-page dataset can be analyzed in comparison with the many datasets already collected by policy-agenda scholars using this same coding scheme, including congressional data on budgets, roll call votes, bills, and laws; executive data on State of the Union addresses and executive orders; Supreme Court decision data; full *New York Times* data (stories sampled from the entire paper); and Gallup "most important problem" survey data. We will see just such a comparison later in this chapter.

At the macro level, the Policy Agendas codebook consists of 27 major topic categories (coded at the two-digit level): Macroeconomics (topic code 01), Civil Rights and Liberties (02), Health (03), Agriculture (04), Labor and Employment (05), Education (06), Environment (07), Energy (08), Transportation (10), Law and Crime (12), Social Welfare (13), Community Development and Housing (14), Banking and Business (15), Defense (16), Science and Technology (17), Foreign Trade (18), International Affairs (19), Government Operations (20), Public Lands (21), Culture and Entertainment (23), State and Local Government (24), Weather and Natural Disasters (26), Fires (27), Sports and Recreation (29), Death Notices (30), Churches and Religion (31), and Human Interest and Miscellaneous (99).[7]

The first 19 of these topics are further divided into a total of 225 subtopics (at the four-digit level), of which 217 appear at least once on the *Times* front page between 1996 and 2006.[8] For example, within Macroeconomics, subtopics include Inflation and Interest Rates (subtopic code 0101), Unemployment (0103), Monetary Supply (0104), National Budget and Debt (0105), Taxation (0107), and so on. The eight major topics that do not contain subtopics (Culture, State and Local Government, Weather, Fires, Sports, Death Notices, Churches and Religion, and Human Interest) are treated as individual subtopics for this book, yielding a total of 225 subtopics, or issues, to be examined (the 217 Policy Agendas subtopics used at least once plus the eight topics that are not subdivided).[9] This dataset, then, provides a rich illustration of which issues have—and which have not—received attention over the last decade.

Just How Big Is the Front Page?

Agenda size matters. The smaller the agenda, the more "competition" between issues, the higher the salience threshold and, thus, the more susceptible the agenda will be to skew and explosive change. Attention scarcity does not produce patterns of skew and explosiveness, but it can certainly exacerbate these patterns. The *New York Times* front page has an average of about eight stories a day, though this number varies (mean = 7.72, standard deviation = 1.22, minimum = 4, maximum = 11). Figure 4.1 shows the frequency of days between 1996 and 2006 that the *Times* front page contained between four and eleven articles. This graphic communicates a simple but powerful fact about the front-page agenda: it is very, very small.

As we can see from figure 4.1, the front page rarely has room for more than eight or nine stories, and often covers even fewer. Perhaps counter-

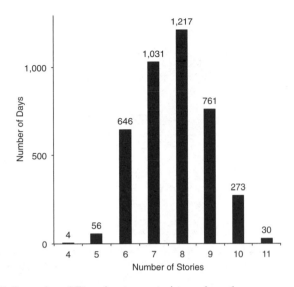

FIGURE 4.1. Daily number of *Times* front-page stories, 1996–2006
Note: N = 31,034 stories across 4,018 days.

intuitively, the front-page agenda tends to be the smallest in the presence of the most (subjectively) important news stories—often stories that contribute to what I call mega storylines. For these big stories, editors want to showcase as much text and photos on page A1 as possible, thereby reducing the total number of stories. During the eleven years studied here, it happened only four times that the *Times* ran only four front-page stories: on September 12, 2001, the day after the attacks of 9/11; on February 2, 2003, the day after NASA's space shuttle *Columbia* exploded, killing all seven crew members aboard; on August 15, 2003, the day after the power blackout that affected an estimated 55 million people across Canada and the northwestern and midwestern United States, representing the most widespread electrical blackout in history; and on April 2, 2005, the day Pope John Paul II died. In general, the larger the story (and encompassing storyline) at play on the front page, the higher the agenda congestion.

What is more, the front-page agenda has literally shrunk over time. On August 6, 2007, for example, the front page was reduced from its long-term size of 13.5 inches wide and 22 inches tall to a new size of 12 inches wide and 22 inches tall. Just an inch and a half—no big deal, right? Yet

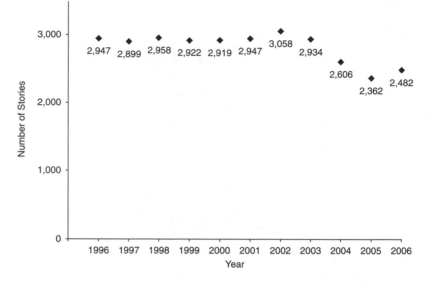

FIGURE 4.2. Size of the *Times* front-page agenda by year, 1996–2006
Note: N = 31,034 stories across 11 years.

this inch and a half equaled 11% of the previous agenda space. While additional pages were added to the full paper to compensate for part of the reduction in space, bringing the overall reduction in the full-paper agenda to 5%, the front page is the front page (Seelye 2006a, 2006b).

Beyond the physical shrinking of the front page, formatting changes have also served to reduce the size of this agenda. For example, although the front page was 13.5 inches wide and 22 inches tall for the entirety of the eleven-year time span I examine, figure 4.2 shows a noticeable decrease in the average number of front-page stories beginning in 2004, presumably a result of shifts toward a "less is more" layout and formatting philosophy that the *Times* undertook around that time. As the newspaper industry continues to struggle, the front-page agenda may be reduced further still by the increasing presence of advertisements. Notably, the *Times* ran a front-page paid advertisement for the first time on January 6, 2009. The full-color ad, purchased by CBS for an undisclosed amount of money, measured two and a half inches high and stretched across the entire bottom of the page, representing a staggering 20.8% of the front-page agenda for that day (Perez-Pena 2009).

How Is Front-Page Attention Distributed across Issues?

Which policy issues hit the front page? Figures 4.3a and 4.4b show how the *Times* front page was distributed across the twenty-seven major topics during the eleven years in this study. The raw values behind these figures as well as basic summary statistics appear in table A.1 of the appendix.

As a pie chart, figure 4.3a is not designed to provide a substantive comparison between the amount of coverage given to each topic area (pie charts are notoriously devious in this regard). Rather, the sole purpose of figure 4.3a is to demonstrate the dramatic degree to which front-page attention is unevenly distributed, or skewed, across topics. In figure 4.3b, we see this same skew but arrayed in more legible format, allowing us to pinpoint the relative amount of front-page coverage given to each topic.

Figures 4.3a and 4.3b show that three topics—International Affairs, Defense, and Government Operations—consume nearly half (48%) of all front-page attention. International Affairs alone consumes 21% of the agenda with 6,354 stories. This topic contains all stories about events foreign to the United States, including stories about domestic issues in other countries (e.g., education in Iraq) that would be categorized elsewhere if happening in the United States. As shown in figure A.1 of the appendix, when the opposite coding approach is applied (e.g., coding education in Iraq under Education, not International Affairs) the portion of the agenda consumed by International Affairs decreases sharply (from 21% to 5%), increasing other topic shares in the process (e.g., Defense goes from 14% to 20%). Yet this alternate approach does not mitigate the main finding here: dramatic skew.

Defense captures 14% of the agenda, with War (subtopic code 1619) accounting for the vast majority of these stories.[10] Considering that more than half the stories examined here were prior to the attacks of September 11, 2001, figures 4.3a and 4.3b offer a sense of just how strong a media presence the war maintained in the years following the attacks, with the front page often saturated with two, three, four, or even five war stories *in a single day*. As figure A.2 of the appendix shows, the post-9/11 agenda devoted nearly four times as many stories to Defense as the pre-9/11 agenda, from less than 8% of the agenda before to more than 22% after. This shift represents a major structural break, narrowing the

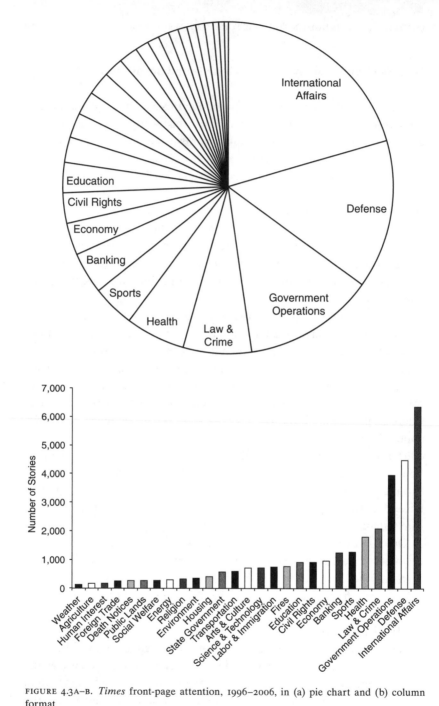

FIGURE 4.3A–B. *Times* front-page attention, 1996–2006, in (a) pie chart and (b) column format

Note: N = 31,034 stories across 27 topics.

agenda space available to other policy topics in the process. Government Operations takes the biggest hit in agenda space after 9/11 compared to before, dropping from 16% to 9%, though much of this decline is due to the high levels of attention paid to the 2000 national election, hanging chads and all. But consider instead a low-level topic like Education. This topic has never received—probably will never receive—a sizable portion of the front page. Still, in the post-9/11 period of the dataset compared to the pre-9/11 period, attention to Education dropped by a third, from 3.4% to 2.4%. For education advocates, this shrinkage of agenda space is significant. War has many costs. One of these is the dramatic reduction in attention available to other important problems.

Government Operations (including subtopics such as Bureaucratic Oversight, Nominations and Appointments, IRS Administration, Presidential Impeachment and Scandal, and—the largest subtopic in this category by far—Elections) received 13% of the agenda, or 3,958 stories, during the eleven years studied.[11] Since the dataset spans 4,018 distinct front pages, this statistic means that, on average, nearly every front page over this eleven-year period had a story primarily focused on the operations of the U.S. national government. An average of one article a day, out of an average of eight, is an awful lot, showing that government—and elections in particular—are at the core not only of political discourse but of the media agenda as well. Again, many of these news stories about government operations were of the horse-race variety (Domke et al. 1997; Iyengar, Norpoth, and Hanh 2004; Lawrence 2000a; Plasser 2005). Nevertheless, these stories cue citizens to think about government at the expense of other topics.

The next five topics in size in figure 4.3b—Law and Crime, Health, Sports, Banking and Commerce, and the Economy—constitute another 24% of the agenda space, meaning that the remaining nineteen topics together consume less than one-third of the agenda. Note how relatively few stories are consumed by topics not directly related to politics or policymaking. While NFL, MLB, March Madness, and other national sporting events certainly maintain a constant presence on the front page, Sports stories consume only 4% of attention. Together, the "nonpolicy" topics of Sports, Fires, Culture, Churches, Death Notices, Human Interest, and Weather constitute just over 11% of the agenda, meaning that nearly 90% of *Times* front-page attention is paid to stories at least implicitly linked to policy and government matters of domestic and international concern.[12] We would likely see a very different pattern in local

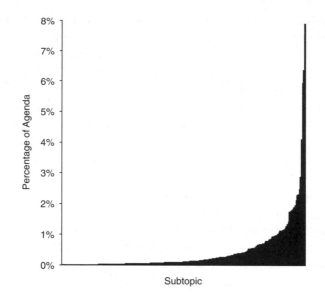

FIGURE 4.4. *Times* front-page attention by subtopic, 1996–2006
Note: N = 31,034 stories across 225 subtopics.

news outlets, where local events (sports and weather especially) receive much more attention. For national news though, the front page is the stuff of policy and politics.

While figures 4.3a and 4.3b show skew in coverage across major topics, figure 4.4 shows an even starker picture at the subtopic, or issue, level. Here, each column represents the total number of stories devoted to each of the 225 issues across the full range of the dataset, with columns arranged in ascending order of size. Consider that if attention was distributed normally, the heights of the columns would increase with a gradual slope carving out the left half of a normal distribution. Instead, we see a long tail of very small counts on the left (but no zeroes, since the eight subtopics in the Policy Agendas Codebook that never received a front-page story during this time range are excluded) before a sudden sweep up to the few subtopics with monstrous counts on the right; these mega subtopics are often, though not always, the issues underlying what I call mega storylines. Of all the 225 issues in the dataset, five received more than 2.5% of attention: Civil Defense (code 1615) including U.S. domestic terrorism such as the Oklahoma City bombings and foreign terrorist attacks on U.S. soil such as 9/11 (3%), Sports (code 2900) (4%),

War (code 1619) (6%), Middle East (code 1920) including all stories about the Middle East where the United States is not a central actor (6%), and Elections (code 2012) (8%). If we were to look at figure 4.4 without knowing what it was, we might think it was a graph of global income disparity, so stark is the skew of front-page attention across issues.

By looking at figure 4.5, we can see how the front-page agenda compares to that of other key agendas in American politics. This figure shows the distribution of the *Times* front page, sorted in ascending order of front-page attention, compared with one measure of the executive agenda (in the form of executive orders), one measure of the legislative agenda (in the form of congressional hearings), and one measure of the public agenda (in the form of Gallup's "most important problem" survey responses). All calculations were run at the major topic level across the first 19 topics of the Policy Agendas Codebook (excluding Sports, Weather, etc.). All datasets have been truncated to the 1996–2006 period to match the NYT dataset, but note that the executive orders dataset ends in 2003. Note also that in order to account for variant versions of surveys in the MIP series and to give equal "weight" to each time period regardless of how many surveys were conducted, the data was first collapsed into a monthly series (with missing months imputed) and then summed by topic before proportions were calculated. Date ranges and observation sizes are listed below:

- NYT Front Page: 1996–2006, N = 26,806 stories
- Congressional Hearings (http://www.policyagendas.org): 1996–2006, N = 1,5681 hearings
- Executive Orders (http://www.policyagendas.org): 1996–2003, N = 339 orders
- Public's Most Important Problem (http://www.policyagendas.org): 1996–2006, N = 132 months of averaged or imputed surveys

Figure 4.5 shows that executive orders and congressional hearings are more evenly distributed than the other agendas. These governmental agendas give large amounts of attention to some of the policy areas that dominate the front page like Law and Crime and, naturally, Government Operations, but they also pay much more attention to policy areas like Transportation, Environment, Public Lands, and Foreign Trade, which the front page all but ignores. The public "most important problem" data, however, shows perhaps the greatest disconnect from the rest of these agendas. The public puts an overwhelming emphasis on Law and

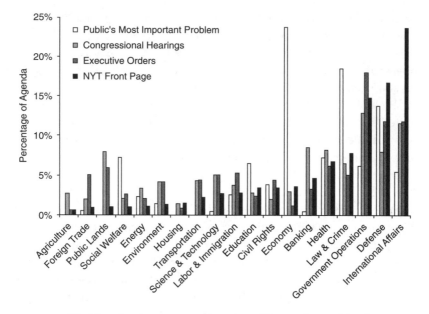

FIGURE 4.5. The *Times* front page compared to other policy agendas, 1996–2006
Note: See online appendix for individual graphs by policy agenda, including the congressional bills agenda using data from the Congressional Bills Project conducted by Adler and Wilkerson (http://www.congressionalbills.org).
Sources: The NYT Front-Page dataset is the one developed for this book. The congressional hearings, executive orders, and Gallup MIP datasets come from Policy Agendas Project (http://www.policyagendas.org). The data used here were originally collected by Frank R. Baumgartner and Bryan D. Jones, with the support of National Science Foundation grant number SBR 9320922, and were distributed through the Department of Government at the University of Texas at Austin and/or the Department of Political Science at the University of North Carolina, Chapel Hill. Neither NSF nor the original collectors of the data bear any responsibility for the analysis reported here.

Crime and, especially, the Economy. For several reasons—not the least of which is the fact that Gallup's poll constitutes a single-issue agenda for each person surveyed—none of the other agendas in figure 4.5 respond to these public concerns in kind; if people were asked to name their top four or five priorities, the public agenda would likely be less skewed (for more discussion on the limits of the most important problem measure, see: Jennings and Wlezien 2011; Wlezien 2005). This and many other caveats accompany the comparison of these very different datasets to one another in this fashion; these agendas surely represent not just apples and oranges, but bananas and kiwis, too.

Figure 4.6 shows a more detailed comparison between the *Times* front page and the full paper. In addition to columns representing the percentage of the front-page and full-paper agendas consumed by each topic, this figure shows a "Difference" line, calculated by subtracting the full-paper percentage from the front-page percentage in each case, with topics sorted in ascending order of this difference measure. Thus, when the difference measure sits on the horizontal line marking the zero point on the right-hand axis, it means that the topic in question takes up exactly the same percentage of attention on both agendas; values below the line represent less front-page attention relative to the full paper; values above the line represent more front-page attention. The difference measure shows that most of the topics (twenty-one out of twenty-seven) receive front-page attention on par with full-paper attention, falling within a 5% difference in either direction. But at the far left, we see three topics

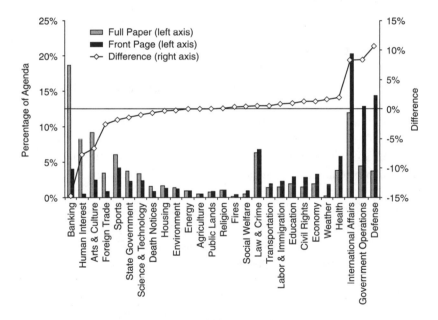

FIGURE 4.6. The *Times* front page versus full paper, 1996–2005
Note: The columns are arranged in ascending order of the gap between the percentage of the front-page agenda and the percentage of the full-paper agenda consumed by each topic. The "Difference" line captures this gap (calculated simply as front-page percentage minus full-paper percentage for each topic). Since the full-paper dataset is only available through 2005, for the sake of comparison the front-page data shown here are truncated to 2005.
Sources: NYT Front Page: 1996–2005, N = 28,552 stories; NYT Full Paper (http://www.policyagendas.org): 1996–2005, N = 9,363 stories (sampled).

that are especially scarce on the front page as compared to the full pa-per: Banking and Commerce, Human Interest, and Arts and Culture. And on the far right, three topics receive much more front-page than full-paper coverage: International Affairs, Government Operations, and Defense—exactly the three topics that consume nearly half the front-page agenda in total.

This comparison reminds us that the front page really is a distinct animal from the full paper (Wolfe, Boydstun, and Baumgartner 2009). Thus, with regard to attention to specific topics, the front-page findings presented here are not generalizable to the full *Times* newspaper, or to other full newspapers for that matter, and this is as it should be. But, again, as the findings in chapters 7 and 8 suggest, the story of how the news-generation process produces systemic patterns of skew and explo-siveness is very much generalizable not just to the full *New York Times* but also to "the" media at large.

How Does Front-Page Attention Vary over Time?

Just as important as understanding the overall distribution of front-page attention across topics is understanding the dynamics of the front page. Figure 4.7 offers a broad view of front-page attention dynamics, showing the distribution of stories across all major topic categories by year. This picture is deceptively smooth. As anyone who follows the daily news knows, the media cycle is much more volatile than the fairly steady lines in this figure imply. Yet, figure 4.7 tells us something interesting and im-portant about the resiliency of front-page attention: in the long-range scheme of things, the agenda is relatively stable. If we pick a topic at ran-dom and follow the thickness of its layer of the agenda over time, in most cases the layer will retain approximately the same thickness from left to right on the graph . . . with a few notable exceptions.

These exceptions appear throughout the range of topic areas, but of course they are most visible in the largest topics toward the bottom of figure 4.7. Most notable is the increase in attention to Defense in 2001 and thereafter, as already discussed and shown in the before/after shots of figure A.2.[13] Also, forming a discernible zigzag pattern, attention to Government Operations rises every other year, namely in years of na-tional elections, and especially the presidential election years. The 2002

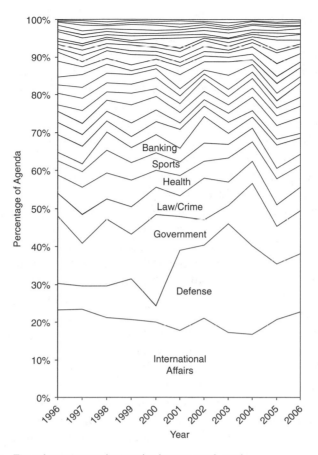

FIGURE 4.7. *Times* front-page topic attention by year, 1996–2006
Note: N = 31,034 stories across 11 years.

midterm election is an exception to this pattern, presumably having been crowded out by discussion of the war.

When we ignore these large-scale changes in attention to Defense and Government Operations and the agenda-narrowing they produce, we can see how the distribution of the agenda across all other topics really is quite stable over time—at the yearly level—although other relative surges are also apparent, such as Energy in 2001 (the rolling California blackouts), Banking and Commerce in 2002 (the Enron scandal), and Law and Crime also in 2002 (when the Catholic priest abuse scandal broke; these stories were coded under subtopic 1207, Child Abuse).

The stability of the agenda, the dramatic shift in attention to Defense following 9/11, the seasonal surges in attention to Elections, and the smaller surges in attention throughout figure 4.7 all support the story of news values and other institutional incentives discussed in chapter 2. Some topics are simply more newsworthy than others. Disproportionate information processing in the news-generation process stabilizes around this baseline equilibrium ordering of newsworthiness, although, as we have seen, this equilibrium can change (as with the structural break induced by 9/11). When storylines involving war, elections, or scandal break, editors give them due agenda space, producing surges in attention. Front-page attention to the topic of Government Operations declines in off-election years not because the workings of government become less important, but because editors are under pressure to return coverage to other newsworthy items. Against the backdrop of this baseline equilibrium, the media frequently goes into alarm or alarm/patrol mode, but the resulting media explosions do not last for long. At the yearly level, it is the powerful equilibrium rather than the punctuations that shows through.

Narrowing in on smaller units of time reveals the punctuations. Figure 4.8 zooms in on one year of data at the monthly level.[14] At this monthly level, even the structural-break shift in equilibrium following 9/11 displays as a sharp punctuation rather than a step increase. Despite sustained levels of public awareness and concern about terrorism and the military action in Afghanistan well into 2002 and beyond, in January 2002 the surge in attention to Banking and Commerce centered on the Enron scandal pushed attention to Defense down to 23% (from 63%, 40%, and 37% in October, November, and December of 2001, respectively). And in the very next month of February, attention to both Defense and Banking and Commerce declined as attention to Sports surged. Given the scarcity of attention and the strategic distribution of newsroom resources to staple seasonal items like elections and major sporting events, even terrorism and banking scandals must make room for the Winter Olympics.

Zooming in further, figure 4.9 shows the first three months of 2002 at the weekly level. Here, we see the strong give and take between the Enron scandal, the Winter Olympics, and the ongoing fallout from 9/11 and subsequent unfolding military actions in Afghanistan. Above all, figure 4.9 shows a picture of a scarce agenda space with a (shifting) base-

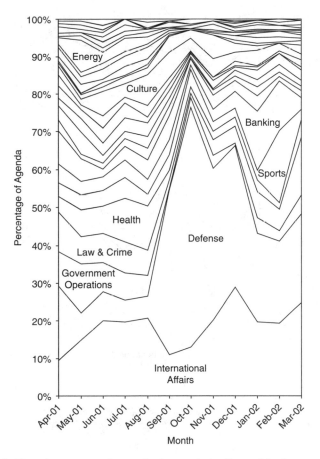

FIGURE 4.8. *Times* front-page topic attention by month, April 2001–March 2002
Note: N = 3,228 stories across 12 months.

line equilibrium punctuated frequently by brief, dramatic surges in attention to key storylines. In short: explosive change.

Which Time Perspective Is Best?

Which temporal unit of analysis is the most appropriate for understanding media dynamics? The yearly level shows at least one major structural
break, but overall resounding stability in the media agenda. The monthly,
weekly, and (not shown here) daily levels of analysis show increasing vol-

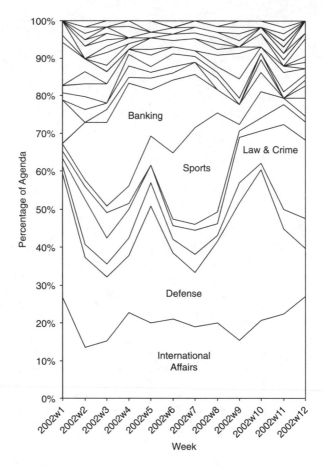

FIGURE 4.9. *Times* front-page topic attention by week, January–March 2002
Note: N = 723 stories across 12 weeks.

atility. At the monthly level, the visible punctuations are produced by those mega storylines that capture the news for several weeks. In general, these monthly punctuations are what I have termed "sustained media explosions," born of the alarm/patrol hybrid mode that news outlets enter under particular (hard-to-predict) conditions, though these sustained explosions exhibit varying durations. At the weekly level, the visible punctuations generally capture what I have termed "momentary" and "timed media explosions," born of the alarm- and patrol-modes of news generation, respectively (though here too the explosions can vary in duration). Of course, punctuations at the weekly level can also fuel sustained media explosions, visible at the monthly level. The daily level exhibits wild fluctuations capturing the day-to-day newsroom decisions underlying these aggregate patterns. But which level tells the true story? Is the media highly stable or highly volatile? Unlike Goldilocks, we have no perfect porridge to choose. The media *is* highly stable over time, with short-term data highlighting the inevitable noise produced by daily decisions of which news items to pursue, in contrast to meaningful long-term trends. At the same time, the media *is* highly volatile, with the daily, weekly, and even monthly levels showing meaningful media explosions, big and small, laid over a (shifting) baseline of issue distribution. In short, the media agenda is, truly, an explosive system of punctuated equilibrium dynamics.

Types of Issue Dynamics

Media explosions come in different forms, as discussed with regard to the news-generation process in chapter 3. The alarm/patrol hybrid mode of news coverage tends to produce sustained media explosions; the alarm mode tends to produce momentary media explosions; and the patrol mode can produce timed explosions when journalistic resources are dispatched to dig into an upcoming important event. All issues are subject to these differing forms of dynamic coverage, depending on the many variables that condition the news-generation process. Yet among issues, some tend to be more susceptible to some types of media explosions than others. Here, I identify three loose (and often overlapping) categories of issues with respect to the dynamics they tend to exhibit, as illustrated by six individual issues displayed collectively in figures 4.10–4.12. Seeing these different dynamic patterns helps us understand how, while news outlets handle coverage of different types of issues in fundamentally different ways, the common mechanisms of institutional incentives in the news-generation process yield some form of explosive change across most issues.

BREAD-AND-BUTTER ISSUES. Some issues, while rarely given large amounts of attention, never fall off the agenda for long. Figures 4.10a and 4.10b show two such issues: Sports and Weather. Like all issues, bread-and-butter issues are shaped by events (and the rest of the eight variables outlined in chapter 2). But unlike other issues, editorial news values dictate that these issues have an all-but-guaranteed position on the front

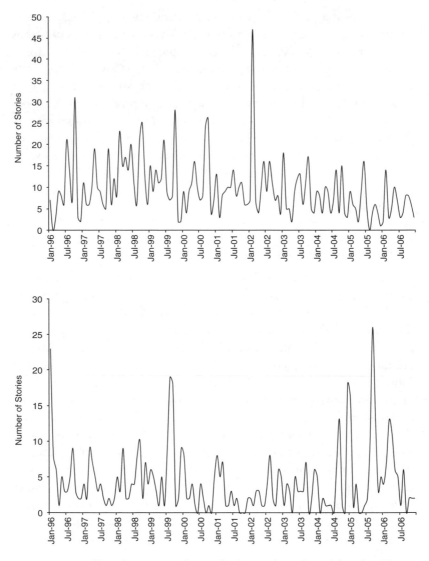

FIGURE 4.10A–B. *Times* front-page topic attention by month, 1996–2006: Bread-and-butter issues

FIGURE 4.10A. Sports and Recreation (Code 2900)
Note: N = 1,273 stories.

FIGURE 4.10B. Weather and Natural Disasters (Code 2600)
Note: N = 573 stories.

page since they are of perpetual interest to readers. These bread-and-butter issues occupy a small minority of the front page, but even in the wake of dramatic and traumatic world events, readers still want to know about baseball scores and storm warnings, and so these issues continue to occupy a small but stable share of the agenda.

Looking at figure 4.10a, the sports coverage shows modest surges in attention around regularly scheduled major sporting events, with timed media explosions occurring with each Summer and Winter Olympics; the biggest spike in attention comes during the 2002 Winter Olympics in Salt Lake City, presumably because the United States hosted these games. Also present in this figure, though more difficult to see, are small timed explosions surrounding each Super Bowl and World Series. And between these timed explosions, sporting events remain constant fixtures in the news. Although the topic of Sports only receives an average of approximately ten stories each month, only twice in this eleven-year period was there a month without a sports article on the front page.

As seen in figure 4.10b, weather events display a similar constant presence on the agenda. On average, the topic of Weather and Natural Disasters receives only four stories per month, yet still nearly every month has weather coverage. The largest spike in the Weather and Natural Disasters series coincides with the sustained media explosion surrounding Hurricane Katrina in August 2005. Also present are the momentary media explosions surrounding the Indian Ocean tsunami, the Haiti earthquake, and major storms (especially those affecting New York).

Other bread-and-butter topics include Death Notices and Culture and Entertainment, which by nature of their subject matter have a firm, though modest, hold on the agenda. Notice that none of these issues are directly governed by governmental decisionmaking, yet they are of perpetual salience to the American public. A constant stream of related events always manages to propel a few articles on these issues each month. Nothing is certain on the front page, we might say, except death, taxes, sports, and snowstorms on the eastern seaboard.

SEASONAL ISSUES.   In the case of some issues, fluctuations in attention are strongly shaped by events that occur regularly and predictably. Figures 4.11a and 4.11b show two such issues: National Elections and Nominations. Note that some bread-and-butter issues—in particular, Sports—are also seasonal issues.

While figure 4.11a shows that elections always have some place on

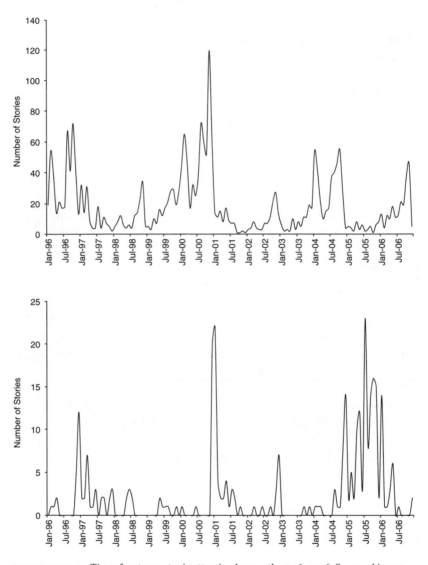

FIGURE 4.11A–B. *Times* front-page topic attention by month, 1996–2006: Seasonal issues

FIGURE 4.11A. National Elections (Code 2012)
Note: N = 2,450 stories.

FIGURE 4.11B. Nominations (Code 2005)
Note: N = 307 stories.

the public agenda, the Elections series also exhibits a telltale, timed explosion leading up to the November elections in each even-numbered year. Unsurprisingly, of the three presidential elections included here, the 2000 election exhibits the largest spike in attention—this timed explosion turned into a sustained one with the recount. News outlets usually dispatch journalistic resources to attend to upcoming national electoral contests (establishing a foundation of patrol-mode coverage); these events can also often kick up unexpected hot news items (like recounts and scandals) that can send the media into alarm mode. As a result, elections are particularly susceptible to all three types of explosions: timed, momentary, and sustained.

Shown in figure 4.11b, the Nominations series follows a similar cyclical pattern to the Elections series, though lagged a few months, with attention to federal nominations usually surging in timed explosion form around December/January following each presidential election; January of 2001 is the largest here. An exception is the timed explosion of July 2005 surrounding President George W. Bush's nomination of federal appellate judge John Roberts to replace Justice Sandra Day O'Connor on the Supreme Court.

Other seasonal issue series include State and Local Government, National Budget and Debt, and IRS Administration, each of which exhibits seasonal spikes in attention surrounding cyclical storylines central to that issue, namely state elections, yearly congressional budget debates, and April 15, respectively. These are very small timed explosions.

PROVISIONAL ISSUES. Most issues, however, are provisional issues, meaning that the level of attention they receive is largely provisional on events, political attention, public concern, the diversity of discussion, and the other variables outlined in chapter 2—including the editorial discretion underlying all these variables. Figures 4.12a and 4.12b show two provisional issues: Tobacco Abuse and Terrorism. These issues are especially notable in that their attention dynamics are largely divorced from the underlying "objective" severity of the problems they involve. When provisional issues explode, they tend to do so in momentary or, sometimes, sustained explosion form.

Echoing the discussion Baumgartner and Jones offer about the shifting nature of the tobacco debate (2009), figure 4.12a shows that front-page attention to smoking is less driven by actual smoking rates than by focusing events, public and political perception of the issue and, relat-

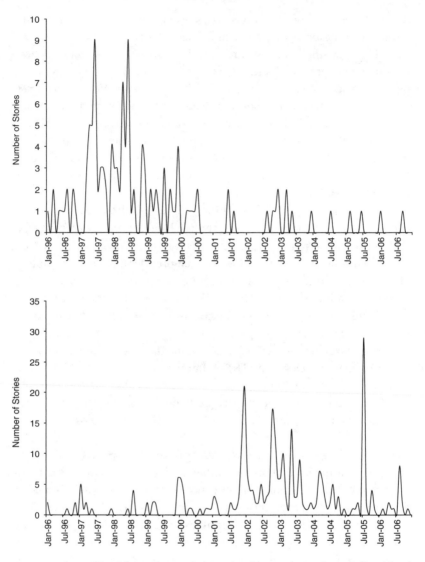

FIGURE 4.12A–B. *Times* front-page topic attention by month, 1996–2006: Provisional issues

FIGURE 4.12A. Tobacco Abuse (Code 341)
Note: N = 125 stories.

FIGURE 4.12B. Terrorism (Code 1927)
Note: N = 305 stories.

edly, how the issue has already been framed in the news. The two tallest spikes visible in this figure (nine stories per month—no small potatoes on the front page) coincide with, respectively, the "tobacco pact" reached in 1997, wherein tobacco companies and antismoking forces agreed to the promise of legislation heightening restrictions on cigarettes in exchange for the lifting of pending and future class-action lawsuits against the tobacco companies, and the tobacco bill of 1998, introduced by Senator John McCain but ultimately voted down, that would have raised cigarette taxes by $1.10 per pack over five years.

Similarly, although international terrorism as we understand it today has been an established threat for decades, looking at figure 4.12b we might think it was invented in September 2001. Note that the Terrorism subtopic (under topic 19, International Affairs) does *not* include stories directly related to the 9/11 attacks, which were coded as subtopic Civil Defense (under topic 16, Defense) because the attacks occurred in the United States. So the events of 9/11 are not responsible for the increase we see here. Figure 4.12b is thus particularly striking, showing that, after the 9/11 attacks, the United States underwent a sharp increase in *awareness* of pre-existing issues related to domestic security, in turn heightening awareness of related international terrorism. The largest spike in the Terrorism series coincides with the London suicide bombings of July 7, 2005.

Other notable examples of always important but provisionally covered issue series include Corporate Management and Fraud, Churches and Religion, Immigration, Nuclear Energy, and Drinking Water.

Conclusion

This chapter sliced the *New York Times* front page in several ways. The slices have revealed three main observations. First, the front-page agenda is small. The scarcity of attention and the issue "competition" it creates exacerbate the already disproportionate nature of how the *Times* and other news outlets process information, contributing to the aggregate patterns in the news observed here. Namely—and this is the second main observation—the agenda is highly skewed across issues. A few issues dominate the front page, while most issues most of the time get little to no coverage. This skew is determined in part by the inherent differences in perceived newsworthiness among issues, but it is also a product of disproportionate information processing (as demonstrated in chapter 7). The inability to attend to issues as they arise in real time, the institutional incentives to attend to issues already on the governmental and public agendas, the established distribution of newsroom resources, and the market-driven mimicking behavior between competing news outlets—all these factors lead to media fixation on hot issues and, thus, a resulting pattern of skew that is even stronger than that seen on many other agendas. Finally, front-page news changes not gradually, but rather explosively, over time. The agenda is strongly rooted in an ever-shifting equilibrium, which is evident at the yearly level. A closer look, however, reveals that this equilibrium is frequently displaced by sudden bursts of attention to the issue *du jour*, resulting in a dramatic pattern of punctuations clearly visible at the monthly and weekly levels. I offer a categorization by which we can think of different types of explosions—timed, momentary, and sustained—driven by different modes of news production, and how they tend to play out in different types of issues—bread-and-butter, seasonal, and provisional. All together, these findings tell us that while the news may seem chaotic, it is in fact strongly governed by systemic forces and the resulting patterns of skew and explosive change.

CHAPTER FIVE

Explaining Front-Page Attention

For people who make the news, write the news, or just read the news, the idea that we can *model* the news may seem absurd. More often than not, each day's news appears complex, sporadic, and surprising; it rarely appears predictable. Is it really possible to predict statistically, even in hindsight, which topics get media attention when?

Yes, to a large extent, it is. When we apply the theoretical understanding of the news-generation process from chapters 2 and 3 to tens of thousands of news stories, we can obtain a large-grained empirical estimation of the rise and fall of each topic on the front page over time. In the grand scheme of things, the news is fairly predictable. This big-picture analysis is a far cry, of course, from predicting the daily news. Again, as former *Times* editor Bill Keller says, "there is no rigid formula to the selection of stories and photographs for the front page" (2006). The composition of each day's front page—and the national media agenda more broadly—is as much an art as it is a science. But daily news predictions are not the goal here.

Rather, the goal of this chapter is to demonstrate that for all its random elements, the news can be explained in large part by accounting for key variables (collectively, hypothesis 1). Although day-to-day events are unpredictable, the incentive-driven journalistic decisions about how to process these events aggregate to distinct patterns of attention and change. And we can indeed model these aggregate patterns as a function of key variables.

At the same time, this big-picture approach also offers at least some predictive power over the news at a finer grained level. Sure, we have no idea what the headline stories will be one year from now. But thinking about what the news held this morning, we can take a pretty good guess about tomorrow. For example, on October 22, 2011, the front page of the *New York Times* reported on the following stories: President Obama's announcement of his plan to withdraw U.S. troops from Iraq by the end of 2011, the shortage of NATO military supplies, the death of Muammar el-Qaddafi, a deal giving World Cup television rights to Fox and Telemundo, a comparison between Occupy Wall Street and the Tea Party, and the current vibrant harvest of mushrooms in New York City. Knowing the composition of that front page, we can fare well in predicting which of these storylines made the front page in the following days (and which did not). It takes a much broader understanding of the patterns in the news and the underlying variables at work to predict what the front page of October 22, 2012, would look like, based only on the front page a year prior. And in fact, the front page of October 22, 2012 bore little similarity to its predecessor of a year before. Yet the variables described in chapter 2 go a long way toward allowing us to estimate the most likely items to appear in the news on October 22, 2012, even without knowing what the previous day's front page held. For example, with the 2012 presidential election barely two weeks away and a presidential debate on foreign policy scheduled for that evening, it should not surprise us that three of the six front-page stories that day were about Obama's and Romney's policy views on the Middle East. Thus, although the model presented here is far from being able to predict specific stories that will run on the front page on any given day, it does explain—to a surprisingly high degree—the relative presence of issues on the agenda at a monthly level at least, and often a more fine-grained level, too.

The particular purpose of this chapter is to explain some portion of the monthly variance in how much media attention policy topics received over the eleven-year period between 1996 and 2006. I use a statistical model to test the effect of each of five key variables on the amount of front-page news given to each topic each month: *prior attention*, *policymaker attention*, *public concern*, *diversity of discussion*, and *agenda congestion*. Of the eight variables identified in chapter 2, then, three are excluded from this analysis: *institutional setup*, *events*, and *context*. Despite their theoretical significance, these variables simply aren't accompanied by data that could be used in this model.[1] Note however, that although events are not included in the model here (lacking a standardized set of nineteen event time series for the nineteen topics examined), the next chapter presents models of two specific policy issues, and these models do include measures of events.

A model that employs only five of the eight key variables I have argued as having influence on the news should only explain a portion of the variance in monthly front-page attention to policy topics. So then, especially considering that the model in this chapter does not account for three key variables, it performs quite well. In the three versions of the model presented below (one for all topics, one for domestic topics only, and one for international topics only), the (imperfect) R squared value suggests that the model explains between 43% and 72% of the variance in monthly front-page attention across policy topics.[2] The model's strong explanatory power points to the importance of the five variables included.

Before turning to more details of the model, it is important to situate the endeavor of modeling the news in the larger context of the political system. In particular, note that many of the five variables employed here are potentially endogenous to events—and to news coverage itself. For instance, public concern for the environment likely increases following the occurrence of environmental disaster events, and specifically those disasters on which the media reports. So, although public concern about a topic should be a leading indicator of news coverage of that topic, in many cases public concern only shifts to a topic when the news covers it first, since news outlets have incentives to follow events of likely interest to consumers. In short, the governmental, public, and media agendas are largely endogenous, and all three are shaped by events. Just as policymaker attention and public concern help drive the news, so too does the news influence these agendas (see chapter 9). The model presented here, showing the unidirectional influences of five key variables on front-page attention, provides important insight into the news-generation process and aggregate patterns in the news. Nevertheless, it is critical that we take the findings in this chapter on their own terms, namely as evidence that the news is indeed shaped in systematic ways, while keeping in mind the much more complicated, and largely mutually reinforcing, nature of the relationships uncovered.

In the sections that follow I describe and then present three models, each of which predicts front-page attention as a function of the same five variables. The first model estimates front-page attention across all nineteen of the major policy topics in the Policy Agendas Project coding scheme (e.g., Macroeconomics, Health, Defense). For the second model, analysis is restricted to the sixteen domestic policy topics. The third model includes only the remaining three policy topics, all related to international concerns (Defense, Foreign Trade, and International Issues). This chapter thus puts concrete values on the theoretical discussion of news generation from chapters 2 and 3 by showing, first, that the news really is shaped by systematic variables and, second, the relative weight of influence that each variable holds.

Method

The goal here is to model statistically the distribution of front-page attention across policy topics and the changes in this distribution over time. Toward this aim, I employ a pooled cross-sectional time series model, in which the major policy topics (as coded at the two-digit level under the Policy Agendas coding scheme) serve as panels that I estimate at a monthly level of analysis.[3] Working at the monthly level allows me to capture the explosive shifts in the agenda we saw in the last chapter without the (meaningful) noise that occurs at the weekly or daily levels. Again, there is no correct time unit to employ here. But the monthly level is, arguably, most appropriate for examining the effects of the explanatory variables in question, such as *policymaker attention*, which operates much more slowly than the media agenda. Moreover, although the news cycle is fast-paced enough to warrant a more fine-grained analysis, the data is not rich enough.

The amount of front-page attention a major policy topic *i* receives at time *t* (in months) is modeled as a function of the five variables discussed above. For all but agenda congestion, which we should expect to operate contemporaneously, I use lagged values in order to assess the effect of each variable in a given month on front-page news in the following month. Formally:

$$Media\ Attention_{it} = \beta_0 + \beta_1\ Media\ Attention_{i\,t-1} + \beta_2 Political\ Attention_{i\,t-1} + \\ \beta_3 Public\ Concern_{i\,t-1} + \beta_4 Diversity\ of\ Discussion_{i\,t-1} + \\ \beta_5 Agenda\ Congestion_{i\,t} + \epsilon_{i\,t}$$

Measures

The sections below detail how all variables in the model are measured. All data series described are utilized at the monthly level of analysis across 132 months, from January 1996 through December 2006. Appendix table A.2 shows summary statistics for all measures.

Dependent Variable: Front-Page Attention

Because front-page coverage is strongly skewed and, thus, not a good fit for a linear model, the dependent variable is set as the log odds ratio of the proportion of total front-page attention that topic i receives at time t.[4] This measure (described below) is cumbersome but appropriate. In order to make the results more intuitive, the figures presented show the findings "backed out" of log odds form, so that we can estimate the size of the effect each explanatory variable has on the number of front-page stories a topic receives.

Calculating the log odds ratio of proportional attention begins by measuring attention as the proportion, rather than the raw count, of front-page stories on each topic in each month (i.e., the number of stories on a topic in a given month divided by the total number of stories that month). If 50 front-page stories appeared on the topic of Defense in a month when 250 front-page stories appeared in total, then Defense received 20% (0.2) of the agenda for that month. This proportional approach is appropriate because it makes theoretical sense (and I carry it through by measuring *policymaker attention* and *public concern* as the proportions of those respective agendas). The whole point of this modeling endeavor is to examine how the *Times* front page—a single (powerful) agenda of a very small, fixed size—gets distributed in a zero-sum way (Zhu 1992). Since the theoretical question is one of proportional coverage, it is good to model it empirically as such.[5]

Next, for each policy topic in each month, the proportion of attention is normalized by calculating the logit of the proportion, accomplished by taking the natural log of the proportion odds, where p_{it} is the proportion of the front-page agenda consumed by issue i at time t.

$$Logit(p_{it}) = \ln\left(\frac{p_{it}}{1 - p_{it}}\right)$$

This formula yields the log of the odds ratio, or log odds, of receiving attention, controlling for the total size of the agenda.

Table 5.1 puts this measure into more intuitive form. As the table shows, whereas proportions (p_{it}) can range from 0 to 1, with .5 as the

TABLE 5.1 **Comparing measurements of attention: The proportion of attention vs. the log odds of attention**

p_{it}	$Logit(p_{it})$
0.01	−4.60
0.05	−2.94
0.10	−2.20
0.20	−1.39
0.30	−0.85
0.40	−0.41
0.50	0.00
0.60	0.41
0.70	0.85
0.80	1.39
0.90	2.20
0.95	2.94
0.99	4.60

mid-point, the log odds transformation of these proportions ($Logit\ (p_{it})$) ranges from negative to positive values centered around 0. Notice that the logit scale magnifies differences in the extremes. For example, the gap between the log odds corresponding with $p_{it} = 0.95$ and the log odds corresponding with $p_{it} = 0.99$ is much larger than the gap between the log odds corresponding with $p_{it} = 0.50$ and $p_{it} = 0.70$.

It is precisely this nonlinearity of the logit scale—linear toward the center of its range but logarithmic at the extremes—that enables a linear model of front-page attention. The proportion of attention is nonlinear to start with, and only becomes linear when it is transformed into the log odds of attention.

For ease of discussion, from this point forward I refer to the dependent variable simply as front-page attention, keeping in mind that this attention variable is in fact measured as a log odds ratio of the proportion of attention. Again, following the results of the empirical models, figures will illustrate the effects backed out of the log odds measurement so that we can understand the size of the effects as measured through front-page stories. The transformation from story counts to log odds and then back again is a circuitous way to tell this straightforward story, but it is both theoretically and methodologically appropriate.

Independent Variables

PRIOR ATTENTION.   I measure *prior attention* by lagging the dependent variable, such that each month's value is set at the log odds ratio of the proportion of attention from the previous month:

$$Logit\ (p_{it-1})$$

In chapters 2 and 3, I discussed how institutional incentives and attention scarcity make the news-generation process highly path dependent. Momentum drives media attention via two main mechanisms: negative feedback (producing periods of equilibrium) and positive feedback (producing punctuations). The single variable of *prior attention* accounts for both these mechanisms, capturing the role of momentum in shaping the news.

To situate the prior attention variable more concretely in our understanding of the news-generation process, let's walk through an explosive cycle from equilibrium coverage through sustained media explosion and back again. Recall that the news fluctuates around a (shifting) baseline distribution of attention across topics; in the pre-9/11 period studied here, for example, education tended to receive 3.4% of the media agenda, while international affairs tended to receive 21.2%. This baseline is stabilized by variance in society's issue priorities but also by the news beat system and other products of institutional incentives. These factors all serve as mechanisms of negative feedback, reinforcing the status quo (i.e., counteracting positive feedback mechanisms that would propel changes on the agenda). But when key variables shift (e.g., the occurrence of a focusing event, a flurry of policymaking activity, a major shift in issue-framing), institutional incentives can instead prompt news outlets to lurch to that new item in media-explosion form. During the alarm-based meteoric rise in coverage to the hot item, institutional incentives now act as positive feedback mechanisms, reinforcing changes on the agenda. Then, during the brief patrol-based equilibrium established during each sustained media explosion, again institutional incentives act as negative feedback mechanisms, reinforcing the current status quo of fixation to the hot item.

In both modes of news-generation—during periods of equilibrium and during surges in attention in between—the best predictor of today's coverage is yesterday's coverage. Once a media explosion has taken hold, it will either be displaced by yet another media explosion or, sometimes, it will gradually fade out (note that these periods of gradual decline mark relatively rare moments of incremental change on the media agenda). During these gradual declines, once again prior attention should be the best indicator of current attention. Thus, the only moments when prior attention should not act as a good predictor of current attention are during the brief transfers of dominance from negative feedback to positive feedback and vice versa (e.g., the morning papers printed on September 12, 2001, looked nothing like those published the morning of September 11, 2001, prior to the 9/11 attacks). In the analyses to follow, I expect that the prior attention a topic received in the previous month should have a strong positive influence on the amount of attention it receives in the current month.

POLICYMAKER ATTENTION.   I use two variables to capture *policymaker attention*: a measure of congressional attention, in the form of the proportion of congressional hearings on each policy topic each month; and a measure of presidential attention, in the form of the proportion of executive orders issued on each policy topic each month. Both datasets come from the Policy Agendas Project (www.policyagendas.org), with each congressional hearing and executive order coded according to policy topic.[6] Both proportional measures are calculated by dividing the number of hearings/orders on a given topic by the total number of hearings/orders in that month.

The Policy Agendas Project's congressional hearings database is drawn from the Congressional Information Service Abstracts. The included hearings are those of committees, subcommittees, task forces, panels and commissions, and the joint committees of Congress. Over the eleven-year period studied here, Congress held an average of 8.4 hearings each month (ranging from a minimum of 0 to a maximum of 43). Hearings can be held on any topic, the only criterion being that a member of Congress must convince the committee chair to hold the hearing in the first place. Previous studies suggest that congressional hearings are the best measure of congressional attention (Baumgartner and Jones 2009; Edwards and Wood 1999), capturing those topics that Congress is taking seriously (Edwards, Barrett, and Peake 1997). Note that legislative attention can be measured in other ways, most notably as the proportion of congressional bills introduced on each policy topic in each month, using data collected by Adler and Wilkerson for the Congressional Bills Project (http://www.congressionalbills.org).[7] In the models presented below (table 5.4), substituting bills for hearings produces the same substantive results, with the exception that bills has an insignificant effect on media attention in the case of international topics.

The Policy Agendas Project's executive orders database contains all executive orders, again coded by topic according to the Policy Agendas Codebook. This data series tends to have low counts; across the eleven-year period studied, presidents issued an average of only 2.4 executive orders per month (ranging from a minimum of 0 to a maximum of 5). Still, this data series is the best available measure of executive attention, serving as a reasonable proxy of those topics to which the president is focusing attention.

I lag both *policymaker attention* variables by one month. As discussed in chapter 2, journalistic incentives—specifically, the principles of indexing theory (Bennett 1990)—suggest that an increase in the proportion of congressional bills/executive orders introduced on a policy topic in the previous month should yield an increase in front-page attention that topic receives in the current month.

Note that missing from this study—but a fruitful topic for other research—would be an assessment of how attention by nongovernmental policymakers, such as lobbyists, influence media attention (e.g., Baumgartner, Berry, et al. 2009).

PUBLIC CONCERN. As a proxy for *public concern*, I use the Gallup Organization's "Most Important Problem" (MIP) series, again as collected and coded by the Policy Agendas Project. The Gallup survey, usually conducted at least once a month in recent decades, asks respondents some variant of the question: "What do you think is the most important problem facing this country today?" Participants give open-ended responses, which the Gallup staff clusters into broad categories. The value of each response category is then presented as a proportion of all respondents for that survey who gave that response.[8] The Policy Agendas Project has coded each response category of each survey according to the Policy Agendas Codebook, thus producing a measure for each month of the proportion of public concern paid to each topic.

The Gallup MIP series is far from perfect. Wlezien (2005; see also 2004) details the shortcomings of the series. Perhaps most notably, the wording of the Gallup question—asking respondents what they think is the most important *problem*—makes MIP a problematic measure of public awareness or interest in issues. Additionally, while respondents are able to offer multiple responses, it is important to know that the composite index contains only the top response per respondent. As a result, the MIP measure shows a much more skewed distribution of public concern across topics than in fact exists; most citizens are concerned about—and interested in—more than one issue. However, the MIP measure remains the best monthly level proxy of the public agenda. I follow past scholars in employing it here (Graefe and Armstrong 2012; Jones 1994; Jones, Larsen-Price, and Wilkerson 2009; Soroka 2003).

In theory, MIP values can range from 0 (not on the public's radar) to 1.0 (complete consumption of public concern). In practice, this measure ranges from 0 to 0.47, with a monthly average of 0.06. For missing months, when Gallup did not conduct the MIP survey, I interpolate values by smoothing the difference between the surrounding observations. For example, the topic of Education received 0.08 (8%) of the public's MIP agenda space in January 2000 and then 0.12 (12%) in March 2000, with no survey conducted in February 2000. Education is thus assigned a value of 0.10 (10%) for that missing month. For rare months in which Gallup conducted the survey twice, the values for that month are averaged.

Again, *public concern* is lagged by one month; the discussion of incentives in chapter 2 suggests that, at least in this context, an increase in the proportion of Gallup respondents identifying a topic as the "most important problem" should produce an increase in front-page attention to that topic in the following month.

DIVERSITY OF DISCUSSION.   In chapter 2, I argued that the diversity of discussion should have a positive (and mutually reinforcing) influence on media attention. News coverage that portrays a policy topic from the point of view of multiple different subtopics (and coverage that portrays a policy issue using multiple different frames) will tend to resonate with citizens and policymakers—and thus with journalists and editors, via news values and other institutional incentives. When news outlets start to pick up on multiple perspectives of a policy area, this coverage can take on a self-reinforcing momentum that helps propel the overall amount of news coverage given to the policy area down the road. Of course, this relationship is mutually reinforcing: strong diversity of discussion helps boost the amount of attention, which in turn helps boost the diversity of discussion. The more issues in the news about a common policy topic last month, the more media attention will be drawn to that topic this month. Likewise, the more frames used to define a policy issue last month, the more attention will be drawn to that issue this month.

The concept of *diversity of discussion* is more nuanced than just a count, however. Specifically, it is concentration or diffusion of news coverage across a topic's component subtopics (or across an issue's component frames). I measure the diversity of discussion using the normalized form of Shannon's H entropy. This measure was originally developed in thermodynamics research, but in the realm of human communication it can be used to capture the diffusion, or diversity, of attention (Boydstun, Bevan, and Thomas 2013). I describe the measure here according to its use in this chapter to capture the diversity of coverage across subtopics within each topic. In the next chapter, I use this same measure, but calculated as the diversity of coverage across frames within each issue. For the current chapter, the diversity of discussion is calculated as follows, where p_{it} is the proportion of discussion about a given policy topic consumed by each composite subtopic i at time t, and n is the number of subtopics available in that topic category.

$$Norm\ Entropy = \frac{\sum_{i=1}^{n} p(x_{it}) * \ln p(x_{it})}{\ln (N)}$$

This diversity measure can theoretically range from 0 to 1, with 0 representing total concentration and 1 representing total dispersion. In the *Times* front-page dataset, the topic-level measure of monthly diversity across issues ranges from 0 to 0.83, with a mean of 0.32. As with the previous explanatory variables, I lag diversity of discussion by one month.

Because this explanatory variable measure of diversity is calculated using the exact same dataset of front-page coverage used to calculate the dependent variable, it is critical to clarify whether the diversity measure might be a mathematical artifact of front-page attention. It is not. Even if the dependent variable was measured as the count or proportion of front-page stories on each topic rather than the log odds of the proportion of attention, the diversity measure would still not be a mathematical function of front-page attention. The diversity measure is not based on the count or proportion of stories within each topic, but rather on how these stories are *spread* across the component subtopics. There does exist a direct mathematical function in the case of small counts, since a topic with only one story (necessarily on a single subtopic) will necessarily have a diversity measure of 0.0—total concentration of attention on that single subtopic. But this function is not an artifact. A single news story within a topic in a month in fact means, meaningfully, that all of the attention to that topic in that month is concentrated on one subtopic; in this case, there is no diversity of discussion.

To get a better sense of how th*e diversity of discussion* variable operates, table 5.2 shows an example of diversity from the front-page dataset, comparing the scope of the coverage on the topic of Health in April, May, and June of 2003. In April 2003 we see that discussion of health care was almost entirely dominated by a single subtopic—Prevention and Communicable Diseases—in reaction to the SARS outbreak during that same time period. In May 2003 front-page coverage of the SARS outbreak declines, but notice how health-care discussion on the front page expands in general, widening from four subtopics to twelve, perhaps in part because policymakers (health officials and interest groups in particular) took advantage of the recent attention to the SARS outbreak by promoting other health policy issues even more strongly. Even though front-page attention to the particular SARS problem declined, the diversity of the larger topic debate expanded—and attention rose from twelve stories to twenty-seven in the process. The increased diversity of discussion in May 2003 is *not* strictly a function of how many stories were available, as we can see in June 2003, when nearly the same number of stories (twenty-six) are more tightly clustered across seven subtopics, producing a lower diversity score.

To reiterate the expectation to be tested in this chapter, I expect that the higher the diversity of discussion across subtopics in the prior month's coverage of a topic, the more media attention that topic will receive in the current month.

AGENDA CONGESTION.   The more the media agenda is congested, the harder it is for all other news items to make it into the news. A highly congested agenda is usually one in which attention is dominated by one or two mega storylines, pushing most other topics off the front page. When items like war, natural disasters, presidential elections, or scandals gain front-page attention, the agenda becomes saturated with coverage of the hot item, leaving very little room for other topics. These mo-

TABLE 5.2 **Example of the diversity of discussion variable: When discussion of a policy topic debate expands, diversity increases**

Health Subtopic	April 2003 Diversity = 0.28		May 2003 Diversity = 0.75		June 2003 Diversity = 0.60	
	Stories	Percentage of Debate	Stories	Percentage of Debate	Stories	Percentage of Debate
Prevention and Communicable Diseases	9	75%	7	26%	3	12%
Insurance Reform	1	8%	2	7%	3	12%
Prescription Drug Coverage and Costs	1	8%	1	4%	9	35%
Infants and Children	1	8%	0	0%	0	0%
Medical Liability, Fraud and Abuse	0	0%	4	15%	2	8%
Health Research and Development	0	0%	3	11%	4	15%
Regulation	0	0%	3	11%	3	12%
Other Health	0	0%	2	7%	0	0%
Mental Health	0	0%	1	4%	2	8%
Long-term Care	0	0%	1	4%	0	0%
Tobacco Abuse and Treatment	0	0%	1	4%	0	0%
Alcohol Abuse and Treatment	0	0%	1	4%	0	0%
Illegal Drug Abuse and Treatment	0	0%	1	4%	0	0%
Total	12	100%	27	100%	26	100%

Note: Due to rounding, individual percentage values do not reflect the 100% total.

ments of high congestion also tend to be prime periods of punctuation. During slower news periods (i.e., between major media explosions), attention tends to be less congested, spread more evenly across multiple topics.

To measure the congestion of the front-page agenda, I turn once more to Shannon's H entropy, but this time calculated inversely, capturing the skew of attention across the entire agenda.

$$Inverse\ Norm\ Entropy = 1 - \frac{\sum_{i=1}^{n} p(x_{it}) * \ln p(x_{it})}{\ln (N)}$$

This measure again ranges theoretically from 0 to 1, with 0 representing total dispersion and 1 representing total congestion. In practice, monthly front-page congestion for the time period studied ranges from a minimum of 0.12 to a maximum of 0.55, with an average of 0.23.

Although the models in this chapter only consider nineteen topics, agenda congestion (here, *front-page congestion*) is calculated across all topics on the front page. Nonpolicy topics contribute to congestion too, affecting the agenda space available for all topics. Thus, for example, when the Red Sox (finally) overcame the curse of the Bambino in 2004, or when Hurricane Katrina hit in 2005, these surges in attention to the topics of Sports and Weather, respectively, are accounted for in the overall congestion affecting attention to the policy topics modeled here.

Table 5.3 shows the quintessential example of how the congestion of the *Times* front page changed following 9/11. In August 2001, attention was spread across twenty-five topics, with seven topics each receiving more than ten stories. In September, front-page attention was still spread across twenty-five topics, but much less evenly than before. Note that on many days in September the events of 9/11 were not only given multiple stories on the front page, but bigger stories too—in total, the *Times* printed eighty-eight more stories on defense in September than in August that year, but twenty fewer total stories.

Sometimes, as with this example, agenda congestion increases because attention shifts to a focusing event as it unfolds. Other times, congestion increases because a topic becomes dominant on the agenda not only on the wave of events, but also as the result of changes in other variables, such as a surge in policymaker attention or a sudden expansion in the diversity of discussion of a topic due to new ways of defining the

TABLE 5.3 **Example of the agenda congestion variable: When a mega storyline like 9/11 hits the agenda, congestion increases**

Policy Topic	August 2001 Congestion = 0.151		September 2001 Congestion = 0.338	
	Stories	Proportion of Agenda	Stories	Proportion of Agenda
International Affairs	53	21%	26	11%
Health	30	12%	6	3%
Government Operations	21	8%	16	7%
Law and Crime	17	7%	5	2%
Defense	15	6%	103	44%
Government Operations	14	5%	1	0%
Macroeconomics	13	5%	15	6%
Banking and Commerce	10	4%	9	4%
Arts and Entertainment	9	4%	5	2%
Sports and Recreation	8	3%	10	4%
Civil Rights	8	3%	6	3%
Education	8	3%	5	2%
Science and Technology	8	3%	4	2%
Environment	8	3%	1	0%
Transportation	5	2%	10	4%
Energy	5	2%	1	0%
Labor	4	2%	4	2%
Housing	4	2%	1	0%
Agriculture	4	2%	0	0%
Social Welfare	3	1%	1	0%
Churches and Religion	2	1%	2	1%
Fires	2	1%	1	0%
Public Lands	2	1%	0	0%
Weather and Disasters	2	1%	0	0%
Human Interest	1	0%	0	0%
Death Notices	0	0%	3	1%
Foreign Trade	0	0%	1	0%
Total	256	100%	236	100%

topic. Whatever the avenue by which policy problems and related policy issues come to dominate the news, once the agenda is congested it becomes very difficult for other issues to gain access. Thus, we should see a *negative* contemporaneous relationship between front-page congestion and front-page attention. Of course, the topic that happens to spur high congestion at a given moment necessarily receives more coverage in that period, but the topic responsible for high congestion tends to change from one congested period to the next. Thus, in general, we should expect that the higher the *front-page congestion* in a given month, the less media attention any given topic is likely to receive that same month.

Results

This section shows results from modeling *New York Times* front-page attention in three contexts: (1) across all nineteen major policy topics; (2) across the sixteen domestic policy topics only: Macroeconomics, Civil Rights, Health, Agriculture, Labor, Education, Environment, Energy, Transportation, Law and Crime, Social Welfare, Housing, Banking and Commerce, Science and Technology, Government Operations, and Public Lands; and (3) across the three international-related topics only: Defense, Foreign Trade, and International Affairs. Table A.2 in the appendix contains descriptive statistics.

In each case, I pool the major topics, such that each topic serves as a panel, and then estimate a pooled cross-sectional time series model of front-page attention. Table 5.4 shows the comparative results from estimating this model in the three contexts listed above. The size of the coefficients here are hard to interpret, as they need to be backed out of the log odds ratio (as I will do below). But looking first at the directionality and the significance of the coefficients, we see strong support for the expectations outlined above.

At the top of table 5.4 we find the results for *prior attention* (front-page attention $_{t-1}$). Recall that this variable is the best single test of the theory that momentum, in its different forms, shapes the news. Across all three models, the prior attention paid to a policy topic has a positive and significant influence on current attention to that topic. In fact, analyses indicate that prior attention explains more variance in front-page attention than any other variable.[9] Moreover, the strong predictive power of front-page attention remains strong (and significant) when conducted using yearly, weekly, and even daily levels of analysis.

Moving down table 5.4, both measures of *policymaker attention*—the proportion of congressional hearings and the proportion of executive orders—display positive and significant effects across all three models, although executive orders exhibit more modest significance levels. *Public concern* as captured by the Gallup MIP series also exhibits a positive and significant influence across all three models. *Diversity of discussion*, too, has a positive and significant effect in all three cases, though its degree of significance is lower in the case of international topics. Finally, as expected, the level of *front-page congestion* in a given month has a *negative* effect across the board (again with more modest significance in the

TABLE 5.4 **Results from pooled cross-sectional time series models of *Times* front-page attention**

	All Policy Topics Coefficients (Std Errors)	Domestic Topics Coefficients (Std Errors)	International Topics Coefficients (Std Errors)
Prior Attention (Proportion of Front-Page Attention $_{t-1}$)	0.457* (0.021)	0.365* (0.024)	0.666* (0.050)
Policymaker Attention			
Proportion of Congressional Hearings $_{t-1}$	4.219* (0.555)	3.686* (0.609)	4.059* (1.249)
Proportion of Executive Orders $_{t-1}$	0.517^ (0.244)	0.401^ (0.282)	0.688^ (0.441)
Public Concern (Proportion of Gallup MIP $_{t-1}$)	3.498* (0.435)	3.309* (0.497)	3.024* (0.899)
Diversity of Discussion $_{t-1}$	0.762* (0.170)	0.777* (0.183)	0.945^ (0.470)
Front-Page Congestion $_t$	−3.145* (0.429)	−3.466* (0.465)	−2.260^ (1.009)
Constant	−3.145* (0.173)	−2.504* (0.186)	−1.436^ (0.443)
N =	2,489	2,096	393
Months =	131	131	131
Policy Topics =	19	16	3
Front-Page Stories =	26,611	15,587	11,024
Adjusted R^2 =	0.427	0.318	0.716
Root MSE =	1.503	1.494	1.363

^ p <= 0.1, two-tailed
* p <= 0.001, two-tailed
Note: The dependent variable is the log odds of the proportion of front page attention each policy topic received each month.

case of international topics), probabilistically decreasing the attention all topics will receive in that same month.

We can visualize the relative size of the effects shown in table 5.4 by looking at figures 5.1–5.4. Each figure presents the log odds results from table 5.4 calculated into story counts so that we can gain a more intuitive understanding of what these results mean for the composition of the actual *Times* front page.[10]

Figure 5.1 shows the relative effect that a one standard deviation increase in each explanatory variable is predicted to have on the amount of front-page coverage a given topic will receive in a month, holding all other explanatory variables at their mean values. In other words, this figure shows how many more (or fewer) front-page stories we should expect to see on a given topic in a given month in the case of each explana-

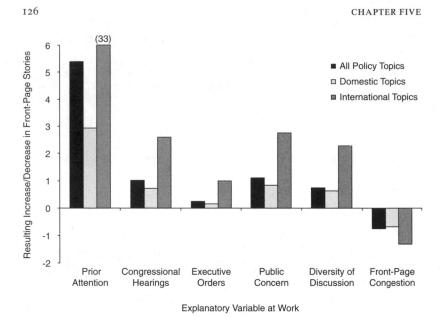

FIGURE 5.1. The change in front-page attention produced by one standard deviation change in each explanatory variable

Note: For each explanatory variable featured across the *x* axis, the bar shows the number of additional/fewer front-page news stories that should be expected when the explanatory variable increases by one standard deviation.

tory variable exhibiting a typical-sized increase. The different columns in figure 5.1 show results for each of the three separate models. As discussed above, a standard deviation increase in *prior attention* has by far the largest impact, yielding an extra three front-page stories the following month in the case of domestic topics, and an extra thirty-three stories in the case of international topics (too big to fit on this graph). But remembering the particular weight that even one *Times* front-page story in a month can bear, all of these variables have meaningful effects beyond their statistical significance.

This figure reveals interesting variance in the relative effects of each variable across the three modeling contexts. For all explanatory variables, a standard deviation increase has a stronger influence on front-page attention in the case of international topics than in the case of domestic topics. For example, a standard deviation increase in the proportion of congressional hearings yields not quite an extra story (0.72) in the case of domestic topics, but nearly three stories (2.76) in the case of international topics. As discussed more below, many factors likely contribute to these discrepancies between domestic and international effects sizes, not the least of which are the strong positive feedback mechanisms associated with foreign news correspondence, such as embedding journalists with troops overseas.

In order to understand the full effects of these variables on front-page attention, we need to consider the range of values that each variable can assume. Figures 5.2–5.4 show—in all three modeling contexts—the predicted number of front-page stories a policy topic will receive across varying conditions of each explanatory variable, holding all other explanatory variables at their mean values. Again, these values are calculated by backing out of the log odds ratio coefficients shown in table 5.4 so that we can see effects in the form of story counts. Notice that most of the lines depicted in these three figures are curvilinear, demonstrating why it was necessary to transform the dependent variable from a count to a log odds ratio in order to employ a linear model.

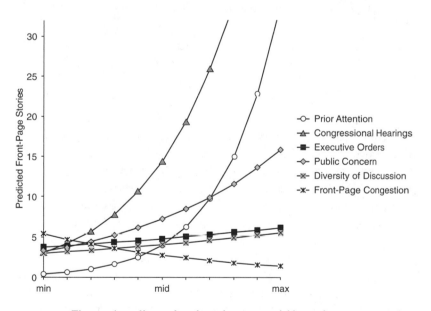

FIGURE 5.2. The varying effects of each explanatory variable on front-page attention across all policy topics
Note: To represent observed values, this figure displays an 11-point *x* axis that ranges, for each variable, from that variable's minimum observed value at the left to its maximum observed value at the right, increasing at each step by 10% of the difference between the two. See book webpage for details.

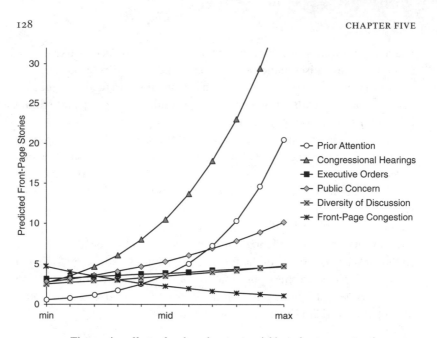

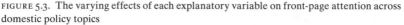

FIGURE 5.3. The varying effects of each explanatory variable on front-page attention across domestic policy topics

Note: To represent observed values, this figure displays an 11-point *x* axis that ranges, for each variable, from that variable's minimum observed value at the left to its maximum observed value at the right, increasing at each step by 10% of the difference between the two. See book webpage for details.

Whereas figure 5.1 displayed the predicted *change* in front-page stories produced by a one standard deviation increase, figures 5.2–5.4 show the total number of front-page stories a topic, on average, is predicted to receive in a single month (remembering that most topics typically receive just a few stories each month or none at all, while a few topics typically receive many). Thus, a value of 10 on the *y* axis means that, on average, when the explanatory variable in question is set at the value indicated on the *x* axis and all other variables are held at their means, a policy topic will receive ten front-page stories that month.

The *x* axes of these figures show an eleven-point scale based on the observed minimum and maximum values of each variable.[11] In other words, each of these figures captures the true range of each variable; nothing is out-of-sample. Scaling the observed range of each variable in this way allows for a more meaningful, commensurate comparison of each variable's relative influence.

Figure 5.2 shows how the influence of each explanatory variable on front-page attention changes over the range of the variable; each relationship behaves very differently at the minimum values of the variable than at the maximum values. For example, the particularly large effect of *prior attention* that we saw in figure 5.1 only begins to distance itself from the rest of the variables around the midrange of its observed values, showing an even more curvilinear shape than the other variables.

The size of the effects shown in figure 5.2 may seem small. But again, these aren't just any news stories; these are stories on the front page of the *New York Times*. And remember that most policy topics, most of the time, get little to no front-page attention in an average month. Looking at *policymaker attention* through the proxy of congressional hearings, for example, we see that when congressional hearings about a topic reach the midpoint of the range of observed values, with all other variables held at their mean, we can expect to see about 14 front-page stories on that topic the following month. But at its maximum, congressional hearings in one month (with all other variables held at their means)

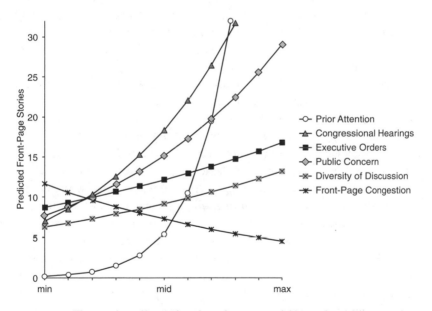

FIGURE 5.4. The varying effects of each explanatory variable on front-page attention across international policy topics

Note: To represent observed values, this figure displays an 11-point *x* axis that ranges, for each variable, from that variable's minimum observed value at the left to its maximum observed value at the right, increasing at each step by 10% of the difference between the two. See book webpage for details.

predicts 57.54 front-page stories the following month. Consider also *public concern*: a midpoint level of concern for a topic in one month (with all other variables at their means) should yield 7.2 stories on that topic in the following month; at its maximum, concern for a topic one month yields 15.85 stories the following month. On the *Times* front page, that's a lot of stories.

Figures 5.3 and 5.4 show the same kinds of results presented in figure 5.2, but this time with values based only on domestic and international topics, respectively. As we saw in figure 5.1, the effects are larger in the case of international topics (fig. 5.4) than in the case of domestic topics (fig. 5.3), suggesting that front-page attention to international policy topics is more susceptible to the influences of all five explanatory variables. For example, looking at the executive orders proxy for *policymaker attention* in figure 5.4, we see that when executive orders on a topic are at their midpoint in one month (and all other variables are at their means), we should expect to see 12.14 front-page stories on that topic the following month. But at their maximum, executive orders predict 16.78 stories the following month. The roles of *diversity of discussion* and *front-page congestion* also come through most starkly in the case of international topics. When these variables are at their midpoints with respect to a given topic in a given month, we should expect to see 9.17 and 7.29 stories on that topic in the following month; when at their maximum values, they yield 13.24 and 4.24 stories, respectively. Thus, as expected, increased *diversity of discussion* prompts heightened coverage, while increased *front-page congestion* prompts lowered coverage.

The higher degree of influence that these variables have in the case of international topics can be explained in many ways. Some likely factors include the overseas beat assignments often associated with international topics, which make *prior attention* a much stronger force in news coverage of these topics. Also, the threshold for policymakers and citizens to perceive a topic as important might be higher in the case of international topics, since they are farther removed. Thus, it may be that institutional incentives to index international topics of *policymaker attention* and *public concern* are stronger once policymakers and citizens are paying attention to an international topic (as opposed to a domestic topic). There is also considerably more leeway available in defining events occurring on foreign soil, perhaps making the *diversity of discussion* more influential on front-page coverage for international topic areas. Additionally, while the front-page agenda generally becomes more congested when stories about major overseas conflicts erupt, in fact most of the periods of high agenda congestion surround domestic mega story-lines. Thus, the negative effect of *front-page congestion* on the estimated amount of *front-page attention* a topic will receive may be exacerbated in the case of international topics. In any case, these findings suggest that, in the case of international topics as opposed to domestic topics, the inertia of news coverage is generally stronger; policymakers and cit-izens have a louder "voice" in shaping front-page news; the diversity of the coverage across component subtopics plays a stronger role; and the degree of congestion on the agenda has a bigger impact.

Conclusion

This chapter put the outlined theory of the news-generation process, and specifically the expectations combining to form hypothesis 1, to a test by modeling the amount of *New York Times* front-page attention that a given topic receives in a given month as a function of five key explana-tory variables: *prior attention, policymaker attention, public concern, di-versity of discussion*, and *agenda congestion*. I tested this model, first, across all policy topics; second, across domestic policy topics only; and third, across international policy topics only.

All three models perform well, explaining a strong amount of the ob-served variance in front-page news. These findings support hypothe-sis 1 from chapter 2, indicating that front-page attention is systematically shaped by institutional variables in the political system. Each of the five explanatory variables demonstrated an effect on front-page attention in the predicted direction.

Additionally, these results reveal interesting variance in how each ex-planatory variable behaves in the context of domestic policy topics as compared to international policy topics. All five explanatory variables exhibit a much greater effect on front-page attention of international topics than of domestic topics. Thus, while front-page coverage in gen-eral is shaped in patterned ways by these key variables, in the case of in-ternational topics the news-generation process appears to be even more susceptible to these institutional forces.

CHAPTER SIX

The Rise and Fall of the War on Terror and the Death Penalty in the News

The last chapter took a broad approach to modeling the news, showing that we can explain statistically how the media agenda (specifically, the front page of the *New York Times*) is divided across major policy topics (e.g., Health, Education, Defense) at a monthly level. The fact that we can model news coverage across policy topics has important implications for how we view the political system, and especially for questions of agenda control. In a nutshell, chapter 5 told us that institutional forces systematically shape the information that policymakers and citizens get from the news. The influence of *prior attention* was especially strong, supporting the alarm/patrol hybrid model of news generation.

In many cases, however, we care less about the macro patterns of attention dynamics than we do about the factors that coincide with the rise and fall of a specific issue in the news. What shapes levels of media attention to immigration, for example, or global warming, or NAFTA? A model that can explain variance in media attention across broad policy topics but not variance in coverage of a particular issue over time is not very useful; we need a model that works at both levels.

This chapter offers further support for the notion that we can explain variance in news coverage as a function of key variables (hypothesis 1) by demonstrating the applicability of the model from chapter 5—but this time also controlling for *events*—to two specific and politically significant policy issues:

1. The U.S.-led military conflicts following the 9/11 attacks of September 11, 2001, beginning in Afghanistan in October 2001 and in Iraq in March 2003 (i.e., the war on terror)[1]
2. Capital punishment in the United States

These two important issues serve as useful test cases, in large part because they are so different. The war is an international issue; U.S. capital punishment is domestic. The war occupied a relatively large proportion of the national agenda for a relatively short period of time. The death penalty, in contrast, receives on average much lower levels of attention, yet it has proven to be an issue of political and social interest throughout U.S. history (Baumgartner, De Boef, and Boydstun 2008). The war is a complex, or "hard," issue with many highly technical considerations that are difficult for both citizens and elites to keep track of and understand. While capital punishment is also complex and highly nuanced, the basic facts of the death penalty and the arguments in the debate are more straightforward than those surrounding the war, producing a more polarized discussion surrounding this "easy" issue (Alvarez and Brehm 2002). Moreover, the complexities of the war changed at a good clip over time, whereas capital punishment shows the signs of a more entrenched policy, moving in general at a much slower pace. One consequence of the distinctions in the technical complexity and pace of these two issues is a difference in the patterns of public opinion about each issue. While most people in the United States are able to voice a strong view on both war and the death penalty at any given point in time, aggregate public opinion about the war on terror was highly volatile during the time period studied (that is, highly volatile as public opinion marginals go). Most survey measures show a change in support for the military operations in Afghanistan of about twenty-five percentage points during President George W. Bush's term alone; support for the military operations in Iraq shifted by about thirty-five points during that administration.[2] Public opinion about the death penalty has also changed in important ways over time, but the shift in opinion of thirty-five percentage points over the period studied took nearly thirty years to occur (though changes in public support for the death penalty were far from gradual over this period).[3]

The war and the death penalty thus serve as stringent test cases for this book's theory of news generation when applied to specific issue areas. In parallel with chapter 5, I begin by outlining the modeling strategy and the different variable measures employed for each of the two issues. Next come the results. If the model of media attention I have developed is worth its salt, it should allow us to explain a considerable portion of the variance in the amount of news coverage each of these issues has received over time as a function of the key variables identified. And indeed, it does, suggesting that this model might also prove useful in helping to explain the rise and fall in the news of other key issues of interest.

Data and Measurement

I model the amount of news coverage to each issue—the war on terror and the U.S. death penalty—as a function of the same key variables used to explain front-page attention across policy topics in chapter 5, with the important exception that in the case of these specific issues we can also account via proxy indicators for the role of *events*, absent from chapter 5. Thus, the explanatory variables studied here are *prior attention*, *events*, *policymaker attention*, *public concern*, *diversity of discussion*, and *agenda congestion*. For each of the two issues under study, the model employed is an autoregressive ARIMA (1,0,0) time series model, estimating the amount of news coverage to the issue at hand at time *t* as a function of different combinations of these explanatory variables. Table A.3 in the appendix provides descriptive statistics for all variables described below.

As with the topic-level model in chapter 5, I model the war at a monthly level of analysis, from September 2001 through December 2006. However, instead of calculating monthly counts using the traditional calendar demarcations of time units (e.g., marking September 2001 as month 1, October 2001 as month 2, and so on), I calculate months as they elapsed from the initial crisis, with the date of September 11, 2001, set as time zero. For example, the first month of the data spans from September 12, 2001, through October 11, 2001.

In the case of capital punishment, the data used here—all *New York Times Index* abstracts on the death penalty, 1960–2005—will not support a monthly level of analysis (with 3,892 stories for this issue in total over forty-six years, the yearly average is about 85 stories, making the monthly average just over 7 stories). For capital punishment then, I model attention at the yearly level, from 1960 through 2005. Although a

finer-grained analysis would certainly be preferable, this approach enables testing the applicability of the model from a different temporal
perspective, and one that is perhaps even more appropriate for an entrenched issue like the death penalty. The explanatory variables under
investigation should affect day-to-day newsroom operations, but then
these individual decisions should aggregate to broader patterns at higher
levels of analysis. As discussed in chapter 4, there is no "right" time perspective to take when thinking about media dynamics. Thus, we should
also see the influence of these variables at the yearly level.

Note that the models presented in this chapter focus on explaining attention to each issue as a function of contemporaneous values of the explanatory variables (with the exception of *prior attention*, which is simply the lagged value of the dependent variable). In other words, the focus
here really is on the correlates of news coverage rather than establishing
leading (i.e., "causal") indicators. In the case of the death penalty, I also
present a model—indeed, a model with a better fit—that explains each
year's news coverage of capital punishment as a function of lagged explanatory variables. But in the case of the war, the monthly level of analysis simply doesn't support this kind of lagged analysis; when lagged values are used, the model fit begins to deteriorate. Why would a lagged
approach be supported in the case of the yearly death penalty analysis but not in the finer-grained monthly study of the war? Most likely
this difference is a consequence of the much slower nature of death penalty policy and the surrounding national discussion. With this kind of
entrenched issue, shifts in key variables like death sentences, related
events, or how the issue is framed (e.g., *diversity of discussion*) can take
months or years to affect news coverage (and vice versa). In the case of
a fast-paced issue like the war, however, the factors that shape the news
operate much more quickly—at a weekly if not a daily level.

Whether the proposed model is used to explain attention as a function
of contemporaneous or lagged values of the explanatory variables, it remains only one snapshot of a much larger, dynamic, largely endogenous
system. We should expect the explanatory variables I describe to have, in
most cases, mutually reinforcing relationships with media attention. So,
as in chapter 5, we must take the findings presented below with a healthy
grain of salt. These findings tell us that news coverage of these two policy issues correlates strongly with key explanatory variables. In the case
of the death penalty, as with the broader model presented in chapter 5,
we can analyze temporal driving forces by lagging these indicators. But

in all cases, these models do not address the important flip-sides of these relationships, which are beyond the scope of this book. For example, it has already been shown that the *tone* (pro- vs. anti-) of news coverage about the death penalty can have a significant influence on public support for the death penalty and on the policy itself, in the form of the number of death sentences handed down in the United States per year—the same variable that I use here as a proxy indicator of *events* (Baumgartner, De Boef, and Boydstun 2008). And chapter 9 shows the effects of media attention on *policymaker activity* and *public concern*. In short, these relationships are complicated. Toward the aim of understanding the news-generation process, focusing on the correlates of news coverage is a critical first step.

Dependent Variable: News Coverage

Both models presented here measure news coverage based on full-paper stories (as well as front-page stories in the case of the war), rather than the exclusive focus on front-page stories in chapter 5. Full-paper news is a different animal from front-page coverage, as we should remember in interpreting the findings below; the statistical relationships shown here may not play out in precisely the same way in the restricted domain of front-page news. That said, incorporating full-paper stories offers as an additional test of the model. That it applies to both front-page and full-paper news speaks to its generalizable usefulness in helping to explain variance in media attention across policy issues/topics and over time.

THE WAR ON TERROR.   To measure news coverage of the U.S.-led military operations in Afghanistan and Iraq following 9/11, I utilize a dataset collected with Rebecca Glazier that tracks front-page *New York Times* (NYT or *Times*) and full-paper *Wall Street Journal* (WSJ) coverage of the war between September 2001 and December 2006 (Glazier and Boydstun 2012). To construct this dataset, we began by identifying the population of NYT front-page stories about the war. This task was made easy by the fact that, in collecting the front-page *Times* dataset already discussed, beyond coding each story by primary topic/subtopic I also used a series of binary variables to record whether or not each story was relevant to each of six specific issues of interest that I knew might not always fit cleanly into a single subtopic code (e.g., Hurricane Katrina, the Israeli/Palestine conflict, the Enron scandal). One of these binary issue codes was for the U.S. conflicts in Afghanistan and Iraq and the war on terror more generally. While stories about the war were predominantly coded as topic code 1619 (Direct War Related Issues) under the Policy Agendas Codebook, some relevant stories were correctly coded elsewhere. For example, stories about the threat of additional terrorist attacks on U.S. soil were coded under 1615 (Civil Defense), international terrorist attacks or the threat of attacks were coded under 1927 (Terrorism, Hijacking), and stories about veteran benefits for soldiers returning from Afghanistan or Iraq were coded under 1609 (VA Issues). The binary variable captured whether each story was directly relevant to the war on terror, allowing us to examine all relevant stories, regardless of primary subtopic. Altogether, 4,227 front-page NYT stories were relevant to the war between September 12, 2001, and December 31, 2006. From these articles, we took a random sample of 2,512 stories (about 60%) to code according to how the war was framed (more on this below).

As discussed in chapter 4, the *New York Times* has been shown to be generally representative of national U.S. news coverage more broadly and, as such, is an appropriate source to use as a proxy of the national media agenda. However, because the debate about the U.S. conflicts in Afghanistan and Iraq was highly partisan in nature, particularly during the time period of the Bush administration that our data encompasses, we felt it important to compare the *Times* data with data from a secondary news source, specifically one perceived to have a more conservative approach than the *Times*. The *Wall Street Journal* fits this bill (Page 1996). We employed LexisNexis archives of WSJ abstracts to identify approximately 9,000 relevant abstracts between September 12, 2001, and December 31, 2006, and from this population we drew a random sample of 901 (about 10%).[4] After excluding 30 irrelevant stories (i.e., false positives), our final dataset contains 871 WSJ abstracts about the war.

Combining the 2,512 NYT articles with the 871 WSJ abstracts yields a total count of 3,383 observations (which I will call stories, collectively). The elapsed system of time measurement described above excludes the last few observations in the dataset, as the last full month in the elapsed series ends on December 13, 2006. Thus, while our starting dataset contains 3,383 observations, the full monthly dataset contains 2,487 NYT articles and 869 WSJ abstracts (for a total of 3,356 stories).

Despite the perception of a liberal bias by the *Times*, NYT and WSJ coverage of the war were highly correlated during the time period in question, not only with regard to the overall level of sampled coverage, but also when evaluating the frame and tone (positive, negative, neutral) employed. For example, looking at the number of stories on the war each month, our NYT and WSJ samples correlate at $\rho = 0.83$. Just as important, the number of stories in each dataset portraying the administration's handling of the war using a positive tone correlate at $\rho = 0.81$. Thus, for the purposes of the analysis presented here, the NYT and WSJ stories are combined into a single set of observations.

These combined 3,356 stories thus provide a solid measure of the fluctuating level of news coverage the war received across this time period. The dependent variable for the war model, then, is the number of sampled NYT and WSJ stories about the war in a given month. Note that this dependent variable is a raw count rather than a proportion of total agenda space. While it is possible to calculate front-page *Times* coverage as a proportion of the front-page agenda, it is very difficult to get an accurate estimate of the shifting total number of full-paper stories (in this case, full-paper WSJ abstracts). Thus, the dependent variable here is the number of stories.

THE DEATH PENALTY.   To measure news coverage of capital punishment, I utilize a dataset collected with Frank Baumgartner and Suzanna Linn (De Boef) comprised of all *New York Times* full-paper stories on the death penalty between 1960 and 2005 (Baumgartner, De Boef, and Boydstun 2008). We identified all relevant NYT stories by collecting all article abstracts listed under capital punishment (and related index items) in the *New York Times Index*. The *Index* yielded a total of 3,939 relevant abstracts (which I will also call stories, for ease of reference), which comprise this database. We validated the use of the NYT as a representative proxy for national news coverage of the death penalty by using tested keyword searches in LexisNexis to compare both levels of attention and the use of specific frames in defining the issue across nine major newspapers: the full *Times* plus eight other newspapers, including the *Houston Chronicle* and the *Washington Post*. Between 1980 and 2005, the yearly level of *Times'* coverage of the death penalty correlated strongly (0.7) with the average yearly level of coverage paid by the other papers. Moreover, the yearly number of *Times* stories utilizing the "innocence" frame correlated even more strongly (0.9) with the average yearly use of this frame by the other papers. In other words, at least for the issue of capital punishment, the *Times* is a strong indicator of national newspaper coverage—both levels of coverage and how these stories are framed (Baumgartner, De Boef, and Boydstun 2008, 127–32). The dependent variable for the capital punishment model I present here is the number of NYT stories about capital punishment in a given year.

Independent Variables

Prior Attention

In both models, *prior attention* is captured simply by lagging the dependent variable. Thus, for each observation, prior attention is set at the previous time period's value of the number of news stories about the issue (monthly for the war, yearly for capital punishment). As with the topic-level model in chapter 5, I expect *prior attention* to have a positive effect on attention.

Events

No single measure can capture all relevant event information that unfolds in a policy area over time. But in the case of specific issues like the war and the death penalty, certain measures can serve as reasonable proxies. Exactly *which* proxy measures to use is a challenging decision. In the case of the death penalty, for example, we might use yearly U.S. measures of homicides, capital-offense trials, death sentences, executions, or the death row population, among other indicators of the underlying varying "severity" of the issue (Baumgartner, Linn, and Boydstun 2009). Specific events not captured by this series matter, too, such as the Abu Ghraib scandal in the case of the war. Measuring events, in other words, is tricky business. Listed below are the indicators I use for each case. While imperfect, these proxy measures help capture the underlying real-world dynamics of the issue as they develop over time. These measures make the most sense given the specific characteristics of each issue and the goal of demonstrating a general and parsimonious model in these two separate cases; other event indicators could certainly be used instead. In the case of both issues, I expect *events* to exhibit a positive and significant relationship with attention.

THE WAR ON TERROR.   As a proxy for events of the war, I use the number
of U.S. military casualties each month, calculated as the total number
of U.S. military casualties in Afghanistan and Iraq, based on data from
the U.S. Department of Defense, Military Casualty Information.[5] This
casualty series serves as a strong objective indicator of the changing situation "on the ground" as the war evolved.

THE DEATH PENALTY.   As a proxy for events surrounding capital punishment in the United States, I use the number of people sentenced to
death each year. This data series uses statistics provided by the Bureau
of Justice Department of Statistics for the years between 1961 and 1972
and data from Snell (2005) for the years 1973 to 2005 (see Baumgartner,
De Boef, and Boydstun 2008). The number of sentences serves as an objective indicator of the application of capital punishment over time.

Policymaker Attention

As with events, we can imagine many potential proxy indicators for *policymaker attention*. Here, I use a proxy that is sensible in the context of
each policy issue. Because both models use count (instead of proportion)
measures of news coverage as the dependent variable, policymaker attention is likewise measured in counts. In both models, I expect *policymaker attention* to have a positive and significant relationship with news
coverage.

THE WAR ON TERROR.   Scholars have argued that Congress takes a less
active policymaking role in the case of foreign policy in general (e.g.,
Wood and Peake 1998), and in the case of the Iraq War in particular
(e.g., Entman 2003; Fisher 2003). Still, these and other scholars recog-
nize the important role of Congress in drawing national attention to policy issues (Baumgartner, Jones, and Leech 1997; Jones, Larsen-Price,
and Wilkerson 2009; Pfetsch 2007; Sellers 2010). As in chapter 5, policymaker attention is captured through congressional hearings—this time
the number of hearings on the war.

THE DEATH PENALTY.   Given the legal groundings of discussion surrounding capital punishment in the United States, it makes sense in this
case to capture policymaker attention through judicial attention. I thus
capture policymaker attention through the number of U.S. Supreme

Court cases decided each year that contained the terms "death penalty" and/or "capital punishment" in the transcript of the decision as archived by LexisNexis.[6] Of course, Supreme Court justices are not "policymakers" in the formal sense, although they certainly influence policy in their own way (e.g., Casper 1976; Segal and Spaeth 2002). In any case, the Supreme Court certainly meets the definition of a policymaker in its relationship to the news-generation process.

Public Concern

The discussion of news generation in chapter 2 suggests that we should also see a positive relationship between the level of *public concern* about an issue and news coverage of that issue.

THE WAR ON TERROR.   The degree of public concern about the war can be estimated using the Gallup most important problem (MIP) series described in chapter 5, coded by the Policy Agendas Project according to topic area. Specifically, I use the proportion of survey respondents who identify a "most important problem" related to defense (topic 16) as an indicator of concern for the war. This measure is less than ideal not only due to the problems with the MIP measure already described (Wlezien 2005) but also because the MIP values on defense capture concern for *all* defense-related issues, not just war. That said, given the fact that most defense-related events during the time period studied related, at least tangentially, to the war on terror, it can be reasonably assumed that most variance in this MIP series is related to the war.

THE DEATH PENALTY.   In the case of the death penalty, public concern is much more difficult to capture using existing measures. Gallup's MIP series can be used to indicate the level of concern about the topic of Law and Crime generally, but this topic is much too broad to use as a proxy of concern for the specific issue of capital punishment. For the sake of parity with the war model, I employ the most sensible proxy of public concern about the death penalty: the percentage of survey respondents, smoothed across all relevant surveys by a range of survey houses, who express a pro–death penalty or anti–death penalty opinion, as opposed to saying "don't know."[7] In essence, then, this measure is an attempt to capture the degree of opinion, one way or the other, about the issue of capital punishment. Still, this pro/anti opinion percentage is a questionable proxy for *concern* about the death penalty, and I exclude the measure from the strongest model presented in table 6.2 below.

Diversity of Discussion

The *diversity of discussion* is the concentration or diffusion of discussion surrounding a policy issue. At the level of a major topic, we can think of the diversity of discussion as the extent to which news coverage of the topic is spread over specific issues within that topic. Thus, in chapter 5 the diversity of discussion for each topic was captured as the diversity of front-page coverage across the composite subtopics of that topic, using the normalized Shannon's H entropy measure. At a finer-grained issue level, we can conceptualize the diversity of discussion as the diversity of attention to an issue across the composite frames that might be used to define that issue.[8] The more diverse the discussion of an issue across alternate frames, the more engaging the debate and the more attention the issue will garner. Thus, I measure the diversity of discussion about each issue as the spread of news coverage about the issue across its possible frames, using the same normalized Shannon's H formula presented in chapter 5, ranging in theory from 0 (total concentration on one frame) to 1 (equal dispersion across all frames and, thus, total diversity).

THE WAR ON TERROR.   Measuring the diversity of discussion about the war is achieved by employing the aforementioned dataset of NYT and WSJ coverage of the war. Each story in this dataset is coded according to the dominant frame used to define the war based on a detailed coding scheme consisting of more than 200 distinct "frames" categorized into twelve broad frameworks, or dimensions of debate: Terrorism, Democratization and Freedom, Government Operations, Soldiers, September 11th, Reconstruction, Weapons of Mass Destruction (WMDs), Civil Unrest, Human Rights and Criminal Abuses, Civilians, Prisoners/Detainees, and Economic Cost. Intercoder agreement was at over 90 percent at both the broad framework and individual frame levels (Glazier and Boydstun 2012). Together, these data provide a detailed view of how media portrayals of the war have shifted over time. The normalized Shannon's H entropy measure was calculated across the 241 specific frames that were used in the news at least once during the period examined.

THE DEATH PENALTY. Similarly, measuring the diversity of discussion about the death penalty is accomplished using the aforementioned dataset of NYT coverage of capital punishment. Each story in this dataset is coded according to the frame(s) used to define the death penalty based on a coding scheme consisting of sixty-five distinct arguments, or "frames," categorized into seven broad frameworks, or dimensions of debate: Morality, Efficacy, Fairness, Constitutionality, Cost, Mode of Execution, and International Arguments. Again, intercoder agreement was at over 90 percent at both the framework and frame levels (Baumgartner, De Boef, and Boydstun 2008). As with the war dataset, the death penalty dataset offers rich documentation of how media portrayals of capital punishment have changed over the years. Here too, I calculate the now-familiar normalized Shannon's H entropy measure across the sixty-four frames (excluding a rarely used "other" frame category) that were used at least once during the period examined.

Agenda Congestion

In chapter 5, I used a measure of *agenda congestion* to track the generally *negative* effect that congestion has on the amount of news coverage an average topic receives. In the case of the death penalty, we would expect congestion to perform exactly this role, pushing capital punishment out of the news to make room for mega storylines, like 9/11. Unfortunately, the measure of congestion I employ for the death penalty leaves much to be desired, as discussed below. But in the case of the war, the war itself *is* a mega storyline serving to push other issues aside. This fact makes using congestion as an explanatory variable problematic, in that front-page congestion during the time period studied is in large part a mathematical function of the amount of attention given to the war specifically. Thus, for both the war and the death penalty, I present findings that include the respective measures of congestion, but then remove these measures in favor of more sensible, parsimonious models.

THE WAR ON TERROR. For the war, I use precisely the same measure of agenda congestion calculated in chapter 5 using the front-page *New York Times* dataset.

THE DEATH PENALTY. Measuring congestion in the case of the death penalty is more problematic. The only existing dataset of news coverage coded by topic—a requirement for calculating congestion—covering the time period in question (1960–2005) is the sample of full-paper *New York Times* coverage collected by Baumgartner and Jones for the Policy Agendas Project. I calculate agenda congestion for the death penalty as the inverse normalized Shannon's H values across all 27 topics in the full paper each year. Unfortunately, this sampled full-paper dataset, while enormous, captures on average about two stories a day (730 per year). Compared with the front-page *Times* dataset, containing an average eight stories per day (2,821 per year), the full-paper dataset supports a much blunter, arguably less accurate, estimate of congestion.

Results

For both issues examined, I describe below the results from modeling news coverage of the issue as a function of the key variables already discussed, using autoregressive (ARIMA [1,0,0]) models.[9] Tables 6.1 (for the war) and 6.2 (for capital punishment) show the results. In each case, I build the model in layers in order to isolate the effects of different combinations of variables. In the final column (column E) of each table, I arrive at a model for each issue that represents the "best-fit" model. In each case, this best-fit model contains (only) the most appropriate variables given operationalization considerations (again, excluding public concern in the case of the death penalty and the problematic congestion measures in both cases). In each case, this model explains the most variance in news coverage (and produces strong white-noise residuals). In parallel with examining tables 6.1 and 6.2, we can get a sense of the data in each case by looking at figures 6.1 and 6.2, which show the time series indicators for the variables contained in each of the best-fit models.

THE WAR ON TERROR.   As we can see in figure 6.1, the war data is fairly noisy at the monthly level. Still, even here we can see common patterns of movement between key variables, although in most instances the leader/follower patterns are difficult to discern; endogeneity is surely at work. In general, we see a great deal of volatility but also common up-and-down movement, most notably with the deployment of U.S. troops to Iraq in March of 2003 (month 19 in the series).

In order to assess these relationships more systematically, table 6.1

TABLE 6.1 **Results from ARIMA models of number of sampled *New York Times* front-page and *Wall Street Journal* stories on the war on terror**

	A Events	B Add Prior Attention	C Add Congress and Public	D Full Model	E Full Model, Minus Congestion
	Coef (Std Err)	Coef (Std Err)	Coef (Std Err)	Coef (Std Err)	Coef (Std Err)
Prior Attention (Number of Sampled NYT and WSJ Stories $_{t-1}$)		0.902* (0.052)	0.765* (0.072)	0.278^ (0.136)	**0.740*** (**0.084**)
Events (Number of U.S. Military Casualties $_t$)	−0.192* (0.092)	0.178^ (0.078)	0.108 (0.097)	−0.055 (0.064)	**0.102** (**0.092**)
Policymaker Attention (Number of Congressional Hearings $_t$)			0.290^ (0.139)	0.112 (0.091)	**0.246^** (**0.132**)
Public Concern (Proportion of Gallup MIP on Defense $_t$)			248.245* (57.478)	111.975* (50.051)	**271.464*** (**60.217**)
Diversity of Discussion $_t$				148.373* (57.518)	**169.683*** (**52.473**)
Front-Page Congestion $_t$				261.207* (34.098)	
Constant $_t$	62.288 (7.948)	58.368* (28.825)	−20.754 (23.896)	−128.030* (35.404)	**−121.989*** (**34.885**)
N (months) =	64	64	64	64	64
Stories =	3,356	3,356	3,356	3,356	3,356
Log Likelihood =	−313.76	−286.95	−279.96	−253.90	−273.74
Akaike (AIC) =	633.51	581.91	571.92	523.81	561.48
Bayesian (BIC) =	639.99	590.54	584.88	541.08	576.59
Portmanteau (Q) Stat =	p = 0.000*	p = 0.578	p = 0.740	p = 0.077^	p = 0.602
Q Stat, Squared Resid =	p = 0.017*	p = 0.975	p = 0.329	p = 0.324	p = 0.844

^ p < 0.1, one-tailed

* p < 0.01, one-tailed

Note: With the exception of the first model, all models are run as autoregressive ARIMA (1,0,0) processes. The first model is run as an ARIMA (0,0,0) process.

TABLE 6.2 **Results from ARIMA models of number of *New York Times* stories on the death penalty**

	A Events	B Add Prior Attention and Events	C Add Courts and Diversity	D Full Model	E All Variables Lagged
	Coef (Std Err)	Coef (Std Err)	Coef (Std Err)	Coef (Std Err)	Coef (Std Err)
Prior Attention (Number of NYT Stories $_{t-1}$)		0.701* (0.132)	0.493* (0.163)	0.606* (0.153)	**0.601*** (0.143)
Events (Number of Death Sentences $_t$)	0.148^ (0.103)	-0.149 (0.227)	-0.094 (0.149)	-0.191 (0.152)	**0.244^** (0.117)
Policymaker Attention (Number of Supreme Court Cases on the Death Penalty$_t$)			4.211^ (2.252)	3.763^ (1.845)	**3.351^** (1.842)
Public Concern (% Pro/Anti Opinion $_t$)				0.827 (8.381)	
Diversity of Discussion $_t$			174.919^ (118.757)	148.452^ (113.851)	**163.382*** (69.659)
Full-Paper Congestion $_t$				519.988^ (228.716)	
Constant	59.047* (21.156)	114.714* (37.660)	-36.382 (82.373)	-150.285 (722.638)	**-88.601*** (54.432)
N (years) =	44	44	44	44	44
Stories =	3,892	3,892	3,892	3,892	*3,892*
Log Likelihood =	-235.51	-225.99	-219.18	-216.97	-217.37
Akaike (AIC) =	477.03	459.99	450.35	449.95	446.75
Bayesian (BIC) =	482.38	467.12	461.06	464.22	457.45
Portmanteau (Q) Stat =	$p = 0.178$^	$p = 0.891$	$p = 0.771$	$p = 0.653$	$p = 0.969$
Q Stat, Squared Resid =	$p = 0.989$	$p = 1.000$	$p = 1.000$	$p = 0.999$	$p = 1.000$

^ $p < 0.1$, one-tailed

* $p < 0.01$, one-tailed

Note: With the exception of the first model, all models are run as autoregressive ARIMA (1,0,0) processes. The first model is run as an ARIMA (0,0,0) process. In the final model, attention at time t is calculated as a combined function of prior attention, along with three variables set at time $t-1$: the explanatory values events, policymaker attention, and diversity of discussion.

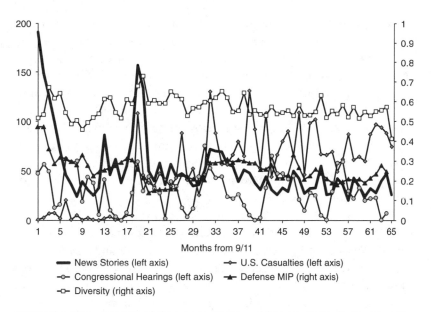

FIGURE 6.1. News coverage of the war on terror, and key correlates, September 2001–December 2006

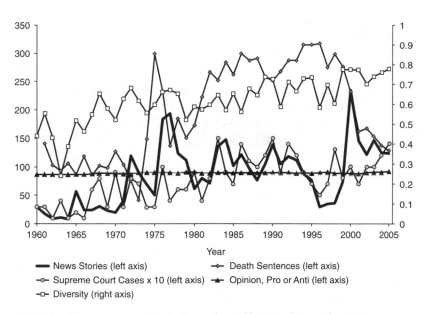

FIGURE 6.2. News coverage of the death penalty, and key correlates, 1960–2005

shows the results of a series of ARIMA models. Because the congressional hearings and Gallup MIP series had no observations during the sixty-fifth month of this analysis, for the sake of comparison all models in table 6.1 are truncated to sixty-four observations. Model A shows the number of news stories modeled as a function of the number of U.S. military casualties only (i.e., using an ARIMA [0,0,0] model). This model is statistically intractable, as can be seen by the highly significant Portmanteau statistics, showing strong autocorrelation (self-reinforcing properties) in both the residuals and the squared residuals of the model. We must account for the autoregressive nature of the news-generation process, above and beyond the role of events.

Model B, then, shows attention modeled using an ARIMA (1,0,0) model. Here, we see white noise residuals and squared residuals, indicating proper fit. As expected, *events* have a positive and significant relationship with news coverage of the war. When we add the indicators of *policymaker attention* and *public concern* in model C, however, both these variables exhibit a significant positive relationship with news coverage while the effects of events disappear. Three measures of fit—the log likelihood, the Akaike information criterion (AIC), and the Bayesian information criterion (BIC)—all indicate (through lower values) that model C explains more of the variance in our dependent variable than the casualties-focused model B.

Model D shows the results from all five potential explanatory variables, including *diversity of discussion* and the problematic measure of *agenda congestion*. Congestion yields a positive and significant coefficient, contrary to our theoretical expectations. However, autocorrelation in the residuals calls into question the integrity of this model.

The best-fit model is model E. Excluding model D as nonviable, model E exhibits the smallest log likelihood, AIC, and BIC values. We can compare these values directly because all models have the same number of observations, meaning that any decrease in these measures indicates a significant increase in model fit. In model E, we see positive and significant relationships exhibited by *prior attention*, *policymaker attention*, and *public concern*, all consistent with the expectations outlined above. As with model C, *events* is positive but insignificant. Again, keep in mind that, unlike the results in chapter 5, these findings are contemporaneous in nature. They document strong, positive relationships between the four variables captured in model E and news coverage of the war on terror, offering suggestive evidence in support of the theoretical story presented about the news-generation process.

THE DEATH PENALTY. Figure 6.2 reveals a much cleaner view of the variables related to the death penalty at the yearly level than the monthly picture of the war we saw in figure 6.1. Here we see stronger evidence of several instances in which news coverage of capital punishment appears to follow the other key variables shown. For example, note that the dramatic uptick in coverage of the death penalty in 2000 came on the heels of an increase in the diversity of the frames used in the news. At the same time, the 2000 increase in attention led a decrease in the number of people sentenced to death—this drop in death sentences has been tied statistically to the rise of the innocence frame in the death penalty debate beginning in the late 1990s (Baumgartner, De Boef, and Boydstun 2008). Again, endogeneity is certainly present.

Table 6.2 helps to sort out the influence of these other key variables on *Times* coverage of the death penalty, whatever the mutually reinforcing nature of these effects may be. In order to compare models A–D with the lagged model E, all models are run across forty-four observations, 1962–2005 (since the sentences series begins in 1961, making 1962 the first observation that accounts for lagged sentences). Again, model A shows attention as a function of *events* only, and again autocorrelation in the residuals indicates that we must account for the autoregressive properties of the news, as shown in model B.

Model C incorporates the role of two additional key variables—*policymaker attention* and *diversity of discussion*—and both these variables exhibit positive and significant relationships with news coverage, as expected. The decrease in log likelihood, AIC, and BIC values indicate an increase in the explained amount of variance in the dependent variable.

Model D incorporates, for the sake of parity, the problematic measures of *public concern* and *agenda congestion*. The coefficient for agenda congestion is significant and positive, as expected, but again the inclusion of this measure is questionable—and perhaps helps explain the decreased p value on the Portmanteau statistic for this model.

Again excluding model D as nonviable, then, we turn to the best-fit model E, which replicates model C but takes a turn by using lagged values of events, policymaker attention, and diversity of discussion, as well as prior attention. This model shows positive and significant effects for all these variables and also exhibits the most explained variance. As with model E in the case of the war on terror, these results suggest that the theoretical expectations presented of the news-generation process can offer statistical traction in identifying the correlates of news coverage to individual issues. But in the case of model E for capital punishment, we can shift from inferring correlation to inferring the directional effects of each lagged explanatory variable on news coverage. Here, we have evidence that these forces truly shape the news.

Conclusion

In this chapter, we have seen the payoffs of modeling two issues—the war on terror and the death penalty—as a function of key explanatory variables, offering compounding support for hypothesis 1 and, more generally, the alarm/patrol hybrid model of news generation from chapter 3. Applied in systematic fashion through layered models in tables 6.1 and 6.2, the theory of news coverage as a (mutually reinforcing) function of these variables has borne out statistically.

But what do these issue-level findings really mean? We can get a sense of the size of the statistical relationships presented in this chapter by comparing the results from models E in tables 6.1 and 6.2 to the summary statistics for these variables (shown in table A.3 of the appendix). In the case of the war, a one standard deviation increase in U.S. military casualties correlates with an increase of 3.77 stories (coefficient of 0.102 × standard deviation of 36.986). This means that, all else being equal in the model, the deaths of thirty-seven soldiers equates to about four stories in the NYT and WSJ dataset—which, remember, is only a small sample of all coverage in these outlets (the actual number of full-paper NYT and WSJ stories would likely be at least ten times larger). By comparison, a one standard deviation increase in policymaker attention (congressional hearings), public concern, and the diversity of discussion (diversity in how the war was framed) correspond with monthly increases of 4.85, 17.65, and 9.33 stories, respectively. Again, considering the small size of our sample, these article estimates are politically as well as statistically significant.

In the case of the death penalty, the effects shown in model E play out as follows: A one standard deviation increase in death sentences, policymaker attention (Supreme Court cases), and diversity of discussion (diversity of how the death penalty was framed) in the prior year produce an estimated increase of 20.42, 13.35, and 18.30 additional stories in the current year, respectively. On a specific policy issue like capital punishment, an increase of thirteen to twenty stories in the *New York Times* is no small thing.

The news-generation process is certainly a complicated one. Yet the variables identified here—including not just events but also institutional forces—provide statistically verified explanations of much of the variance in how much traction each issue receives in the news over time. These findings speak directly to past work investigating how variables—including issue-framing—combine to drive attention cycles (Baumgartner, De Boef, and Boydstun 2008; Baumgartner and Jones 2009; Downs 1972; Sellers 2010). What is more, the model shows promise of being one that could be applied to studies of multiple different policy issues.

CHAPTER SEVEN

How Institutional Mechanisms Lead to Media Skew and Explosiveness

As chapters 5 and 6 illustrated, the news is systematically influenced not only by events, but also by forces that derive from the institutional incentives under which news outlets operate. We can capture some of these incentive-driven forces through measurable variables, such as proxy indicators of *policymaker attention* and *public concern*, providing a considerable degree of explanatory power in modeling the rise and fall of broad topics and specific issues in the news. Yet, while the effects of these individual variables are important, it is just as important to understand the roles these forces play as mechanisms of positive and negative feedback (as described in chapters 2 and 3), producing aggregate patterns of skew and explosiveness in the news.

The crucial variable of *prior attention*, examined in chapters 5 and 6, captures general momentum driving the news-generation process. This variable encapsulates momentum in the form of positive feedback during periods of punctuation: at the beginning of media explosions (big and small), when the media is in alarm mode. This same variable also captures momentum in the form of negative feedback during periods of equilibrium: during "quiet" periods between explosions and during the brief patrol-driven periods of fixation on a storyline in the context of sustained media explosions.

In fact, though, all the explanatory variables examined in chapters 5 and 6 can influence news coverage via self-reinforcing (and mutually reinforcing) momentum. For example, take the media's institutional incentives to index elite issues and opinions (Bennett 1990). These incentives are what enable *policymaker attention* to an issue to influence media attention to that same issue. But the incentive-driven variable of policymaker attention can act as either a positive feedback or negative feedback mechanism of momentum. Consider again instances when policymaker attention to an issue surges, and the media follows suit by giving more coverage to that issue. Policymakers will then often (though certainly not always) give even more attention to that issue still, seeking to capitalize on the opportunities for awareness (and political gains) the increased news coverage can present. In turn, increased policymaker attention drives media attention even further, and the cycle continues, often culminating in an attention cascade. This is positive feedback. By contrast, sometimes policymaker attention to an issue is relatively stable, as in the case of routine attention to fixture issues on the executive or legislative agendas (e.g., foreign policy) or in the case of sustained concentration to an issue of lasting salience but not usually on these agendas (e.g., the 2010 Affordable Care Act). During these periods, the influence of policymaker attention on media attention acts as a negative feedback mechanism, reinforcing the status quo level of news coverage to that issue. As I demonstrate below, the result of the give-and-take between positive feedback and negative feedback—not only in the form of prior attention, but also policymaker attention and the other key variables I have discussed—produces a media agenda marked by skew (hypothesis 2) and explosiveness (hypothesis 3).

Positive feedback, in particular, is critical to our understanding of the news-generation process. It is positive feedback that underpins the two most dramatic forms of media explosion: alarm-driven momentary explosions and alarm/patrol-driven sustained explosions. Both types of media explosions exacerbate the agenda's degree of skew across policy issues, not because the explosions are initiated by extreme change, but because they direct so much attention to just a few issues. Thus, because positive feedback is the driving mechanism behind these types of explosions, we can attribute to it a strong amount of the skew in the news. Note, of course, that the patrol-driven timed media explosions, such as those surrounding the Olympics, are driven by negative feedback, pulling the media's attention consistently back toward the planned news item at hand. And timed media explosions also exacerbate the skew in the agenda by "over"-representing the issues around which they center, since major planned news items are certainly not randomly distributed across policy areas. But without positive feedback, the media agenda would be much more evenly spread across issues.

To conceptualize positive feedback in context, consider again the 2002 surge in U.S. news coverage surrounding the sexual abuse of parish children by some Catholic priests. This surge in media attention was not the result of an increase in the underlying severity of the problem. In fact, a rigorous study conducted by researchers at John Jay College indicates that sexual abuse by Catholic priests has largely been on the decline since 1985 (Terry et al. 2011). Rather, the surge in media attention in 2002 was triggered by a series of *Boston Globe* stories based on five months of in-depth investigation by eight of its reporters. This investigative journalism entailed many components, including an ultimately successful legal battle over the release of church documents detailing abuse allegations (containing some 10,000 pages related to eighty-four different lawsuits about Father John Geoghan alone). Beginning in January 2002, the *Globe* stories revealed that over the preceding decade the Boston archdiocese had covered up sexual abuse claims made not just against Father Geoghan, but "against a staggering 70 of its priests" (Henley 2010).

This single initiative of investigative journalism—which certainly constituted a major "event" in the form of revealed information—fostered a flurry of media attention across news outlets. For example, in all of 2001, across three national newspapers (*New York Times*, *USA Today*, and *Washington Post*) and five television news outlets (ABC, CBS, CNN, Fox, and NBC), just eleven stories appeared that were relevant to alleged sexual abuse by U.S. Catholic priests. In 2002, this story count jumped to 802.[1] The *Boston Globe* journalists and editors, of course, had strong incentives to generate as many stories as they possibly could, since they had poured considerable time and resources into the investigation. And as the storyline grew, other news outlets had strong marketplace incentives to jump on board as well, both by reporting the same details already uncovered and by launching follow-up investigations to unearth information and sources unique to their own news outlets. The result: a sustained media explosion.

Unlike many other cases we might consider, in the case of the Catholic priest abuse scandal, policymakers were slow to jump on the attention bandwagon. President Bush raised the issue with Pope John Paul II in May 2008, but otherwise policymakers remained relatively quiet, perhaps because the issue—as a valence issue—offered no clear "side" on which to take a constituent-approved stand (Baumgartner and Jones 2009). Some policymakers might also have worried that in calling attention to the issue they would risk tripping over political (and financial) ties to the Catholic community.

Citizens, by contrast, reacted strongly to the news. While no polling data are available to compare attitudes before and after the *Boston Globe* series broke, an ABC News poll conducted in February 2002 found that 58% of sampled Americans reported that the issue of sexual abuse of children by priests had hurt the overall reputation of the Catholic Church in their eyes.[2]

Yet the biggest positive feedback mechanism of all in this case was the response from the victims of abuse who had remained silent, in many cases for decades. The John Jay College study cites 10,667 individual reports of sexual abuse by Catholic priests against minors that allegedly occurred between the years 1950 and 2002. Fewer than 50 of these reports involved abuse said to have taken place in 2002; the vast bulk of the abuse reported as of early 2003 occurred in the 1960s, 1970s, and 1980s. Yet of the 10,667 reports of abuse spanning back to 1950, nearly one-third (3,399) were brought forward in 2002 alone. This flood of victim reports almost certainly was due in large part to the surge in media attention—and a corresponding surge in social awareness. In turn, the wave of abuse reports further fueled media attention. In these ways, multiple forces of positive feedback contributed to the sustained media explosion surrounding the scandal.

In the case of news coverage of this abuse scandal and in media attention in general, it is the combination of both positive and negative feedback that produce systemic patterns of skew and explosiveness in the news. In this chapter, I test the media agenda for the presence of skew and explosiveness, discussing and showing why these patterns—to the dramatic degree they appear in the news—cannot be explained by events and attention scarcity alone. Instead, we must understand skew and explosiveness as largely products of momentum derived from the media's institutional incentives.

The rest of this chapter proceeds in three main sections. The first section is a more detailed discussion of how the news-generation process yields the specific patterns of skew in attention across issues as well as explosive change over time. In the second section, I demonstrate empirically just how skewed and explosive front-page news coverage really is. The statistical measure of skew serves to test the expectation (hypothesis 2) that front-page attention is not distributed normally across policy issues; rather, some issues receive the vast bulk of news coverage while most receive very little. The statistical measure of explosiveness tests the expectation (hypothesis 3) that front-page attention does not change gradually over time; rather, the front-page agenda lurches between periods of relative stability and periods of dramatic change.

The statistical measure of media explosiveness presented here is especially important, because it represents the best single test of the alarm/ patrol hybrid model of news generation. If news generation was strictly patrol-based, the media agenda would be dominated by periods of relative stability (equilibrium) and, probably, incremental change over time. If news generation was strictly alarm-based, the media agenda would be in dramatic upheaval nearly all the time, with very few periods of stability (equilibrium). The measure of explosiveness that I employ—called l-kurtosis—measures the agenda for the presence of *both* stability and dramatic change. The high l-kurtosis values of the *Times* front page demonstrates, empirically, that this is an agenda of both (alarm-driven) attention overhaul *and* (patrol-driven) sustained attention. Again, it is the dual presence of these alarm (positive feedback) and patrol (negative feedback) forces that produces the level of dramatic skew we will observe. Applying these measures of skew and explosiveness consistently across datasets, I also compare the patterns on the front page to those exhibited by other key agendas. Of the several political agendas examined here, the front-page agenda is one of the most skewed and most explosive.

In the third and final section, I use simulation evidence to show how the degree of skew we see in the news not only *can* be explained by the kind of news-generation system I have described in theory—one that includes positive feedback as well as negative feedback—but in fact can *only* be explained by this kind of system. The only way to understand the behavior of the media in a case like the Catholic priest abuse scandal is to account for the influence of positive feedback, offering support for the alarm/patrol hybrid model.

Let me underscore, again, why investigating the endemic nature of these patterns in the news is worth our time. The notion that the news is patterned in some way should not be surprising: instinctively, we probably expect some degree of skew, some degree of explosiveness, simply by virtue of how information tends to unfold in society. Yet the notion that these patterns stem not only from the media's general proclivity to focus on dramatic and evocative events, but are necessary products of institutional incentives, should give us considerable pause. Skew and explosiveness directly shape the likelihood that any given news item, on any given day, makes the news (and especially the front page). The likelihood, then, that citizens will see a particular item in the news depends only partially on the item itself; it also depends strongly on the U.S. media system as an institution. That the news is shaped in this way is neither good nor bad, per se, for our democratic ideals. But it does mean that in addition to being able to explain (sometimes even predict) which items are most likely to become news and when, we can also conclude that the media's institutional incentives produce a very particular form of media agenda: one that changes explosively over time and to which most issues have scarce access. The systemic nature of skew and explosiveness in the news affects us all.

The Institutional Dynamics of Media Attention

The combination of positive and negative feedback leads institutions (and the human beings that comprise them) to process information disproportionately. This disproportionate information processing system is further exacerbated by attention scarcity. The purpose of this section is to unpack in more detail the precise mechanisms at work in this process.

The core of this discussion is generalizable across institutional agendas, but of key concern here, of course, is how these mechanisms play out in the context of the U.S. media. While disproportionate information processing is common across agendas, specific institutional incentives can exacerbate or mitigate this process and the resulting patterns of skew and explosiveness. In the case of U.S. news outlets, most incentives are of the exacerbating variety. Theoretically, then, we should expect the news not only to exhibit skew and explosiveness, but to do so to a *stronger* degree than many other agendas.

To reiterate, institutional incentives can serve at different times as momentum elements of negative feedback (that dampen change) or positive feedback (that reinforce change). Negative feedback elements serve to reinforce the current equilibrium of an agenda. But when positive feedback elements come into play, they can propel the system into hyperdrive, prompting news outlets to swarm (individually and collectively) to a news item. Sometimes the resulting attention cascade can draw much-needed attention to a latent problem of high severity (like the Catholic priest abuse scandal). Other times, it can draw an amount of attention that is arguably way out of whack with the problem's importance (like the "balloon boy" storyline in October 2009). Moreover, the positive feedback that propels an enormous amount of attention to a few issues only means that most issues of arguable importance generally receive little to no attention. Thus, with rare but important exceptions—usually in the form of sustained media explosions stemming from both alarm and patrol modes of journalism—news coverage rarely attends to events and related policy problems in proportion to the (unmeasurable) importance of those events/problems. Thus, disproportionate information processing.

Generally speaking, the stronger the negative feedback mechanisms embedded in an institution's incentive structure, the less often change will occur. Conversely, the stronger an institution's positive feedback mechanisms, the more susceptible the institution will be to dramatic, self-reinforcing change. Thus, the stronger the positive *and* negative feedback mechanisms of an institution, the more explosive the institution's dynamics will be (Jones, Sulkin, and Larsen 2003). And with explosive change comes overall skew in attention across issues. Whatever the (shifting) baseline distribution of agenda space, explosive dynamics lead to increased skew: first, by reinforcing any baseline degree of skew during periods of equilibrium; second, and critically, by diverting significant amounts of attention to only one or two issues during periods of explosion—both the initial surge in attention *and* the sustained attention that sometimes follows.

Of key significance in understanding the interplay of negative and positive forces in the news is to think of negative and positive feedback mechanisms as just that—*feedback* mechanisms. Operationally, both types of mechanisms shape the current pressures on the agenda based on past agenda performance. These mechanisms, in opposite ways, make the front-page agenda at time t highly conditional on the agenda at time $t-1$, above and beyond the degree to which the most (subjectively) pressing real-world events at time t are connected to those that were most pressing at time $t-1$. Thus, in order to capture the positive and negative feedback mechanisms at work on the front page, we need to account for the forces that reinforce past behavior—both the standing equilibrium and deviations therefrom. Together, these "underreacting" and "overreacting" forces produce the dramatic degree of skew and explosiveness in the news.

Mechanisms of Momentum

Jones and Baumgartner (2005) identify three major types of self-reinforcing processes at work in disproportional information processing systems that can generate explosive change and skew: sieves, cascades, and friction. These three processes can happen alone or simultaneously, although they can be very difficult to parse out in the real world. Regardless, understanding sieves, cascades, and friction can provide a better view of the gears and cogs behind the news.

SIEVES. Sieve processes, Jones and Baumgartner write, "come about when decision makers apply ever greater constraints to a decision-making process. Adding constraints rules out options, causing greater changes from the status quo when adjustments finally do occur" (2005, 139). When decisionmakers, such as journalists and editors, are faced with a problem such as how much attention to pay to an issue, they tend to review the possible options using "serial judgment" as opposed to comprehensive, incremental review (Padgett 1980, 1981). They begin by identifying the constraints (and resulting incentives) of the situation, such as retaining readership or maintaining favor with the White House, and then they "cycle through the available options until one option satisfies the constraints of the situation" (Jones and Baumgartner 2005, 143). In applying serial judgment, these decisionmakers tend to begin by considering options close at hand that would mean a small step away from the status quo, and only begin to consider more radical options after cycling for a while. If the constraints are small, often it does not take long to arrive at a satisfactory solution. The more demanding the constraints, however, the more cycling will be required before arriving at an acceptable solution.

In general, then, simple constraints will lead to decisions that fall close to the status quo, while complex constraints will require larger deviations from the status quo. In this way, the constraints that instigate a sieve process act as negative feedback, dampening the likelihood of change in the system. At the same time, stronger constraints force decisionmakers to look to increasingly more dramatic options in order to satisfy the criteria, meaning that when change occurs it will be much more explosive than if no constraints existed or if decisionmakers used incremental rather than serial judgment. Since journalists and editors must satisfy a number of (mostly informal) constraints in making their daily decisions about the news, media attention is highly susceptible to sieve processes and to the disproportional patterns of change that result.

CASCADES.   Cascade processes are those "in which one action begets other actions, independent of the nature of the external event stimulating the initial action" (Jones and Baumgartner 2005, 140). Once started, cascades take on lives of their own, propelling a snowball-like sequence of reactions that are often out of proportion with whatever the original seed of the cascade may have been. Often the wave of positive feedback to the initial stimulus will decay and die out, but in other instances it cascades. At the core of the cascade process is positive feedback—an all-too-familiar mechanism in financial markets, when a drop in stock prices can lead to a chain-reaction series of drops ending in a market crash. Cascades have been documented in numerous other domains, including social fads (Bikhchandani, Hirshleifer, and Welch 1992), overcoming collective action problems (Granovetter 1978), human herd behavior (Shiller 1995), residential segregation (Granovetter and Soong 1988; Schelling 1972), economic trends (Shiller 2000; Sornette 2003), restaurant patronage (Banerjee 1992; Becker 1991), presidential primaries (Bartels 1988), and the success of the QWERTY keyboard (David 1985).

In politics, we see positive feedback in action every time bandwagoning occurs around a popular political candidate or policy issue (Baumgartner and Jones 2009). Another cascade example is the "spillover" effect that can occur in policymaking, where policymakers use the inertia of an initial policy innovation to push through their own versions of the policy initiative and, as a result, the policy spreads like wildfire (Kingdon 1995). Many factors influence how dramatic and far-reaching a cascade will be, including threshold effects (Granovetter 1978) or what Malcolm Gladwell has termed "tipping points" (2000), the embeddedness of human networks (Barabasi 2003; Granovetter 1985; Penn 2007), and "microtrends" (Penn 2007). Given the many cascade mechanisms at work in the news, and especially the tipping point nature of reader/viewer interest in unfolding hot news items, we should expect frequent media cascades.

FRICTION.   Institutional friction is a sticky resistance to change that, when overcome, produces change that is lurching rather than gradual.

Institutional friction occurs "when institutions retard change, but result in a large-scale 'jump' when the built-in friction is overcome" (Jones and Baumgartner 2005, 139). Many institutional constraints and incentives serve as negative feedback mechanisms, reinforcing the status quo and resisting change. As already discussed, in the case of the media incentive-driven newsroom patterns, such as beat routines and storyline follow-up reporting, operate as negative feedback mechanisms, reinforcing the current equilibrium distribution of attention across issues and deflecting attention from other (important) issues.

We might think of this kind of resistance to change through negative feedback mechanisms in an institution, including the media, as gridlock. Yet whereas gridlock implies stasis, the concept of friction implies dynamism. Even high levels of friction will eventually be overcome (resulting in institutional change) because while an institution is busy processing the small number of problems it can handle at any one time, information inevitably builds up in other problem areas as events in those areas continues to unfold. Sooner or later, a problem will become too large to ignore, and/or a major event (usually focusing or triggering) will occur, and the institution will lurch focus to attend to it. During these moments of dramatic change, positive feedback mechanisms serve to compound additional attention to the new problem in a self-reinforcing, spiraling manner.

Because the media is governed by considerably fewer formal institutional constraints than Congress, the presidency, or the Supreme Court, we might think that it operates under less friction than these traditional institutions and, thus, expect it to exhibit a lower degree of explosiveness and skew (Jones, Sulkin, and Larsen 2003). However, the media is unusual among U.S. institutions in that its incentives operate on a much quicker-paced cycle. The decisionmaking process of journalists and editors is measured in hours and minutes, not days, weeks, or months. So, in terms of cycle duration, we should expect the media to be even more susceptible to punctuation than other institutions. In some cases, the media may demonstrate less pronounced patterns of punctuated equilibrium (i.e., less dramatic punctuations) than higher friction institutions. Yet, its equilibria will generally be shorter and its punctuations more frequent than institutions with longer decision-making cycles, leading ultimately to high degrees of explosiveness and skew.

Testing Skew and Explosiveness on the Front Page

If the news-generation process operates via the dual momentum forces of positive and negative feedback as argued, we should see dramatic skew and explosiveness in the media agenda. In chapter 4, we saw visual evidence of skew (figs. 4.3–4.4) and explosiveness (figs. 4.8–4.9) on the *New York Times* front page. But the presence of skew and explosiveness can be evaluated to a much more precise degree using established measures. In this section, I test statistically the degrees of skew and explosiveness on the *Times* front page.

Skew

Part of the skew exhibited in figures 4.3–4.4 can be attributed, of course, not only to the inherent differences in human prioritization of issues but also to the coding system employed. When Baumgartner and Jones (2006) developed the Policy Agendas Codebook, they never claimed to be creating topic and subtopic categories of equal size. Still, given a subjective understanding of the topics and subtopics in this coding scheme, it would be reasonable to consider the "importance" of these topics and subtopics as being something close to normally distributed, since event severity tends to be normally distributed (Jones and Baumgartner 2005). Instead, we see a highly skewed distribution. That the front-page agenda is so dramatically skewed reinforces the alarm/patrol hybrid model of news generation—disproportionate information processing played out in the context of the media, where news outlets "over"-attend to a few issues while wildly "under"-attending to most.

We can test the idea that the skew on the front-page agenda is only partially attributable to the coding scheme employed by comparing the front page to other institutional agenda datasets coded using the same Policy Agendas codebook. Table 7.1 shows two normalized measures of skew—the inverse Shannon's H entropy measure, as well as an alternate measure, the Herfindahl-Hirschman Index—across several different agendas. Both measures can range, in theory, from 0 to 1, with increased values representing heightened skew.[3]

Both measures presented in table 7.1 tell the same story. Of the datasets examined, only three—Supreme Court cases, public laws, and Gallup's most important problem measure—exhibit stronger agenda

TABLE 7.1 **A comparison of skew across major topics by institutional agenda**

Agenda	Measures of Skew	
	Inverse Normalized Shannon's H Entropy	Normalized Herfindahl-Hirschman Index
Supreme Court Cases	0.271	0.131
Congressional Public Laws	0.235	0.123
Gallup Most Important Problem	0.214	0.073
NYT Front Page	**0.169**	**0.062**
NYT Full Paper (1996–2005)	0.147	0.048
President's State of the Union Address (1996–2005)	0.141	0.051
Congressional Roll Call Votes (1996–2004)	0.114	0.048
Executive Orders (1996–2003)	0.094	0.036
Congressional Hearings	0.062	0.022
Congressional Quarterly Almanac	0.056	0.021
Congressional Bills	0.053	0.018

Note: Interpreting the numbers: The higher the skew of an agenda, the more concentrated the agenda is on one or more topics. For both measures used, a value of 0 would indicate that each topic receives exactly the same amount of attention; this is perfect dispersion, zero concentration. A value of 1 would indicate that one topic receives 100% of attention; this is perfect concentration, zero dispersion.

Sources: The NYT Front-Page dataset is the one developed for this book. The Congressional Bills data comes from the Congressional Bills Project (http://www.congressionalbills.org). All other datasets come from Policy Agendas Project (http://www.policyagendas.org). All calculations were run at the major topic level, with the number of topics ranging from 19 (in the case of the executive and some of the congressional datasets; some include 20) to 27 in the case of both NYT datasets. All datasets have been truncated to the 1996–2006 period to match the NYT front-page dataset (with some datasets not spanning this full range, as noted).

skew than the *Times* front page. These findings makes sense: the salience threshold a topic has to pass in order to appear on the front page, while high, should still be lower than the salience thresholds required to land on the Supreme Court's exclusive docket, to survive the entirety of the legislative process, or to appear on the very top of Americans' minds (remembering the problems with the MIP measure discussed in chapter 5; Wlezien 2005). Moreover, each of these three agendas is marked by a virtual lack of attention to entire topic categories, which strongly contributes to the skew of that respective agenda. For example, in the Gallup surveys Americans almost never mention the topics of Banking and Commerce, Transportation, Housing, Agriculture, or Public Lands as the most important problem facing the country. Compared to all the other agendas examined, however, the front-page agenda shows the highest measures of skew. These findings suggest not only that the front page is highly skewed (supporting hypothesis 2), but also that this skew is not just an artifact of the coding system employed. As a result of the disproportionate information processing by which events and their associated

policy issues become news, the front page is one of the more dramatically skewed agendas coded under the Policy Agendas rubric.

Explosiveness

While figure 4.8 showed us a portion of the monthly changes in the *Times*
front page, we can see the full distribution of monthly changes across the
1996–2006 dataset in figure 7.1. The values in this histogram represent
the frequency of changes (increases, decreases, or no-change observations) across all major topic categories.

For example, if 100 stories on Defense appeared in month t_1, then 70,
80, and 80 in months t_2, t_3, and t_4, respectively, the change values would
be $t_2 = -30$, $t_3 = +10$, and $t_4 = 0$. While the x axis of figure 7.1 shows the
level of change, the y axis represents the frequency of observations with
that degree of change. Thus, each column in the figure shows the number of instances of each level of change (clustered in "bins," with each

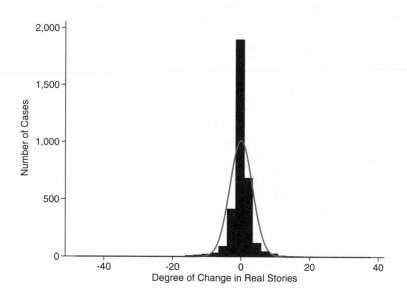

FIGURE 7.1. Histogram of major topic change on the front-page agenda, by month, 1996–
2006
Note: This figure shows the frequency of different degrees of change in the number of
front-page stories captured by a given topic in a given month, pooled across all topics/
months. L-kurtosis = 0.383. Overlaid on the histogram, the gray line shows a normal distribution curve.

bin represented by a column), arrayed from lowest (negative) to highest (positive). So as not to inflate the findings, all zero observations (i.e., instances when a major topic received exactly the same number of stories two months in a row) are excluded, making this test of explosiveness more stringent.

A normal distribution line, drawn from the same mean and standard deviation as the data, is overlaid on the histogram. Note that figure 7.1 is formatted so that the x axis accommodates large values on both sides: beyond −40 on the left and 40 on the right, though in fact the range is even larger than this axis suggests. The last column on each end of the x axis includes all remaining tail observations; the farthest column on the left contains the most extreme observed change value of −113, while the farthest column on the right includes the largest positive change value of +88. Because the x axis is shown across such a large range, the normal distribution line in the figure looks taller and thinner than we are used to seeing it. If changes in the media agenda were normally distributed, the dark columns in figure 7.1 would fit under (and fill out) the normal distribution line. Again, the null hypothesis here—that changes in the media agenda are normally distributed—is not a straw man hypothesis, since changes in events tend to be normally distributed (Jones and Baumgartner 2005).

But, by contrast to the normal distribution line shown, the multitude of small changes on the front page produces an even taller, thinner central peak, while the key moments of tremendous change push the x axis to a much wider range. We see very little incremental movement here, as shown by the weak shoulders of the histogram (the empty sections between the black columns and the normal curve); instead, we see a predominance of equilibria (the tall central peak), broken by dramatic periods of agenda overhaul (the small but important fat tails). This is no normal distribution, but a highly explosive one. Remember that instances when attention to a topic did not change from one month to the next are excluded from this histogram, providing a stricter test of the agenda's explosiveness. Thus, this tall central peak represents only those observations where attention to a topic changed very slightly between months. The wide tails of the histogram, far off to the left and right sides of the graph, are difficult to discern because the frequencies of those extreme observations are too low to register on the y axis. But, in fact, figure 7.1 contains 149 instances in which *a single topic* increased or decreased by more than fifteen stories (i.e., more than two standard deviations) in *a*

single month—these instances are spread out across both tails of the figure. Considering that figure 7.1 represents only 131 months of change
values, these 149 instances of extraordinary change point to strong and
frequent punctuations in the front-page agenda.

We can capture the precise degree of explosiveness using the l-
kurtosis statistic.[4] L-kurtosis values can range from zero to one, with
higher values representing more explosiveness (i.e., punctuated equilibrium behavior). A Gaussian (normal) distribution has an l-kurtosis value
of 0.123. L-kurtosis values below 0.123 indicate platykurtic distributions
(flat central peak, thick shoulders). Higher l-kurtosis values indicate lep-
tokurtosis (tall central peak, weak shoulders, wide tails). The real lit-
mus test of the alarm/patrol hybrid model is whether change values in
the news exceed the established l-kurtosis value of a normal distribution (0.123). At least with the *Times* front page, they certainly do. The
distribution of change values shown in figure 7.1 has an l-kurtosis value
of 0.344 (when zeroes are included, l-kurtosis = 0.383). Alternatively,
when calculated as changes in the *percentage* of the agenda captured by
each topic in each month, front-page agenda change during this time period has an l-kurtosis value of 0.372 (0.384 when zeroes are included). All
these measures point to a highly explosive agenda (supporting hypothesis 3 and the alarm/patrol hybrid model more broadly).

In contrast with comparing the skew of the *Times* front page to that
of other agendas (shown in table 7.1), comparing the level of explosiveness is made more challenging by the fact that different agendas move
at different speeds. It makes little sense, for example, to compare the
monthly change on the front page with monthly change in the Supreme
Court—or any other nonmedia agenda, for that matter. By way of general comparison though, when changes are calculated as percentages at
the yearly level, the *Times* front page shows an l-kurtosis value of 0.48
(even higher than at the monthly level, driven in large part by the large
topic-level changes resulting from the events of September 11, 2001).
Jones, Larsen-Price and Wilkerson (2009) report the l-kurtosis values
for several agendas calculated at the yearly level. Their calculations employ datasets spanning several decades rather than the eleven years of
the *Times* front-page dataset used here, meaning that the 9/11-driven
change observations hold less weight in these other datasets. But with
that caveat, at the yearly level the *Times* front page is more explosive
than these other agendas.[5]

In short, the *Times* front-page is highly skewed, and highly explosive. These patterns are not only stark in the abstract, but also when compared to other political agendas.

Evidence from Computer Simulations

It is not at all a given that front-page attention should be skewed and explosive in these ways. Random events are a strong driving force behind the news. But random events, by definition, would not produce the dramatic levels of skew and explosiveness we observe on the front page.

We can use computer simulations to model the idea that, beyond the role of events, institutional momentum drives the news. Computer simulations allow us to work backward from the patterns we observe in the news to identify what kind of influential forces need to be in place in order to produce them. Simulations reduce real-world complexities to a much smaller number of moving parts, which we can control. By tinkering with these moving parts until we arrive at a version of the world that looks like reality, we can estimate the variables that drive the actual news-generation process. Specifically, computer simulations begin with a (simple) formal model that explains the dependent variable of interest as a function of key explanatory variables. By specifying the exact rules by which the system updates over time, we can see how different starting assumptions about the way the world works lead to different results as the system plays out over time. Multiple simulation runs, each based on different starting seed values, produce a large N of unique outcomes centered around a core finding, allowing us to generalize the behavioral patterns that result from each arrangement of assumptions and variables.

I focus on the pattern of skew by developing a simulated front-page agenda and then adjusting its input variables until we see a degree of skew that matches that of the real front page. Events alone, we will see, are not enough to produce these patterns in the news. Neither are events in combination with institutional negative feedback. There must be some positive feedback, too, and quite a lot of it, to produce the level of skew we actually observe in the news.

We can imagine many different scenarios by which media attention might get allocated across issues. In the discussion that follows, I begin with the simplest possible model, in which front-page news is determined solely by random events (drawn from different distributions, as I describe) and an error term. The resulting front page, as we will see, demonstrates hardly any skew at all. Then I add the additional influence of a baseline (skewed) distribution of attention to account for the fact that not all issues are of equal (subjective) importance. This baseline skew captures the role of negative feedback in the news-generation process. The resulting agenda is mildly skewed, but nothing like the real news. Finally, I add a force of positive feedback—a placeholder for the many institutional incentives that often drive news outlets to pay additional attention to issues already in the news, thus initiating media explosions. Only here, and only with a strong amount of positive feedback, do we observe skew of the same degree in the real news. These findings demonstrate that positive feedback is a necessary (and, at high enough levels, sufficient) condition for producing skew in an agenda. Since we observe strong skew in the news, there must be (strong) forces of positive feedback at work in the news-generation process. Thus, these simulations provide direct evidence in support of the alarm/patrol hybrid model.

Simulation Design

To test the mechanisms underlying systemic skew in the news, I present here the results of a computer simulation designed to formally model the news-generation process—in vastly oversimplified terms. The simulation begins with a very basic world of *ten issues*, but room for only *three stories* on each day's front page. Each day, which issue(s) land in these three story spots is determined by one or more variables. The variables in this system can be manipulated—using systematic adjustments based in theory—to identify how the different "levers" of this simulated news-generation system affect patterns of simulated news coverage that result. The goal here is to see what combination of forces are required to produce the same degree of skew across issues on the artificial front page that we see on the real front page. While the simulation allows for more sophisticated combinations, here I show results from modeling artificial front-page news as a function of three conditions.[6]

Condition A: News coverage driven by random events and error

Condition B: News coverage driven by negative feedback, random events, and error

Condition C: News coverage driven by positive feedback, negative feedback, random events, and error

Each simulation run lasts for 100 time points, allowing us to see how the distribution of simulated front-page news shakes out across issues in the long run. The simulation does not account for exogenous shocks (though outlier values can occur in each variable in the model), and so is not designed to capture agenda dynamics. Scholarly understanding of agenda dynamics would certainly be enhanced by a more sophisticated simulation—beyond the scope of the current study—designed to replicate the give-and-take of positive and negative feedback forces that yields dynamic patterns of punctuated equilibrium of different rates and different degrees of explosiveness. But the simulation presented here is designed simply to evaluate the type of overall attention distribution across issues (evenly distributed, highly skewed, somewhere in between) that each parameter specification produces.

Results

At the end of running the simulation under each condition for 100 time points, we can evaluate the distribution of front-page attention produced. The first step is to calculate the *cumulative* percentage of the agenda each issue received: that is, out of all 300 stories available (3 stories per time point × 100 time points), what percentage did each issue capture? Then, turning again to the inverse normalized Shannon's H entropy measure, the total degree of skew on the agenda is calculated for that simulation run. Because each simulation run is different (seeded by random values), each condition (A, B, and C) is run 1,000 times. The mean level of skew for each condition is then calculated by averaging across all of its 1,000 runs.

Table 7.2 shows these results as well as, for reference, the cumulative percentage of the agenda captured by the largest issue. Using the observed degree of skew across ten representative issues on the *Times* front page (0.197) as a benchmark, we see that Condition C alone comes close at 0.194. It is a lot of work for a few values, but the results are clear: only by accounting for positive feedback can we replicate the degree of skew observed on the real front page (and, as chapter 8 shows, on the U.S. media agenda in general).

Each of the figures 7.2, 7.3, and 7.4 shows a single simulation run for the respective three conditions: A, B, and C. Although each simulation run plays out in a different way, with different issues rising to the top, these figures are representative of the general findings for each condition. Only in condition C does the agenda become highly skewed.

TABLE 7.2 **It takes positive feedback to produce skewed attention**

	Condition A	Condition B	Condition C
	Random Events and Error	Negative Feedback (Attention Baseline), Events, and Error	Positive Feedback, Negative Feedback (Attention Baseline), Events, and Error
Skew (Inverse Normalized Shannon's H Entropy)	0.007 (sd = 0.003)	0.037 (sd = 0.011)	0.194 (sd = 0.091)
Cumulative percentage of a genda captured by largest issue	13% (sd = 1%)	16% (sd = 1%)	32% (sd = 6%)

Note: Each value in table 7.2 is the average of values across 1,000 simulation runs. Standard deviations are displayed in parentheses. For reference, ten issues drawn from the spread of *New York Times* values in table A.1 have a skew (inverse normalized entropy) value of 0.197. See the book webpage for details.

The ten issue proportions drawn from the *Times* values in table A.1 to fuel the "attention baseline" variable have a skew value of 0.197. Condition A produces an agenda that is barely skewed at all, exactly as we would expect if the news were simply a representative sample of real-world events. In condition B, we see that even when the model is designed to "pull" issues into a skewed alignment by virtue of negative feedback (imagine, for example, an assumed skewed degree of perceived issue importance), the agenda will not unfold in a similarly skewed manner; rather, the system gravitates toward a less-skewed equilibrium. It takes positive feedback to produce a level of skew that approaches what we see in the news. And a lot of it! In order to achieve these results, the "updating" values in the simulation were set so that the "agents" influencing the news via positive feedback (e.g., policymakers/citizens) increased their attention to issues that in the previous time point received one, two, and three front-page stories by 60%, 80%, and 100%, respectively. In other words, these results indicate that the degree of skew we see in the news is not due to journalists, policymakers, and citizens shifting a bit more political attention to hot issues when they hit the news and positive feedback kicks in. When a media explosion breaks, political attention is consumed and most other issues are dropped.

This simulation model is, again, a dramatic simplification of the very complicated news-generation process. Yet the findings are stark enough to leave little wiggle room in concluding that the news is not simply a

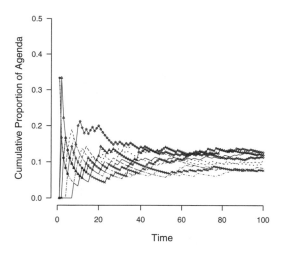

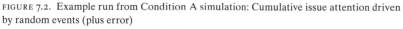

FIGURE 7.2. Example run from Condition A simulation: Cumulative issue attention driven by random events (plus error)
Note: Inverse normalized entropy for this run = 0.007.

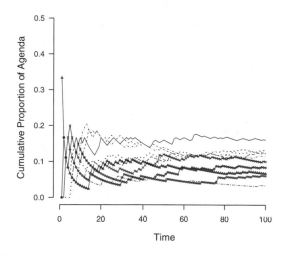

FIGURE 7.3. Example run from Condition B simulation: Cumulative issue attention driven by negative feedback and random events (plus error)
Note: Inverse normalized entropy for this run = 0.031.

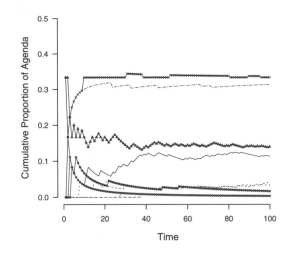

FIGURE 7.4. Example run from Condition C simulation: Cumulative issue attention driven by positive feedback, negative feedback, and random events (plus error)
Note: Inverse normalized entropy for this run = 0.194.

function of random events. Rather, the dramatic skew that we observe empirically in the news means that the news-generation process necessarily includes strong positive feedback mechanisms. Note that the simulation findings presented here hold regardless of what type of event series is used to seed the simulations—Gaussian distribution; poisson distribution; or even seasonal real-world event series in the form of suicide rates or highway driving patterns (see book webpage for more details). Institutional positive feedback *must* be at work in order to produce the skew we observe in the news. These findings thus offer further support for the alarm/patrol hybrid model.

Conclusion

Under investigation in this book is how the news-generation process operates and what patterns, if any, are produced by this process. While data on news stories and interviews with journalists offer sharp insights into the black box of news generation, it is difficult to attribute the patterns that we see produced to specific mechanisms at work. But this chapter allowed us to look directly inside a (wildly simplified) model of the black box itself.

The chapter began with the argument that skew and explosiveness in the news are produced by the dual mechanisms of positive and negative feedback. Media explosions are what exacerbate skew, and positive feedback is required to produce explosions. Thus, institutional mechanisms not only of negative feedback (reinforcing the current distribution of media attention across issues), but also positive feedback (reinforcing change to a different issue) should be required to produce the degree of skew (and explosiveness) observed in the news. A discussion of the sieve, cascade, and friction processes underlying forces of positive and negative feedback iterated the precise ways in which skew and explosiveness can unfold.

Exactly how much skew and explosiveness is in question here? The chapter contained findings showing the specific degree to which the front-page agenda is skewed in coverage across topics and also explosive in how it changes over time. In short, the front page is highly skewed, and highly explosive—more so than many other political agendas.

But where do these patterns come from? Are they flukes of journalistic whims, or are they inescapable products of the news-generation process? A simple computer simulation shed light on these questions. Varying the mechanisms driving the selection of each day's issues onto an artificial front page allowed us to see under the hood of the news-generation process in simplified form. The simulation results showed that positive feedback is required to produce the degree of skew observed in the real news. In other words, the skew we see in media attention is neither a fluke nor the (exclusive) product of biased journalism. Rather, even in a world of perfect journalistic ethics, the institutional nature of the media means that news coverage will necessarily be explosive and, thus, skewed.

Are these patterns of skew and explosiveness unique to the *New York Times* front page, the *Times* more generally, or even just newspapers? The next chapter offers a resounding answer in the negative. Because skew and explosiveness are driven by institutional mechanisms that cross-cut news outlets in at least some form, these patterns embedded in the *Times* front page are, in fact, to be found throughout the media system—from old-school broadsheets, to online blogging, and everything in between.

CHAPTER EIGHT

Skew and Explosiveness in the Shifting Media Landscape

The Web is a vast agenda space. Thinking strictly of its sheer room for information, the problem of attention scarcity simply does not apply to online news. I have pointed to scarce agenda space as exacerbating the skew and explosiveness we see on the *New York Times* front page. If space is no issue, then in theory news outlets should have the room to give more attention to underrepresented issues (resulting in less skew) through a more gradual system of issue replacement (resulting in less explosiveness) and, thus, online news should exhibit less skew and explosiveness than broadsheet news. Moreover, if that's the case, then the social and political implications of skew and explosiveness in the news are only relevant for citizens who exclusively get their news from actual newspapers (or maybe just the *Times*). And really, how many of us still do that? Perhaps online news is a new frontier of news generation, bringing citizens much closer to real-time, proportional information processing. As Vinton Cerf, one of the founders of the Internet, says: "The Internet was designed with no gatekeepers over new content or services" (2005). If there are no gatekeepers, then shouldn't we see more proportionally representative, even-keeled news online?

In fact, that's not at all the case. Without question, online news represents a new frontier of news generation in many respects. But as demonstrated through the simulations in chapter 7 (with room for only three stories on the artificial news agenda!), skew and explosiveness are not only a matter of agenda space; they are the necessary result of positive feedback forces that stem from the media's institutional incentives.

While online news outlets operate under slightly different institutional incentives than traditional broadsheets, still institutional incentives are strongly at play—ones that induce tremendous forces of positive feedback. Thus, the patterns of skew (hypothesis 2) and explosiveness (hypothesis 3) should not be unique to the *Times* front page. They should not be unique to front pages more generally, or to broadsheet newspapers as a medium. As shown in this chapter, online news (and television news, too) exhibits even *stronger* patterns of skew and explosiveness than newspapers, including the *New York Times*. In short, all the discussion in the preceding chapters regarding skew and explosiveness on the front page applies across media types. And in the case of television and online news, these patterns play out in spades.

I begin this chapter by spelling out why these exacerbated patterns make sense, that is, why television and online news should be expected to produce news that is even more skewed across issues and explosive over time than broadsheet news. In television and online news outlets, just as in newspaper newsrooms, institutional incentives shape the news-generation process. In particular, television and online outlets have more direct access to breaking information but, because of their (current) institutional setups, are less equipped to *generate* new information in the form of investigative journalism. Instead, television and online news outlets are strongly incentivized to mimicry, running close versions of news stories from other outlets or often just reposting stories in their original form. Thus, we should expect television and online news outlets to operate more in alarm mode than in patrol mode, meaning that television and online news outlets should also exhibit even stronger explosiveness than broadsheet news by virtue of more frequent media explosions. Momentary media explosions are prevalent in television and online news, and sustained media explosions are as well. The difference between these sustained media explosions and those we see in broadsheet news is that in these newer medium contexts (and online news especially) the propelling force behind sustained media explosions is less frequently investigative journalism and more frequently the echo chamber effect of the insular media environment. I explain how, between this different variety of sustained media explosions and the prevalent momentary media explosions, we should expect television and online news to exhibit stronger, not weaker, aggregate patterns of skew and explosiveness than in newspaper coverage.

Next comes a discussion of some of the interesting ways in which the shift in the media landscape is unfolding for newspapers, as these declining—but arguably not endangered (Keller 2007)—outlets evolve to keep up with the migration of consumers from traditional to "new" media. From strategic timing of stories online and in print to new patterns of information gathering, newspapers are evolving in many ways, both troubling and exciting.

Then I test the degree of skew and explosiveness across the media system, using a massive dataset of news coverage representing more than two million news stories from newspaper, television, and online media outlets. These findings demonstrate, conclusively, that skew and explosiveness are not unique to the *Times* front page. Rather, skew and explosiveness are endemic across the U.S. media system. In fact, these patterns are most extreme in television and, especially, online news.

Finally, a discussion of the implications of these findings centers on citizen information consumption in light of our collective increasing reliance on electronic news. The heightened skew and explosiveness in online news are not necessarily normative ills. As some research indicates, the focus on hot news items interrupted by frequent agenda overhaul—combined with the increased agency that citizens have in selecting their own news diet—may in fact help stimulate knowledge, political participation, and feelings of political efficacy.[1]

At the same time, however, skew and explosiveness in an online context may also prompt citizens to become more fragmented in their interests and more polarized in their views. And, of course, the other normative problems of skew and explosiveness already discussed in the context of newspaper coverage apply in the television and online contexts, too—perhaps even more so, given the stronger degree of skew and explosiveness in those contexts. Across all media types, the skewed nature of news coverage makes it very difficult for most issues to gain media attention. And the explosive nature of news coverage makes it very difficult for citizens and policymakers to respond in meaningful ways to the policy problems in the news. As I discuss in more detail in chapter 9, these patterns hold many implications for policymakers wanting to keep up with the news and for citizens wanting to consume a healthy information diet (see Johnson 2012). In any case, the current chapter shows that these patterns of skew and explosiveness in the news are not disappearing with the shifting media landscape; they are becoming more pronounced.

The News-Generation Process across Media Types

In 1981 Winter and Eyal wrote of the *New York Times*: "It is the elite U.S. newspaper," by which they really meant that it was the elite U.S. news source of any kind. Over the intervening years, the U.S. media system has undergone dramatic changes. Readership of the *Times* and most other newspapers is on the decline, and it is still uncertain whether a TV or online source will take its place as the epicenter of American media (Dimmick, Chen, and Li 2004); whether Americans will continue to draw their news from both traditional and electronic sources (Ahlers 2006); or whether the diffusion of news outlets across media types—newspapers, television, radio, talk radio, online news, blogs, social media—will continue into the future, producing a marketplace of news consumption that would be barely recognizable to us today. Clearly, these different media types generate news in different ways, and these differences will undoubtedly fuel important research for decades to come.

With particular regard to skew and explosiveness, what should we expect? The key is to determine whether these "new" media types—television and, especially, online news—are similarly subject to the twin mechanisms of positive and negative feedback that we believe to be at work in broadsheet news. Although positive and negative feedback mechanisms may take different forms in different media types, if they are present (and, more specifically, if positive feedback is present) then we should see aggregate patterns of skew and explosiveness.

We can expect that media outlets of different types vary widely in the specific institutional incentives affecting news-generation decisions on a day-to-day level. For example, blogs have a fundamentally different set of constraints than national newspapers like the *New York Times* or *Washington Post* with regard to source credibility and professional advancement. Yet, for nearly any news source we might consider, we can identify likely mechanisms of positive and negative feedback. In all cases, even if the agenda space of a news outlet or broader media format is unlimited, cognitive space is not. The people behind each news agenda, regardless of the medium, process information disproportionately, which in turn exacerbates skew and explosiveness.

Additionally, all news outlets employ some form of incentive-based news judgment in order to filter the onslaught of incoming information, thereby focusing on key items of interest. News judgment surely varies across media type, but news judgment, regardless of form, gives unequal weight across different types of events and related policy issues, resulting in heightened skew—as well as heightened explosiveness produced when events with strong news values arise. In a study of news coverage of the 2006 midterm elections, Baum and Groeling found that blogs and cable-news outlets in particular filtered incoming information using much stronger partisan news judgments than newspaper wire services (2008). This kind of polarized news selection should further exacerbate skew across issues—giving stronger weight to those issues best suited to the partisan slant of the outlet.

But, most important, all news outlets are incentivized, at least in part, by marketplace competition and scarce resources. Marketplace competition need not be financial in nature; even volunteer online news sites and blogs compete for audience attention. Recall from chapter 2 that competition is one of the main positive feedback forces behind mimicking behavior across news outlets (Walgrave and Vliegenthart 2010). This mimicking behavior helps to explain intermedia agenda setting, the process by which news outlets influence one another's agendas (e.g., Boyle 2001; Golan 2006; Vliegenthart and Walgrave 2008). More broadly though, mimicking helps to explain the cascades of media attention (Jones and Baumgartner 2005), often in the form of multimedia swarm behavior that contribute to agenda explosiveness and, ultimately, to agenda skew.

Competition is especially fierce among television and online news outlets, by virtue of the radically faster pace at which consumers expect these outlets to produce the news, almost in line with real-time events. Indeed, Livingston and Bennett suggest that event-driven news is much more prevalent in the case of online news (2003). Traditional newspapers suffer from these pressures, too, especially in keeping their websites in synch with breaking news while still leaving themselves with original content to run on the following day's front page. But the marketplace incentives to keep up with event-driven news apply more acutely to television and online-only news outlets, pressuring these outlets to update their agendas on an hour-by-hour or even minute-by-minute basis.

Additionally, at least in the current media marketplace, online-only news outlets generally lack the financial and staff resources needed to support hard-hitting, patrol-based investigative journalism. For example, as described by Andrew Nusca (2010), in 2010 the online news source *Business Insider* produced an in-depth story on how Facebook was founded. This story was based on two years' worth of investigative reporting, including interviewing more than a dozen sources. The *Business Insider* reporters also unearthed original IMs and emails that shed light on the conflicting stories told by Facebook founder Mark Zuckerberg and three former Harvard classmates who claimed he stole the idea from them and that he used deceit to delay their production of a competing site (Carlson 2010). After this story appeared online, Business Insider editor-in-chief Henry Blodget offered a "tweetfesto" on the challenges of producing this kind of in-depth reporting with limited staff and resources, suggesting that the current model of online news is simply not conducive to investigative journalism. Blodget concludes: "So that's the truth about investigative journalism. It's important. It's great. But it is also fantastically expensive and time-consuming" (2010). With notable exceptions then (including *Business Insider* and other sites like *ProPublica*), we should expect online-only news outlets to spend less time on in-depth reporting than their traditional counterparts.

Together, these heightened marketplace pressures and (in the case of online news) more limited resources suggest that, in general, television and online news should offer less original informational content than can be found in investigative-based national broadsheet newspapers. Research supports this notion, pointing to the "echo chamber" effects of online news especially (Boydstun, Moody, and Thomas 2013). Television and online news tend to cover breaking news about each hot news item but then recycle the same basic information about that news item in saturated bursts (until the next hot item hits). For example, think of the repeated news flashes that television outlets broadcast. In the case of online news, consider the pervasive blog posts about blog posts about online editorials about blog posts . . . about newspaper stories.

With these considerations in mind, we can see how the alarm/patrol hybrid model applies to television and online news generation as well as traditional broadsheets, but in different form. We should expect to see television and online sources go into alarm mode more quickly and more often than newspapers, especially in response to event-driven news. We should also expect television and online sources (at least under the current media system) to pay less attention to the kind of patrol-driven background and follow-up reporting that digs up additional information beyond the facts of the main event. Thus, television and online outlets are more susceptible than newspapers to momentary media explosions. And, somewhat paradoxically, television and online outlets should be more susceptible to sustained media explosions, too. However, while sustained media explosions in these outlets sometimes occur through investigative journalism, more often they arise via incentive-driven mimicking behavior of television and online news. As described above, this mimicking behavior can lead to a deluge of identical or highly similar stories, especially online where stories can be reposted and morphed between outlets. Although these stories provide very little new information, the resulting echo chamber phenomenon will present as a sustained media explosion, with information ricocheting around the media for several days if not weeks (Boydstun, Moody, and Thomas 2013).

In short, television and online news will be even more explosive and, thus, more skewed because these outlets foster more moments of alarm-driven surges *and* more (relatively) stable periods (during echo chamber fixations). Recall that the l-kurtosis measure employed in chapter 7 measures the total explosiveness of an agenda—both punctuation and equilibrium. The more volatile the spikes (and drops) in attention and the more stagnant the periods in between, the more explosive the agenda (and the higher the l-kurtosis value). In the tests below, we should expect to see both television and online news exhibit clear patterns of skew and explosiveness. What is more, we should expect these patterns to be even stronger in these media types than in broadsheet news.

The Increasing Role of the Media Consumer

The institutional incentives underpinning the alarm/patrol hybrid process are not the only driving forces behind the skew and explosiveness we should see in the news. Additionally, the way that people tend to *consume* news can further exacerbate the skew and explosiveness in the media signals they receive. This fact is true of all news outlets to some extent but especially true of online news. Hindman and colleagues, for example, show that of the millions of politically relevant online sites, site traffic follows a power law distribution, with a few sources providing the vast bulk of information to which citizens are actually exposed. In particular, Hindman shows how online news audiences gravitate toward a mere twenty top online news outlets, ignoring a plethora of independent web sites (Hindman 2009; Hindman, Tsioutsiouliklis, and Johnson 2003, 2004).

The concentrated distribution of audience attention across online news sources is not only a function of the popularity and quality of each source. Online news audiences have greater agency in selecting their news à la carte as compared with audiences of traditional news, and evidence suggests that they use this agency to focus on more narrowly focused news (Althaus and Tewksbury 2002). For example, in their network analysis of blogs, Farrell and Drezner show that readership across blogs follows a power law distribution, and that this concentration is largely driven by users' practices of linking between sites of similar political content (2008).

Finally, the online medium is an interactive one. This fact is of key importance in understanding skew and explosiveness on the Web. So, when citizens select their news online in a way that narrows their focus, online news outlets respond; in other words, the variable of *public concern* examined in earlier chapters (and, relatedly, public *interest*) drives online news coverage in a much more immediate, direct way than it influences broadsheet news. Mullainathan and Shleifer (2005) use game theoretic modeling to demonstrate this concept, showing how—on topics where audience opinions diverge (e.g., politically divisive issues that are likely to shape news consumption)—we should expect news outlets to divide the market, slanting toward (and reinforcing) the polarized views of their smaller constituencies. As Delli-Carpini and Keeter write, "once chosen, producers of information are likely to give these consumers more and more of the same, creating very different information environments for different segments of the public. The deliberative, interactive aspects of the Internet will only serve to reinforce this fragmentation as citizens self-select or are exposed to only those chat groups or other venues that are frequented by like-minded people" (2002, 145).

In this way, news outlets face escalating tension between what news media consumers "want" to see and what they "should" see. For example, the *Washington Post*'s decisions about what stories to put on a newspaper's home page are, according to Bzdek, "driven much more by traffic and number of clicks we get—and to an astonishingly new degree—and that makes some people in the whole enterprise uncomfortable."[2] Whatever the normative implications for a free press, these changes make good business sense. And this consumer tailoring is exactly the kind of positive feedback process that leads, in the aggregate, to dramatic skew and explosiveness, even beyond what we see in traditional newspapers.

What the Shifting Media Landscape Means for Newspapers

The heightened patterns of skew and explosiveness that we should see in online news are increasingly relevant as the U.S. media market shifts toward online formats; newspapers, too, are affected by this evolution. As online news outlets have proliferated, this increase in competition for audience attention has forced traditional news outlets to adjust the way they do business. Individual news outlets, especially local ones, have learned to stay afloat by becoming increasingly specialized, learning how to play to—and market—their particular strengths. This type of specialization strategy has long been at work in the U.S. news industry, but we can see it in sharp relief by looking at changes news outlets have made since the spread of online news, beginning in the mid-1990s. This shifting media landscape has forced many local newspapers to shut their doors. Among those traditional news outlets that have survived (and additional local news outlets that have developed for this explicit purpose), many survive by pulling their focus inwards to that portion of the information commodity system over which they have a near-monopoly: local news (Tewksbury and Rittenberg 2012).

National newspapers, too, have shifted their operations. Many changes have been procedural in nature, yet they affect the news-generation process nonetheless. For example, in concert with the fast-paced timing pressures under which television and online news outlets operate, the rate at which editors must develop the news agenda has increased dramatically. *Washington Post* news editor Vince Bzdek describes the changes this way:

> Because of the web, and how people read the coverage of the news, given the web, there's a lot more focus on driving the conversation during the day. So newspapers, media outlets, are devoting a lot more resources to finding out what people are going to be talking about and doing all sorts of different media about that. Not just a story, but getting a panel of experts assembled to talk about that, having an interactive chat for our readers or viewers about the subject, figuring out a bunch of ways to leverage that one story so that we can maintain an interest level all day long. Economics is behind that; the more clicks we get on our websites, the more advertising we can sell and the better our advertising does. So there's very much a new impetus to drive

the conversation so that people come to your site to find out what's new about this particular subject.[3]

Bzdek points, in other words, toward the increasing influence that factors like *public concern* and continuing storylines (i.e., explicit *prior attention*) have on the selection of the news, with an increasing reliance on news judgment geared toward the marketplace. This more rapid updating of news based on what's hot and what's not suggests that newspapers like the *Post* are now employing news-generation processes that are even more strongly shaped by positive feedback mechanisms, leading to more skew, more explosiveness.

As newspapers learn to balance the need to cover breaking news in real time on their websites with the need to have original stories in each morning's hard-copy paper, competition between news outlets has made the strategic timing of the day's news cycle especially important. Often, if a newspaper has a scoop on a story that is big but does not mandate immediate online reporting, the newspaper will hold onto the story until after around 10 pm so that, as Cohen says, "the next day everyone else has to reference your story."[4]

The shift to online media affects not just the timing, but also the content of the news. For example, the journalists and editors who prepare each day's hard copy of a newspaper tend to be the same journalists and editors who prepare and update the corresponding website for that paper. But because these venues operate under different marketplace incentives, the two agendas often look subtly but importantly different. Even titles, which serve as critical information short-cuts for readers, often differ between the online and print versions *of the exact same story.* A print headline needs to fit the physical space (i.e., column inches) allotted to the story, and good copyeditors (reporters rarely title their own stories) can devise a title within seconds that fits the allotted space down to the exact character. Online story titles, on the other hand, need to contain descriptive keywords that make the stories easy to identify through electronic searches.[5] A quintessential example: Penelope Green's 2010 *New York Times* story on President Obama's redecoration of the Oval Office originally appeared online (and is indexed electronically by the *Times*) under the search-friendly title "The President's New Office" but appeared in print under the much more alluring title "The Audacity of Taupe" (Green 2010).

Other strategic changes in the newsrooms of papers like the *Times* and the *Post* have resulted in important shifts in newsroom strategy. For example, cuts in staff have forced even large newspapers to focus, in part, on those stories of particular interest to their main consumer base. As Bzdek says, "we have to do more triage [now] on the stories we are going after and [our] focus has been for and about Washington . . . So it's mainly a resource issue."[6] At the same time, the dual use of print and online media has allowed major newspapers to expand their consumer base. *Washington Post* executive editor Marcus Brauchli puts it this way:

> In the past, whether we put a scandal or a political process story on the front page, the same number of newspapers hit the same number of driveways. Today, though, the vast majority of our online audience comes from outside of Washington. We are in control of our destiny in the sense that we have a lot to do with how many readers we attract and how many eyeballs connect to our journalism. (Schmitz and Schulz 2010)

Additionally, newspapers such as the *Post* have adopted a strategy of attending to major storylines with a high volume of focused coverage—what Bzdek calls the "breaking waves" approach to news coverage. "This is actually a conscious policy here at the *Post*, where, okay, there's a big story . . . [like] this foreclosure crisis here," says Bzdek, speaking of the housing foreclosure crisis in the fall of 2010. "We've sort of seized on this story as a story that's important to our readers and important to the moment. And we've flooded the zone with coverage, so we've had a page one story after page one story on the subject."[7]

This breaking waves policy holds real market benefits. Flooding a newspaper with stories in this way incentivizes readers to return to the *Post* in particular to see how a given storyline develops, potentially fostering the kind of loyalty that television series promote through ongoing story threads that viewers can only keep up with by watching each episode. And thus, journalists are incentivized to follow up on the storyline, thereby allowing them an *incentivized* chance to go into patrol mode, digging beneath the surface of a story to give readers a richer understanding of the issue (and perhaps discovering key facts that might have been missed with a more cursory or intermittent treatment).

In short, the shifting nature of the U.S. media landscape means that news outlets' incentives are shifting, too. As the marketplace becomes increasingly competitive and consumers shift their attention online, the momentum-driven dynamics of news coverage—in particular, the influence of *public concern* and *prior attention*—are becoming even more pronounced. This trend plays out differently in newspapers (with perhaps an increasing incentive-driven potential for patrol-based coverage) than it does in television and online news outlets (geared much more strongly for alarm-based coverage, as well as echo-chamber-style fixation). In all cases, it appears that changes in the U.S. media marketplace, still unfolding, make the news more skewed and more explosive. The idea that increased marketplace competition leads to greater skew and explosiveness is not tested here, but it is an idea worth exploring in future research.

Measuring Skew and Explosiveness across Media Types

I compare the aggregate patterns of skew and explosiveness across three main types of media—newspapers, television news, and online news—using data collected as part of a larger collaborative project.[8] This dataset contains the daily frequency of news stories in outlets across these different media types on each of forty-five issues (i.e., subtopics from the Policy Agendas Codebook). These forty-five issues were drawn randomly from a larger set of ninety-two issues selected across all nineteen major policy topic categories of the Policy Agendas codebook as well as four of the media-only topics (Weather and Natural Disasters, Fires, Arts and Entertainment, and Sports and Recreation). The original ninety-two issues were picked randomly, but filtered to include only issues for which accurate keyword searches could readily be constructed in two databases: the LexisNexis collection of newspaper stories and television news transcripts, and the Google News Archive collection of news stories appearing in online news outlets (more on these datasets below). In the case of issues drawn from the major topics without component subtopics (e.g., Sports and Recreation), we came up with specific items that seemed appropriate and searchable (e.g., World Cup). For feasibility, we then randomly selected approximately half of the issues (forty-five) for the purposes of the data presented here.

For each of the forty-five issues studied, we began by developing a keyword string that we vetted through multiple searches, narrowing in on the search terms that would optimize the percentage of relevant hits each search produced (i.e., true positives) while minimizing the percentage of irrelevant hits (false positives) and relevant misses (false negatives). Some keyword searches were straightforward. For example, we captured subtopic 707 (Recycling) through the single keyword "recycling" and its variants, and we captured attention to the World Cup (under topic 29) through the search term "World Cup." Other searches ended up requiring more detailed or sophisticated keyword strings in order to optimize accuracy. For example, a systematic test of different keyword strings designed to capture subtopic 1807 (Tariff and Import Restrictions, Import Regulation) showed that we received the most accurate results by using two different terms (and their variants): "tariff" and "import quota."

Due to the differences in search mechanisms between LexisNexis and the Google News Archive, in some cases we were forced to use different forms of the keyword strings in the two archives. For instance, for subtopic 335 (Prescription Drug Costs and Coverage), the keyword string that retrieved the highest accuracy of results in LexisNexis was as follows: <BODY("prescription drug!" w/5 (cost! OR price! OR coverage))>. Google News does not support Boolean searches, however, and so we performed the following five isolated searches, after which we combined the results and used date and title fields to eliminate duplicates: <prescription drug>, <prescription drugs>, <cost of prescription drugs>, <price of prescription drugs>, <prescription drug coverage>. Sample tests across issues indicated that our Google News search strings yielded high accuracy in retrieving the same newspaper stories (appearing in electronic form on newspaper websites) as were retrieved by the Lexis-Nexis Boolean searches in the print versions of those newspapers.

Even with the care taken to maximize the performance of our keyword strings, this keyword search approach is far from perfect. Still, our method minimizes the chance of nonrandom error in our results, allowing us to treat the data as strong indicators of the relative frequency of news coverage across topics and the changes in coverage over time. As large-N media research methods go, this approach offers about as close to an apples-to-apples look across media types as we can hope to get, given available research tools.

We used these tested keyword strings to trace the rise and fall in attention to each of our forty-five issues across the different types of media outlets over the same eleven-year period captured by the NYT front-page data examined in earlier chapters (1996–2006). (For the sake of simplicity, I refer to all news items collected—blog posts, online articles, television news report transcripts, newspaper articles—as stories.) For hard-copy newspaper stories and television stories, we ran our searches through the LexisNexis archives. We identified the frequency of stories on each issue in each of five television news outlets and fifteen newspapers ranging from broadsheets with a national readership to newspapers with a more local audience (full list is below). These searches yielded 413,049 newspaper stories and more than 100,000 television stories. For electronic news, we ran the corresponding keyword searches through the Google News Archive, yielding hits across 8,392 sources, ranging from newspaper websites where most stories are identical to those found in print (e.g., nytimes.com), to online-only sources including news outlets as well as blogs.[9] To reduce noise in the Google News Archive data, we eliminated all sources that had only a single story (out of all forty-five issues), reducing the total number of Google News sources to 7,141, representing a total of 354,479 stories appearing in print as well as online and more than one million online-only stories.

In the results section below, I focus on six mutually exclusive categories of outlets that together represent the entirety of the LexisNexis and Google News data as described above:

National newspapers: *New York Times, USA Today, Wall Street Journal,* and *Washington Post*

Local newspapers: *Albuquerque Journal, Ann Arbor News, Atlanta Journal and Constitution, Boston Herald, Charleston Gazette, Chicago Sun-Times, Houston Chronicle, Philadelphia Inquirer, Pittsburgh Post-Gazette, St. Louis Post-Dispatch,* and *St. Petersburg Times*

TV news: ABC, CBS, CNN, Fox, and NBC

National online and print news: businessweek.com, newsweek.com, forbes.com, nytimes.com, time.com, usatoday.com, wsj.com, washingtonpost.com

Local online and print news (e.g., dailycal.org, fairfaxtimes.com, valdosta dailytimes.com)

Online-only news (e.g., NewsChannel5.com, bloomberg.com, huffington post.com)

Of course, we can imagine several ways to categorize media outlets, and in many cases categorization choices are not clear-cut (e.g., *Chicago Sun-Times* is commonly among the top ten U.S. newspapers in terms of circulation, but is it a national newspaper?).[10] The above categorization is one good way to compare outlet behavior across different types of media.

Results

These LexisNexis and Google News Archive searches thus produced daily counts of the number of stories on each of the forty-five sampled issues between 1996 and 2006. To give a sense of the size of this dataset, table 8.1 offers the total number of stories retrieved across all forty-five issues by source type, along with the counts for three specific issues by way of illustration.

This dataset can be used to address many questions, including the relative degree of attention a particular issue receives across news outlets and, excitingly, the conditions under which different types of media tend to "lead" coverage of specific issues. I scratch the surface of the data with simple correlations. For example, looking at the distribution of attention across all issues, national newspapers correlate with television news at $\rho = 0.52$, national newspapers correlate with online-only national news at $\rho = 0.49$, and television news and online-only national news correlate at $\rho = 0.41$. Examining dynamics, the mean correlation (averaged across all forty-five issues) in monthly coverage between national newspapers and television news is $\rho = 0.51$, between national newspapers and online-only national news is $\rho = 0.38$, and between television news and online-only national news is $\rho = 0.25$.

The goal of this chapter, however, is to test one simple, important claim: The aggregate patterns of skew and explosiveness shown on the *New York Times* front page are in fact multimedia phenomena, which all media types should exhibit.

I test this claim by employing the same calculations of skew (inverse normalized Shannon's H entropy) and explosive change (l-kurtosis) described in chapter 7. We saw in chapter 7 that the *Times* front page displays a skew value of 0.169 and an explosiveness value of 0.344. For reference, when restricted to stories on the forty-five issues studied in this chapter, the *Times* full paper as archived by LexisNexis displays a skew value of 0.086 and an explosiveness value of 0.327. Recall that one baseline reference point for interpreting these values is to consider the skew and explosiveness measures that a normal distribution would produce—that is, for skew, an agenda that is normally distributed across all issues

TABLE 8.1 **Story frequencies across media types, 1996–2006**

| | From LexisNexis Archive | | | From Google News Archive | | |
	National Newspapers (N=4)	Local Newspapers (N=11)	TV News (N=5)	National Online and Print News (N=8)	Local Online and Print News (N=533)	Online Only (N=6,600)
Issue 202	2,727	1,573	963	2,464	1,342	6,794
Issue 1409	9,727	6,682	7,364	8,234	17,252	63,792
Issue 2902	17,106	11,483	2,081	6,648	28,065	128,130
⋮	⋮	⋮	⋮	⋮	⋮	⋮
All 45 Issues	232,663	180,386	106,668	138,074	216,405	1,068,790

Note: Values in table 8.1 indicate the number of stories retrieved by media type. The three example issues are as follows: Issue 202: Gender and Sexual Orientation Discrimination; Issue 1409: Homeless Issues; Issue 2902: World Cup.

and, for explosiveness, an agenda that changes over time in a largely incremental way such that the change values are normally distributed. A
normal distribution has a skew value that approaches 0.000 and an explosiveness value of 0.123. Any values higher than these numbers indicate
true skew and explosiveness. The *New York Times*, then, is both highly
skewed and highly explosive (and the front page more so than the full
paper). But are these patterns generalizable across other media types?

Yes, they are. Figure 8.1 shows the skew of each type of media outlet, along with—for reference—the skew of the *New York Times* full paper alone based on this same forty-five-issue data. These values are produced, first, by calculating the skew value for each individual news outlet
based on the proportion of attention given to each of the forty-five issues (treating the total agenda size as the sum of all stories across these
forty-five issues, for want of a better measure) and, second, by averaging
the skew values across all news outlets in that media type. All zero observations (individual news outlets that contained no stories on a given
issue) were treated as missing so as not to inflate the skew values. Here,
we see that not only does the skew we see in the *New York Times* gen-

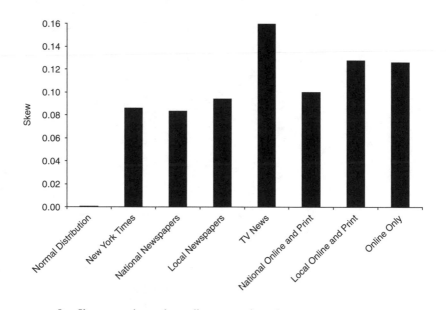

FIGURE 8.1. Skew across issues, by media type, 1996–2006
Note: The values represent the inverse normalized Shannon's H entropy calculated for
each media type across the 45 sampled issues.

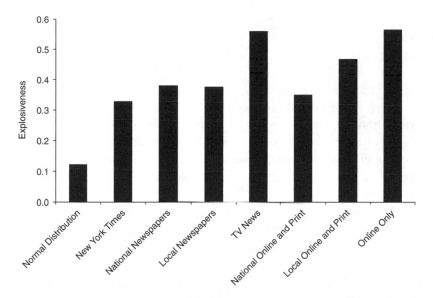

FIGURE 8.2. Explosive change, by media type, 1996–2006
Note: The values represent l-kurtosis calculated for each media type across the 45 sampled issues.

eralize to other national newspapers, but this pattern is even stronger in the case of local newspapers, television news, and all forms of online news.

Figure 8.2 compares levels of agenda explosiveness across these same categories. In this case, the values are produced by pooling the monthly change values across all forty-five issues in each media type (again treating zero observations—months in which no change occurred—as missing) and then calculating the l-kurtosis value of these pooled change values. Similar to figure 8.1, we see that the agendas of new media outlets change even more explosively than those of traditional broadsheets.

Implications

The fact that skew and explosiveness are multimedia phenomena has important implications. These findings suggest that, at least for now, the expansive agenda space of the Web exacerbates rather than mitigates the disproportional nature of media information processing. To the extent

that our normative notion of the news involves important policy problems having proportional access to the agenda and citizen and policymaker attention, national newspapers fall short of this notion, and television and online news fall even shorter. While online agenda space is
all but limitless, the constraints of human cognitive limits, institutional
incentives, and limited resources combine to propel all media—but especially online outlets—toward fixating on hot issues and then lurching toward new ones. And because citizens can individualize their news
consumption more in the online context, personal preferences further
contribute to patterns of skew and explosiveness in the information
received.

The exact effects of heightened skew and explosiveness in the particular context of online information are still unclear. Yet studies do show
that citizens respond differently to online news than to newspapers.[11] For
instance, in a study of exposure to print versus online versions of the
New York Times, Althaus and Tewksbury (2002) find that both media
serve to influence people's perceptions of which issues are most important. However, due to the heightened ability to select and filter news stories in the online format, readers of the hard-copy news ended up being exposed to a much broader range of issues than readers of the online
version. Consequently, even though the total population of news stories
available in online and print versions of the *Times* tends to be nearly
identical, the broadsheet readers came away with very different perceptions from the online readers regarding *which* issues were most pressing
(Althaus and Tewksbury 2002).

Specifically, readers of online news tend to select stories that hit clos-
est to home, both geographically and politically. As compared to readers
exposed to hard-copy newspapers, online news readers will have less exposure to—and thus less knowledge of—information regarding national,
international, and political events (Tewksbury and Althaus 2000). International issues, in particular, are more likely to register as important
issues with hard-copy readers than with online readers (Althaus and
Tewksbury 2002).

Of course, because online users have significantly more control over
the content they select, the type of news citizens receive is strongly influenced by the type of user—these variables are endogenous. For example,
citizens who are more interested in politics are more likely to approach
online news with "seeking/surveillance" reasons and, consequently, are
more likely to be exposed to informational-rich content (though perhaps

polarized in nature) as opposed to entertainment content, for example (Kaye and Johnson 2002).

Similar to Althaus and Tewksbury, de Waal and Schönbach (2008) find that readers of broadsheet news generally walk away with a broader understanding of the number of important political issues. Yet, in line with Kaye and Johnson's work, these findings are conditional in part on the reader being generally interested in news in the first place. Note, however, that this study also finds that some online sources serve to broaden people's perceptions of the range of important issues, regardless of the level of reader interest (de Waal and Schönbach 2008). In a separate study, Schönbach, de Waal, and Lauf (2005) find evidence that the effect of news exposure on people's perceptions of the range of important issues depends not only on interest but also on education levels. Both print and online news outlets can have broadening effects on the perceived issue agendas of the highly educated. Yet, unlike online news, print news can also broaden the agendas of readers who have at most an average level of news interest (Schönbach, de Waal, and Lauf 2005). Thus, at least with respect to the effects of media agenda setting, the differences between traditional and new media tend to vary across individual citizens and individual news outlets. In general though, extant studies and the findings from this chapter suggest that the signals people receive from online news are even more skewed and more explosive than those they receive from traditional print news. And in the online medium, this skew appears to take the form of fragmentation, posing potentially significant challenges for democracy (Selnow 1998).

In summary, whether these heightened patterns of skew and explosiveness in new media are good news or bad news for democracy and citizens of various stripes is still unclear. A heightened agency in selecting online news exposure may help citizens feel more politically empowered in general. At the same time, more focused (skewed) exposure to information limits the diversity of perspectives a citizen receives, potentially increasing polarized attitudes in general. And it is possible that an increased frequency in agenda explosions can distort citizens' perceptions of the relative gravity of events—both in the news and in their own lives. Again, the explosive nature of the media makes it exceedingly difficult for citizens (or policymakers) to process and respond to issue information before the issue is out of the news, replaced by another.

In any case, these patterns of skew and explosiveness—and their effects on citizens and politics—are important to account for and under-

stand, especially in light of the system-wide shift to online news. As Tim
Berners-Lee, inventor of the World Wide Web, is credited as saying,
"Whether it is a turning point in societal evolution depends not only on
the technology . . . but also how we use it! The web does give us lots more
choices about how we organize ourselves."[12]

CHAPTER NINE

Implications for Politics and Society

In the political system, where problems and perspectives are many and attention is scarce, the media is a powerful arbiter of what is important and what is ignored. The news-generation process determines access not only to the media agenda but also to nearly every corner of the political system, from citizens' living rooms to Pennsylvania Avenue. News coverage can make events and their underlying policy issues the stuff of hallway conversations, lobbying leverage points, and the nation's general to-do list.

The preceding chapters have offered fine-grained and big-picture views of the distribution of media attention across policy issues and across time, assessing patterns of attention distribution and change in this scarce but important resource. This chapter serves to summarize the findings presented and extend the discussion further. I address the critical issue of agenda endogeneity, describing how the agendas considered in this book are part of a large system of mutual reinforcement. Having demonstrated the particular effects of policymaker attention and public concern on media attention in chapters 5 and 6, I show here that media attention drives these same variables in turn. I also discuss some of the questions this book leaves open—questions that warrant future study. Finally, I close with a discussion of the normative and practical implications that we can draw from the study at hand.

What We Have Learned

The central findings of this book are (1) media attention is inherently skewed across issues, and (2) the media agenda changes in inherently explosive ways over time. These patterns are produced by the media's institutional incentives and, most important, momentum.

Specific variables, such as *policymaker attention* and *public concern*, help predict (probabilistically) how much news coverage a given issue receives at a given point in time. But more than static forces, these variables operate in turns as positive feedback mechanisms reinforcing change in the agenda, and as negative feedback mechanisms reinforcing agenda stability. The alarm/patrol hybrid model describes how these alternating processes map theoretically onto alternating modes of reporting. The lurching shifts between alarm and patrol modes of news generation produce dramatic explosiveness in the news. And, as the simulations in chapter 7 demonstrate, it is by means of this positive-feedback-fueled explosiveness that dramatic skew results. In this way, the alarm/patrol hybrid model brings the significance of dynamics to bear on existing approaches to the news-generation process, honing our understanding of how momentum drives the influence that key variables have in making the news.

Not all aspects of the theoretical arguments presented have been tested here, but I have offered extensive supporting evidence. Specifically, I have demonstrated the effects of several key variables in the case of front-page news coverage across policy topics over time, as well as in the specific cases of news coverage of the war on terror and capital punishment. According to the alarm/patrol hybrid model, these self-reinforcing variables should produce aggregate patterns of skew and explosiveness. I have tested two very different media environments for the presence of these patterns, finding high degrees of skew and explosiveness in each case: first, the *New York Times* front page and, second, looking broadly across nearly two million newspaper, television, and online news stories. These patterns are strong and ingrained.

Questions of Endogeneity

Considering media attention as a dependent variable begs questions of causality, especially given this book's reliance on past studies of agenda setting and indexing. Indeed, the media agenda is by no means a passive receptor of influence. In the excitingly messy system that is politics, causal arrows run in many directions. It is extraordinarily difficult to get a theoretical or empirical handle on how the media affects and simultaneously is affected by other political forces. Taking a cue from Mayhew

(1974), I have focused here on only one causal direction: looking strictly at the determinants of news coverage. The lines of influence I have identified are surely mutually reinforcing in many cases. But this exercise has allowed us to see what kind of theoretical and empirical mileage we can gain out of considering, just for the duration of this book, media attention as a dependent variable.

And here is what we have seen: The statistical models of media attention in chapters 5 and 6 point to the significant influence that several key variables have on the news. These models also show that lagged media attention strongly drives current attention, suggesting the strong role of momentum dynamics—both positive and negative feedback—in driving the news. The alarm/patrol hybrid model suggests that these results derive from a mutually reinforcing, symbiotic network of relationships and should be interpreted as such.

The tests I have provided of the alarm/patrol hybrid model do not rest on a causal argument. At the core of this model is the notion that momentum propels the influence of key forces on the news. The model holds that forces of positive and negative feedback—captured by proxy through the key variables employed here—will produce patterns of skew and explosiveness. Endogeneity concerns about the models in chapters 5 and 6 are important, but they do not undercut the additional tests of the alarm/patrol hybrid model, which came in chapters 7 and 8, showing conclusive evidence of skew and explosiveness in the news. This evidence, in tandem with the suggestive findings of key variable influence on the news, offers strong support for the model.

The Effects of Media Attention

Beyond the evidence I have provided showing the effects of key variables on media attention, it is also worth documenting that these effects often run both ways, as in the case of *policymaker attention* and *public concern*. We can use precisely the same datasets of congressional hearings, presidential executive orders, and Gallup "most important problem" data as employed in chapter 5 to model each of these variables as a function of media attention (as well as the other variables and a lagged version of the dependent variable in question).[1]

Table 9.1 shows the results of these cross-sectional time series models. In each model, media attention in one month has a significant

TABLE 9.1 **The effects of media attention on policymaker activity and public concern**

	Dependent Variable		
Explanatory Variable:	Proportion of Congressional Hearings	Proportion of Executive Orders	Proportion of Public Concern
Proportion of NYT Front-Page Stories $_{t-1}$	0.237*	0.236*	0.019*
	(0.018)	(0.043)	(0.006)
Proportion of Congressional Hearings $_{t-1}$	0.295*	0.091^	−0.003
	(0.019)	(0.046)	(0.006)
Proportion of Executive Orders $_{t-1}$	0.020^	0.114*	−0.001
	(0.008)	(0.020)	(0.003)
Proportion of Gallup MIP $_{t-1}$	−0.023^	−0.101^	0.966*
	(0.015)	(0.035)	(0.005)
Constant	0.027*	0.022*	−0.001^
	(0.002)	(0.004)	(0.001)
N =	2,489	2,489	2,489
Months =	131	131	131
Policy Topics =	19	19	19
Front-Page Stories =	26,611	26,611	26,611
Adjusted R^2 =	0.221	0.037	0.949
Root MSE =	0.051	0.122	0.017

^ p <= 0.1, two-tailed
* p <= 0.001, two-tailed
Note: Each model in figure 9.1 is a pooled cross-sectional time series model run across all policy topics using the dependent variable specified. The grey cells thus represent the lagged dependent variable in each case. The first explanatory variable listed uses the complete *New York Times* front-page agenda dataset (i.e., domestic and international topics combined). Cells display coefficients (and standard errors).

and positive influence on the next month's value of the given dependent variable (hearings, executive orders, or public concern). In each case, the agenda under study shows strong path dependency (via the lagged dependent variable), just as disproportionate information processing would suggest.

Figure 9.1 allows us to visualize the effects of media attention on these other agendas.[2] While the models in table 9.1 are based on proportional measures of all variables, figure 9.1 helps us see the size of the effects of media attention on congressional hearings and executive orders by showing these effects in real values (the Gallup MIP measure is already a proportional measure). The x axis ranges across observed proportions of front-page attention. For example, we see that, holding all other variables at their mean values, the difference between a midrange amount of media attention and a maximum amount of media attention on a given topic in a given month is expected to produce: almost double the number of executive orders on that topic the following month

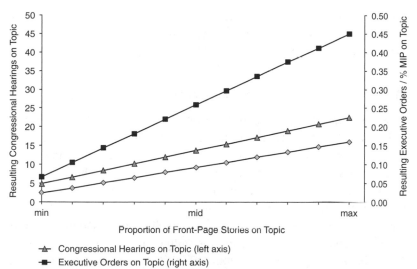

FIGURE 9.1. The political effects of front-page coverage
Note: This figure shows how three agendas—congressional hearings, executive orders, and the public's "most important problem"—are influenced by the front-page agenda. As the proportion of front-page attention to a given topic increases from its minimum to its maximum, these other agendas pay the topic more attention, too.

(from 0.26 to 0.45 orders); nearly ten additional congressional hearings (from 13.67 to 22.45) and an additional 7% of citizens citing that topic as the most important problem facing the country (from 0.09 to 0.16). Such large shifts in media attention don't occur often, but figure 9.1 offers a sense of the degree of impact media attention can have on these other agendas. As with the analyses presented in chapters 5 and 6, with media attention as the dependent variable, these findings need to be taken with several caveats. Still, the results suggest (in line with past research) that while key variables including policymaker attention and public concern significantly affect news coverage, news coverage significantly affects policymaker attention and public concern.

Remaining Questions

While this book has advanced our understanding of the news-generation process and the role that media dynamics plays in the political system, the question of endogeneity is just one of several questions I have not fully resolved. I identify some of these questions here, noting the advancements that could be made by their future study.

Variance across Media Contexts and Over Time

One question left unanswered is exactly how the alarm/patrol hybrid model and, specifically, the influence of the key variables examined here, applies differently across newspaper coverage, television news, online news, and social media. While the findings in chapter 8 offer strong evidence of the generalizability of skew and explosiveness across broadsheet, television, and online news, I leave untested how the specific forces driving attention vary across media venues. As indicated by the rich growing literature examining online media in particular, these questions hold considerable potential for advancing our understanding of media dynamics and, just as importantly, media effects.

Additionally, the bulk of the empirical evidence presented here covers a limited time frame: 1996–2006. Only the capital punishment analysis in chapter 6 extends further (1960–2005). There are good reasons to expect that the news-generation process, the forces that influence it, and its resulting patterns have varied over time as the U.S. media system has evolved. Evolutions in the news-generation process are worth studying in their own right and in order to shed light on the varying role of the media in the political system at important points in time, both historically and in the future.

Thankfully, the rapidly expanding field of automated and semiautomated text analysis facilitates the collection and topic coding of much larger datasets of news coverage, stretching both over media type and over time, than had previously been afforded. The development of these datasets will enable more wide-ranging examination of media dynamics (as well as the mutual influence between the media agenda and other political agendas), thereby supporting more generalizable conclusions.

Institutional Setup

I have discussed but have taken no steps toward testing the influence of *institutional setup* on the news-generation process. Past work has advanced our understanding of this influence, showing how agenda setting operates differently in different institutional contexts, specifically media systems in different countries (Hallin and Mancini 2004). Thus, I hope readers will consider how the theory and implications presented here may apply to other media environments (and other institutions altogether) beyond the U.S. media. Journalistic norms, for example, vary widely by country (e.g., Plasser 2005; Yoon and Boydstun 2011). Nevertheless, all media systems face the problem of attention scarcity, and the specific variables described here exist to varying degrees in most media systems. Most of all, dynamics are always present. Still, variance in institutional setup should affect exactly how the alarm/patrol hybrid model applies to each media system.

Event, Issue, and Framing Variance

I have talked in loose form about how event characteristics, issue characteristics, and framing help determine how much media attention an event/issue receives. Woefully absent from this book, however, is any specific test of these ideas. The data used simply don't support such analyses. But such tests are critical to our understanding of media attention—and media effects.

Endogeneity is surely at play. For instance, issue-framing can drive levels of attention, as the *diversity of discussion* effects in chapter 6 suggest and as past work has indicated. And event and issue characteristics surely influence not only how much coverage the event/issue receives but also how it is framed. Yet, at the same time, past research shows explicitly that how much coverage an issue receives and how it is framed can affect societal understandings of the event/issue characteristics (Baumgartner and Jones 2009; Lawrence 2001; Rochefort and Cobb 1994). The "characteristics" of events and issues, in other words, are subject to interpretation and, thus, media definition.

Largely as a result of these unanswered questions, this book also gives us a lot to chew on regarding the forces that drive media attention over time (temporal variance). I have shown, empirically, that positive feedback is the key force responsible for high degrees of skew across issues in the news. But beyond theoretical positing about news judgment, I have offered little by way of explaining the forces that drive media attention across specific issues (cross-sectional variance). In other words, what drives overall levels of attention to one issue versus another?

Soft News and Media Bias

The alarm/patrol hybrid model holds implications for the prevalence of soft news (vs. hard news), as I discussed briefly in chapter 3 but did not investigate any further. We might expect that the alarm mode of news generation lends itself to soft news more than does the patrol mode. But while the patrol mode often involves investigative, in-depth, hard-news reporting, it can also involve soft-news fixation and regurgitation, scanning an identified "neighborhood" with an eye for sensation rather than information. In the echo chamber context of online news in particular, heightened degrees of skew and explosiveness suggest a higher prevalence of soft news. While the benefits or drawbacks of soft news to society are still debated, understanding the role that soft news plays is central to our understanding of the media system.

Relatedly, this book has not advanced our understanding of the important phenomenon of media bias, whereby news outlets consciously or subconsciously tailor the news with a partisan slant: namely, how prevalent is media bias, what factors produce it, and what are its effects? However, we can draw some inference from what we have learned about skewed news coverage across policy issues. Seeing that skew in the news results not only from incentive-driven news judgment by editors and journalists but, more directly, from positive feedback momentum suggests that, where media bias does exist, it may be due to institutional forces (including citizen demand) as much if not more so than the individual agendas of some journalists and news outlets.

Causal Mechanisms

The tests offered in chapters 7 and 8 show, conclusively, that media attention exhibits strong patterns of skew and explosiveness. Furthermore, the simulations in chapter 7 demonstrate the formal link between positive feedback and skew (via a simulated one-time explosion). Skew is a necessary product of positive feedback, and positive feedback is a necessary antecedent to the degree of skew that the news exhibits. This evidence offers strong support for the alarm/patrol hybrid model. Still, a range of causal mechanisms and relationships remain untested.

Specifically, for the purposes of theoretical tractability I have suggested that periods governed by positive versus negative feedback stem from the media responding to an event in alarm versus patrol modes, which modes are governed by institutional incentives and the characteristics of the event. This is a complicated story. I have provided only anecdotal evidence to suggest that periods governed by positive and negative feedback are in fact embodied in the alarm and patrol modes of journalism as we understand them. In other words, I have not tested the argument that the aggregate dynamics we observe in the news indeed stem from the media system shifting between qualitatively different styles of reporting. The counterargument would be that these stark aggregate patterns somehow emerge from a uniform news-generation process. And even if it is fair to equate positive and negative feedback dynamics with, respectively, alarm and patrol modes of reporting, to what extent are these reporting modes simply aggregate patterns of coverage across the media as opposed to intentional newsroom-level decisions about how to gather and craft the news?

My interviews with journalists and editors suggest that the aggregate patterns of skew and explosiveness are unintended consequences of the news-generation process. Newsrooms do indeed tend to adopt an alarm mode of coverage for some stories and a patrol mode in other instances. Underneath these modes, however, is a maintained degree of editorial and journalistic agency in the nature of each story's pursuit and the mode of reporting employed. For instance, while the media may appear frenzied when news outlets swarm around a hot news item, this is a different mode of reporting than investigative journalism. Yet the alarm mode, like the patrol mode, is the product of (mostly) reasoned and considered newsroom decisions. For future study, then: to what degree might the lurching dynamics of media attention reflect a particular kind of news judgment—news judgment with a calculating eye toward the best pace and depth of reporting—that channels newsroom efforts into different modes of reporting under different circumstances?

Normative and Practical Implications

These lingering questions notwithstanding, we can draw several implications from the evidence presented in support of the alarm/patrol hybrid model. Below, I discuss what I consider to be the most important of these implications, specifically those that impact the media's role as the fourth branch of government and the effects of media coverage on citizens and the political system.

The Role of the Press in the Political System

To begin on a bright note, the alarm/patrol hybrid model points to the watchdog media as a surviving (if endangered) species. Patrol-mode reporting does not occur all the time—it may not even be the norm—but it does occur. That it occurs as often as it does, and often in spite of institutional incentives, supports the notion that surveillance journalism is still deeply ingrained (Shoemaker 1996). Yet this intermittent patrol mode of news-generation carries unintended consequences that are at odds with the normative ideal of a watchdog press. Specifically, because the media frequently kicks into patrol mode only in particular geographic or policy neighborhoods designated by a preceding alarm, these modes of surveillance serve to further exacerbate skew (and explosiveness) in the news, thereby restricting agenda access to many of the important policy problems that an idealized watchdog media would catch.

The findings presented here also imply that the disproportionate nature of media attention is not just a coincidental parallel to disproportionate policy attention shown in other agendas. The disproportionate nature of media attention is, in fact, a likely culprit of exacerbating disproportionate policy responsiveness—since, as scholars such as Cook (1998) and Baumgartner and Jones (2005) make clear, the media agenda is central to policymaker efforts to craft policy. This book lays a foundation for future work examining the effects of disproportionate media attention on government policymaking.

Agenda Control

The findings I have presented also speak to the tension between the influence of policymakers in shaping the news on the one hand, and press independence on the other. Past research has supported both notions, and this book helps to untangle this apparent paradox. In line with indexing theory, I have shown that policymaker attention indeed has a significant influence on media attention. This finding is consistent with what we know of the organizational incentives under which news outlets operate. It is nonetheless normatively troubling.

At the same time, however, the findings presented here suggest that the news is very difficult to control, even for the most powerful elites. This book has demonstrated the explosive nature of media attention. It has also shown the significant effect that the *diversity of debate* can have on the amount of attention an issue receives. Specifically, we saw in chapter 6 that increased spread of media coverage across frames of an issue goes hand-in-hand with increased levels of attention to that issue. Together, the influence of diversity of discussion and the ingrained explosiveness suggest that policymakers who try to control the framing of an issue for an extended period are likely to be disappointed. When competing issue frames come into play, this framing diversity can prompt a media explosion, often not in the direction that the elites had planned.

By way of illustration, consider the case of President George W. Bush and the U.S. military operations in Afghanistan and Iraq. Given the context of the post-9/11 world and the sophisticated communication strategies the Bush administration developed, the U.S. conflicts in Afghanistan and Iraq offered prime opportunities for executive media control. Throughout the war, President Bush's communications kept tight rein of the frames used to define the issue and focused on those frames that lent themselves most readily to positive portrayals of the administration's policy, such as considerations of democratization, human rights, and weapons of mass destruction. In contrast, the president steered clear of discussing the war in terms of troop deaths, economic cost, the treatment of detainees at Guantanamo Bay or Abu Ghraib, or the effects of the war on local citizens in Iraq. And for a long period at least, the press followed the president's lead (Glazier and Boydstun 2012). Bennett, Lawrence, and Livingston have pointed to this period as a critical instance of the press failing in its watchdog duties (2007).

Early executive control over media coverage of the war took many forms. In a decision of arguable political genius, the president and his staff allowed journalists to cover the fighting in Afghanistan and Iraq from the highly newsworthy—but highly controlled—perspective of being embedded with U.S. troops. Not only does being embedded with troops give journalists a perception of the war that aligns more closely with troop perceptions, simply by virtue of sharing living conditions, but these extreme situations can foster a strong sense of camaraderie that, understandably, shapes journalists' reports back home (Brandenburg 2005; Pfau et al. 2005). The administration also channeled its framing of the war directly into U.S. media outlets by offering a hand-picked group of retired military officers to serve as independent military analysts able to offer expert and unbiased assessments of the war. An investigative report by *Times* journalist David Barstow describes this integration of administration-controlled military analysts into the news-generation process as "a kind of media Trojan horse" (2008).

The effort to control media attention is nothing new to the White House (or the Pentagon). For example, according to Laurence Moskowitz, chairman and chief executive of Medialink, which serves as a major producer of promotional news segments, "the Clinton administration was probably even more active than the Bush administration" in advancing news segments promoting its policies (Kirkpatrick 2005). Yet the Bush administration's handling of the war offers a stringent test of the notion that the news is difficult to control. If ever such an elite attempt to control media coverage could succeed, it probably would have been this one. Indeed, these strategies worked well for a time.

Eventually, however, new frames began to enter the debate. As early as 2003, members of Congress began to make public statements about the financial cost of the war, and the public showed signs of unease about these costs. Bush diverted a portion of his attention to heading off these concerns, but as criticisms mounted it became increasingly difficult for the administration to neutralize them (McCarthy, Campbell, and Norton-Taylor 2003). In 2004, during a meeting with Donald Rumsfeld publicized as a visit to boost troop morale, Spc. Thomas Wilson asked about troop body armor (Schmitt 2004), and the press swarmed to cover the encounter. In 2005 Cindy Sheehan, the mother of a soldier killed in Iraq, staged a protest outside the Bush ranch in Texas, focusing a surge of attention on the deaths of U.S. soldiers (Associated Press 2005). That same year, photos of detainees being tortured at Abu Ghraib were released, drawing sensationalized and critical news coverage (Jacobs 2004). And even the same military analysts who had proven invaluable in helping to frame media attention to the war in pro-administration terms began to speak out against how the conflict was being handled (Barstow 2008).

As events unfolded and the war's rally effects deteriorated, the media operated under its incentives to cover the growing diversity of elite perspectives (e.g., Bennett 1990) and to define events using an increasing diversity of frames. The increase in diversity of discussion drew continued media coverage, by this point highly negative in tone. Ultimately, news coverage spun out of the administration's control, presumably contributing in mutually reinforcing fashion to decay in public support (Glazier and Boydstun 2012). Depending on the measures considered, between

2003 and 2007 public approval for the war dropped between thirty-five and fifty percentage points (Franklin 2007). In the world of relatively stable public opinion marginals, and even accounting for the large rally effect the war initially inspired, this change is staggering. The rise and fall of the Bush administration's handling of media coverage of the war is strong anecdote for understanding how media explosiveness puts a severe shelf life on elite abilities to control the news.

Issue Access

Systemic skew in the news means that most issues have scarce access to the media agenda. This finding is bad news for advocates of any policy issue that is socially significant but that lacks the particular characteristics—or surrounding events—that make it more likely to gain media attention. At the same time, the alarm/patrol hybrid model shows how media explosions can occur. And I have offered several examples of how the particular media phenomenon of sustained media explosions can draw dramatic attention to issues that often would otherwise have been missed. Often, sustained media explosions can pass a critical mass of salience, leaving a meaningful impact on citizen awareness and even policymaking.

These findings suggest that issue advocates must rely largely on timing, waiting for a media explosion—big or small—to surround their issue of concern. Specifically, they should make strategic use of scarce resources. Their resources are perhaps best used by trying to link the given policy issue to related issues currently in the media spotlight—especially if those issues are at the center of a period of alarm coverage likely to be followed by media surveillance. Through attention bandwagoning, many issues in the surrounding policy/geographic neighborhood can gain traction in the news.

Additionally, advocates can potentially take advantage of the same *diversity of discussion* concept that makes the agenda difficult to control. For advocates unhappy with the status quo distribution of power in a policy debate, introducing additional frames into the discussion can draw more attention to the issue while also realigning the debate. This realignment can widen the scope of the debate, redistributing power between the conflicting camps. In other words, in order to draw attention to an underserved issue, advocates might spend time and money not on saying their message louder, but on reframing the issue. This strategy applies exclusively to debate "losers" though, since reframing the issue and drawing in more attention can only spell trouble for the status quo majority in the form of potential media explosions (Baumgartner and Jones 2009; Downs 1972; Schattschneider 1960).

Information Flow

For policymakers, the skew and explosiveness embedded in the news can make life very difficult. Policymakers have strong incentives to keep up with the items in the news, but the media's explosiveness renders this goal infeasible; they cannot possibly respond to items in the news in a meaningful way before the media lurches to the next issue. Periods of sustained media explosions offer perhaps the best opportunity for substantial policymaker response. But even here, "sustained" in the world of the media is a couple weeks (which equates, in congressional time, to approximately a nanosecond).

Thus, policymakers hoping to provide meaningful response to policy problems may need to maintain two parallel agendas. Policymakers may have little choice but to stay active in public discussions surrounding hot issues in the news that are of key concern to their constituents, namely through public versions of their agendas (e.g., press statements, websites). But realizing that this public discussion will move too fast to facilitate real policy improvements, they should—and indeed, often do—reserve attention and resources for a second, behind-the-scenes agenda comprised of those policy problems toward which they can make the greatest difference through slow and difficult day-to-day work.

For citizens, the alarm/patrol hybrid model bears weight on the nature of the information gained from the news and on prescriptive ideas for how to balance one's information diet. The findings in this book imply that news coverage portrays real-world problems as being vastly less diverse than they in fact are and as resolving much more quickly than they in fact do. Society's shift to digital media may enhance political engagement under some conditions, but it also means that skew and explosiveness and, thus, the disparities between news signals and "reality" are becoming more pronounced.

Moreover, increasing marketplace competition in the U.S. media is leading to increased fragmenting of news outlets; many news outlets— especially online news outlets—now target news coverage toward their narrow consumer bases. Plus, with the ability to select our news, we citizens are further skewing the media signals we receive, sending strong cues to news outlets that we want more of the same. Thus, in line with other studies, this book suggests that we should maintain a keen awareness of our information diets, striving for a well-grounded pyramid of information consumption. Specifically, we should reference multiple news sources—including traditional broadsheet newspapers especially—in order to consume as diverse an array of stories as possible (Johnson 2012).

Closing Thought

I close by stressing, again, that the alarm/patrol hybrid model describes how the news-generation process behaves in the aggregate; it does not capture journalists' and editors' intentions. As Bennett (2003) points out, even under the increasing strains of a shifting media marketplace, newsroom decisions largely map on to news standard ideals. In picking stories to pursue and in presenting those stories, most news outlets aim to serve the public by alerting society to those threats on the horizon. Yet these decisions are subtly but significantly shaped by institutional incentives and, most of all, by the momentum these incentives induce. The resulting skew and explosiveness are products of institutional forces, not bad or biased journalism. Thus, the alarm/patrol hybrid model helps explain the apparent paradox of how the mostly noble intentions of journalists can result in a media agenda that is far from most normative ideals. These noble intentions get filtered through a complicated system of organizational and marketplace incentives and disproportionate information processing. As a result, such intentions are not always reflected in the news and its patterns. I have suggested that we citizens account for systemic patterns of skew and explosiveness in the news by being more proactive in diversifying our information diets. This prescription is not on account of journalists not trying to do their jobs. If anything, it reflects our deteriorating media consumption habits, which make journalists' job descriptions increasingly slippery.

What is amazing, we might say, is that we see as much "true grit" news coverage as we do. Newsrooms around the country work hard to deliver informative, insightful news. These efforts are clearly shaped by the many incentive-based pressures that news outlets shoulder. But it is also clear that journalists and editors often buck these pressures for the sake of better reporting. As *Washington Post* news editor Vince Bzdek

says, the surveillance model of journalism may be impossible, but it still
motivates the newsroom. That's "the life blood of this place," he says,
"being the watchdog." He goes on to riff on the Rolling Stones: "you
can't always get what you want, you know, but we'll try to get you what
you need."[3]

Supplementary Tables/Figures

An online appendix is also available.

TABLE A.I *Times* **front-page attention by topic, 1996–2006, with monthly summary statistics**

Code	Major Topic Category	Total, 1996–2006	Percent Total	Monthly Summary Statistics			
				Mean	Std Dev	Min	Max
19	International Affairs and Foreign Aid	6,354	20.5%	48.1	12.7	21	100
16	Defense	4,479	14.4%	33.9	27.3	2	150
20	Government Operations	3,958	12.8%	30.0	20.4	1	124
12	Law, Crime, and Family	2,088	6.7%	15.8	8.1	3	49
3	Health	1,799	5.8%	13.6	5.3	4	30
29	Sports and Recreation	1,273	4.1%	9.6	6.8	0	47
15	Banking, Finance, and Domestic Commerce	1,249	4.0%	9.5	7.1	0	44
1	Macroeconomics	964	3.1%	7.3	5.1	0	27
2	Civil Rights, Minority Issues, and Civil Liberties	914	2.9%	6.9	3.9	0	25
6	Education	912	2.9%	6.9	3.9	1	30
27	Fires	769	2.5%	5.8	3.0	1	15
5	Labor, Employment, and Immigration	749	2.4%	5.7	4.3	0	25
17	Space, Science, Technology and Communications	719	2.3%	5.4	4.7	0	45
23	Culture and Entertainment	715	2.3%	5.4	4.3	0	21
10	Transportation	594	1.9%	4.5	4.1	0	30
24	State and Local Government Administration	573	1.8%	4.3	4.6	0	26
14	Housing and Community Development	410	1.3%	3.1	2.6	0	15
7	Environment	354	1.1%	2.7	2.1	0	9
31	Churches and Religion	329	1.1%	2.5	2.9	0	30
8	Energy	299	1.0%	2.3	3.5	0	22
13	Social Welfare	273	0.9%	2.1	2.2	0	13
21	Public Lands and Water Management	269	0.9%	2.0	1.6	0	8
30	Death Notices	268	0.9%	2.0	2.2	0	15
18	Foreign Trade	254	0.8%	1.9	2.4	0	16
99	Human Interest, Other, and Miscellaneous	172	0.6%	1.3	1.4	0	7
4	Agriculture	168	0.5%	1.3	1.5	0	10
26	Weather and Natural Disasters	129	0.4%	1.0	1.7	0	10
	Total (mean across 132 months)	**31,034**	**100%**	**(8.7)**	**(5.5)**	**(1.2)**	**(34.9)**

Note: Due to rounding, individual percentage values do not reflect the 100% total.

Descriptive statistics for chapter 5 models

All Policy Topics	Obs (Months)	Mean	Std Dev	Min	Max
Dependent Variable					
Front-Page Attention (log odds of proportion of front-page agenda) $_t$	2508	−4.113	1.988	−9.210	0.545
Independent Variables					
Front-Page Attention $_{t-1}$	2489	−4.113	1.988	−9.210	0.545
Proportion of Congressional Hearings $_{t-1}$	2489	0.053	0.058	0	0.760
Proportion of Executive Orders $_{t-1}$	2489	0.037	0.125	0	1
Proportion of Gallup MIP $_{t-1}$	2489	0.048	0.074	0	0.473
Diversity of Discussion $_{t-1}$	2489	0.323	0.239	0	0.834
Front-Page Congestion $_t$	2508	0.231	0.071	0.119	0.549

Domestic Policy Topics	Obs (Months)	Mean	Std Dev	Min	Max
Dependent Variable					
Front-Page Attention (log odds of proportion of front-page agenda)	2112	−4.283	1.814	−9.210	0.343
Independent Variables					
Front-Page Attention $_{t-1}$	2096	−4.284	1.816	−9.210	0.343
Proportion of Congressional Hearings $_{t-1}$	2096	0.050	0.056	0	0.760
Proportion of Executive Orders $_{t-1}$	2096	0.032	0.117	0	1
Proportion of Gallup MIP $_{t-1}$	2096	0.046	0.071	0	0.404
Diversity of Discussion $_{t-1}$	2096	0.308	0.235	0	0.834
Front-Page Congestion $_t$	2112	0.231	0.071	0.119	0.549

International Policy Topics	Obs (Months)	Mean	Std Dev	Min	Max
Dependent Variable					
Front-Page Attention (log odds of proportion of front-page agenda)	396	3.208	2.553	−9.210	0.545
Independent Variables:					
Front-Page Attention $_{t-1}$	393	−3.203	2.541	−9.210	0.545
Proportion of Congressional Hearings $_{t-1}$	393	0.068	0.065	0	0.500
Proportion of Executive Orders $_{t-1}$	393	0.066	0.157	0	1
Proportion of Gallup MIP $_{t-1}$	393	0.060	0.091	0	0.473
Diversity of Discussion $_{t-1}$	393	0.403	0.247	0	0.816
Front-Page Congestion $_t$	396	0.231	0.071	0.119	0.549

War on Terror	Obs (Months)	Mean	Std Dev	Min	Max
Dependent Variable					
Number of Sampled NYT and WSJ Stories $_t$	65	52.031	33.492	20	191
Independent Variables					
Number of Sampled NYT and WSJ Stories $_{t-1}$	64	52.438	33.595	20	191
Number of U.S. Military Casualties $_t$	65	51.769	36.986	0	131
Number of Congressional Hearings $_t$	64	29.453	19.719	0	75
Proportion of Gallup MIP on Defense $_t$	64	0.254	0.065	0.198	0.473
Diversity of Discussion $_t$	65	0.567	0.055	0.412	0.731
Front-Page Congestion $_t$	65	0.257	0.082	0.162	0.566

Death Penalty	Obs (Years)	Mean	Std Dev	Min	Max
Dependent Variable					
Number of NYT Stories $_t$	46	85.630	53.679	8	235
Independent Variable:					
Number of NYT Stories $_{t-1}$	45	84.800	53.986	8	235
Number of Death Sentences $_t$	45	197.733	83.702	42	317
Number of Supreme Court Cases on the Death Penalty $_t$	46	7.652	3.985	1	15
% Pro/Anti Opinion $_t$	46	88.976	1.445	85.967	91.579
Diversity of Discussion $_t$	46	0.620	0.112	0.241	0.776
Full-Paper Congestion $_t$	46	0.152	0.029	0.102	0.212

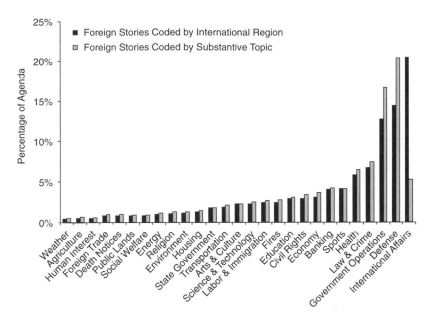

FIGURE A.I. *Times* front-page attention using different topic categorizations

Note: The figure shows how results differ when foreign stories (e.g., about higher education in Iraq; English Premier League football) are categorized by International Affairs regional subtopic codes (e.g., 1920 for Middle East; 1910 for Western Europe) rather than by substantive subtopic/topic codes (e.g., subtopic 601 for Education; topic 29 for Sports). This book uses the former approach, restricting all stories *not* primarily focused on the United States to within topic 19, International Affairs. N = 31,034 stories across 27 topics.

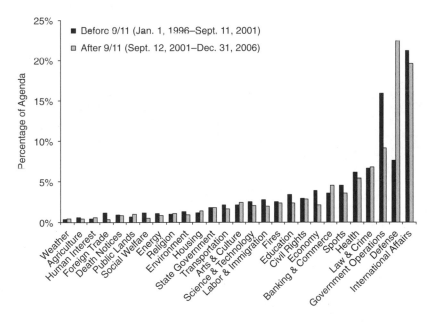

FIGURE A.2. *Times* front-page attention before and after 9/11

Notes

Chapter One

1. Supporting legislation and judicial rulings include the Patient Self-Determination Act passed by Congress in 1990, the New Jersey Supreme Court's *In re* Quinlan decision in 1976, and the U.S. Supreme Court's *Cruzan v. Director, Missouri Department of Health* decision in 1990. For more information, see: http://www.uslivingwillregistry.com/.

2. One in eight Americans age sixty-five or over—and nearly half of Americans age eighty-five and over—exhibit the symptoms of Alzheimer's, and many more cases go unrecorded since the disease is so difficult to diagnose. Accounting for the aging baby boomer generation, by 2030 it is estimated that nearly 20 percent of Americans will be at least 65 years old, including 7.7 million Alzheimer's patients (Alzheimer's Association 2012).

3. Pew Research Center, "Strong Public Support for Right to Die: More Americans Discussing—and Planning—End-of-Life Treatment," http://www.people-press.org/2006/01/05/strong-public-support-for-right-to-die/, released January 5, 2006. The PDF version of the full report shows findings from both surveys: http://www.people-press.org/files/legacy-pdf/266.pdf.

4. Hereafter referred to as the *Times* or *NYT*.

5. Based on LexisNexis archives of the following sources: ABC, CBS, NBC, CNN, Fox, *Chicago Daily Herald*, *Denver Post*, *Houston Chronicle*, *New York Times*, *Philadelphia Inquirer*, *San Francisco Chronicle*, *USA Today*, and *Washington Post*.

6. My primary data source is the front page of the *New York Times*. While certainly not devoid of soft news, the *Times* is as packed with hard news as any other single media agenda that can be measured. Moreover, studies suggest that even soft news serves to send citizens key policy cues (e.g., Baum 2002, 2003; Baum and Groeling 2008; Prior 2003).

7. Note that the term "skew" refers not to journalistic bias or slant but rather

to the distribution of news coverage across policy issues. Under any model of news generation, there is no reason to expect a media agenda that is equally distributed across issues; air pollution might simply be perceived as less important than poverty or terrorism. Yet both the alarm and patrol models individually suggest that we should see a media agenda that is distributed across policy issues roughly in proportion with their perceived (if not objective) severity. It is difficult to say exactly what this distribution of "proportional" attention would look like, of course, but it stands to reason that it might approximate a normal distribution, with a few issues getting a lot of attention, a few issues getting very little attention, and most issues getting some amount in between. Events, after all, tend to be normally distributed in severity and change over time (Jones and Baumgartner 2005). By contrast, the alarm/patrol hybrid model suggests dramatic skew across policy issues and dramatic explosive change over time.

8. An "agenda" is the finite amount of attention that any given body has at its disposal. Each person has an agenda, for example, in the form of time and cognitive capacity available to devote to problems, considerations, activities, and so on. The political system contains many different agendas: the congressional agenda, the presidential agenda, the agenda of public opinion, the media agenda, and so on. We can measure attention on each of these agendas in many different ways, such as through the number of bills on a particular policy issue, the number of times the president mentions the issue, the percentage of Americans who name that issue as important, or the number of news stories on the issue. "Agenda setting," then, is the process by which attention is distributed on a given agenda, though "agenda building" is perhaps a more accurate term (Hänggli 2013). It is through this process that some policy issues (e.g., prescription drug benefits, political corruption, gas prices) gain position on an agenda at the necessary exclusion of other policy issues (e.g., farming subsidies, schizophrenia, third world genocides).

9. Supreme Court statistic taken from Carrington and Cramton 2009; note that the U.S. Supreme Court decided about eighty cases on average in the 2000s, down from an average of about 150 cases per year in the 1980s (Strauss 1987; Tyler 2010). Bill signing statistic calculated by taking the average number of public laws passed per Congressional session as recorded in the Library of Congress Public Laws archive and then dividing this number by two to arrive at a yearly average (http://thomas.loc.gov/home/LegislativeData.php?&n=PublicLaws). Statistic on time the average American spends thinking about politics taken from Lake and Sosin 1998. *New York Times* statistic taken from the dataset presented in this book.

10. For instance, the same issue can make a different mark depending on whether it is framed as a thematic (systemic) or episodic (isolated) issue (Iyengar 1991), in terms of potential gains or potential losses (Kahneman and Tversky 1979; Ledgerwood and Boydstun 2013), along one substantive dimension of the

given issue debate as opposed to alternate framing dimensions (e.g., Baumgart-ner, De Boef, and Boydstun 2008; Chong and Druckman 2007b; Hänggli 2013; Nelson, Clawson, and Oxley 1997), or in the context of competing frames (Chong and Druckman 2007a).

11. Readers who recognized the name Terri Schiavo may be interested to see how many of the items in this list they also remember. All of these events were important; only a small number received attention.

12. Jon Stewart, "Weathering Fights," *Daily Show with Jon Stewart*, Comedy Central, October 26, 2011, http://www.thedailyshow.com/watch/wed-october-26 –2011/weathering-fights.

13. Sarah Cohen, interview by author, Washington, DC, September 3, 2010.

Chapter Two

1. For excellent examples, see Baumgartner and Jones 2009, Bennett 1990, Entman 2003, Graber 2006, Iyengar and McGrady 2007, Lawrence 2000b, and Wolfsfeld and Sheafer 2006.

2. See Diermeier and Krehbiel 2003 for an excellent treatment of institution-alism as theory and methodology.

3. Mark Leibovich, telephone interview by author, November 17, 2010.

4. Sparrow refers here to the so-called iron triangle of policymaking, in which Congress, the bureaucracy, and interest groups operate in a closed network (e.g., Heclo 1978).

5. Institutional powers and constraints vary across countries, within each country across media submarkets, within submarkets across individual news out-lets, and within a given news outlet over time. As a quick thought experiment, consider the same country in two parallel universes. The two versions of this country are identical in every way—even the events that occur—except for the institutional setup of their media markets (e.g., the level of news outlet competi-tion, level of government subsidization). Based on these institutional differences alone, the two news systems would process the same events in slightly different ways, producing two different agendas with different patterns of change.

6. Anne E. Kornblut, telephone interview by author, October 5, 2010.

7. Sarah Cohen, interview by author, Washington, DC, September 3, 2010.

8. Vince Bzdek, telephone interview by author, October 5, 2010 (hereafter Bzdek interview).

9. See also Berkowitz 1990, Lewin 1947, Livingston and Bennett 2003, and on the collapse of gatekeeping see Williams and Delli Carpini 2000.

10. Alan Sipress, telephone interview by author, September 29, 2010,

11. From this point forward, I use the term "event" as a catch-all for any bit of new information: a speech, a trend, a protest, an opinion, a bombing, a partner-

ship . . . the *finding out* of a speech, a trend, and so on. An event, in other words, is any occurrence or development "out there." Thus, every news story contains information about an event, but only a fraction of events receive news coverage.

12. Based on city-level homicide data provided by the Department of Justice, Bureau of Justice Statistics, e.g., *Crime in the United States 2005* (http://www2 .fbi.gov/ucr/05cius/), correlated with yearly counts of newspaper stories archived in LexisNexis for the following newspapers: *Oregonian* (Portland), *Seattle Post-Intelligencer, St. Louis Post-Dispatch, San Diego Union Tribune,* and *San Francisco Chronicle.* Correlations were run from 1985 to 2005 except when newspaper archives were not available back to 1985, in which case correlations were run on as many years as were available (never less than sixteen).

13. See also Baumgartner and Jones 2009, Grossman 2011, Hallin and Mancini 2004, Strömbäck and Kiousis 2010, Wolfsfeld 1997, Yagade and Dozier 1990, Zucker 1978.

14. These different issues also exhibit different strengths and directions of influence between real-world events, news coverage, public attention, and policy attention (Soroka 2002).

15. That said, while disruptive protests generally receive prominent coverage, anticorporation claims-making events tend to receive worse page placement (Rafail et al. 2008).

16. For example, had the failed terrorist attempts of December 22, 2001 (when Richard Reid, aka Abdul Raheem, tried to detonate explosives hidden in his shoe on American Airlines Flight 63), or December 25, 2009 (when Umar Farouk Abdul Mutallab tried to detonate explosives hidden in his underwear on Northwest Airlines Flight 253), been successful, we can imagine that they would have received more media attention than they did, and for a longer period of time.

17. Such studies include Behr and Iyengar 1985, Iyengar and Kinder 1987, McCombs and Shaw 1972, Price and Tewksbury 1997, Shaw and McCombs 1977, Scheufele 2000, Scheufele and Tewksbury 2007, and Winter and Eyal 1981.

18. Bzdek interview.

19. The idea that diversification is beneficial to the success of an endeavor has been explored in other contexts. For example, Surowiecki's (2005) work on decisionmaking and Page's (2007) work in the realm of human organizations in particular show that a diversity of perspectives offers an even greater advantage in group tasks than high levels of intellect or experience do. Given two groups of people trying to accomplish the same goal, for example, where one group is more skilled for the task at hand but homogenous and the other group is less skilled but heterogeneous, all else being equal, the latter group will be more likely to succeed (Page 2007).

20. The term "debate" refers here to political, public, and media discussion

of an issue/topic, whether or not it the issue/topic is easily divisible into two (or more) sides.

21. On framing, see also Baumgartner, De Boef, and Boydstun 2008, Callaghan and Schnell 2005, Druckman 2001, Iyengar 1996, Nelson, Clawson, and Oxley 1997, and Sellers and Schaffner 2009, just to name a few.

22. Bzdek interview.

23. To estimate the number of front-page *Times* stories reporting on civilian casualties during the Soviet-Afghan War, I searched within document text for the search string [(Afghan* AND civilian* AND (death* OR died OR kill*)) AND Soviet] between December 27, 1979, and May 15, 1988. To estimate the number of *Times* stories reporting on civilian casualties in Afghanistan and Iraq during the U.S. conflicts there since 2001, I searched within document text for the search string [((Afghan* OR Iraq*) AND civilian* AND (death* OR died OR kill*)) AND (U.S. OR "United States" OR "American")] between October 7, 2001, and December 31, 2007. I also performed a simple comparison of overall coverage of the wars by searching for the string [Afghan* AND Soviet] between December 27, 1979, and May 15, 1988, and for the string [(Afghan* OR Iraq*) AND (U.S. OR "United States" OR "American")] between October 7, 2001, and December 31, 2007. Based on these general search strings, there were a total of 660 front-page *Times* stories on the Soviet-Afghan War during its nine years, whereas the first six years of the U.S. conflicts in Afghanistan and Iraq produced 2,535 front-page *Times* stories.

24. Sarah Cohen, interview by author, Palo Alto, CA, June 24, 2010.

25. Alan Sipress, telephone interview by author, September 29, 2010.

26. Ibid.

27. Sarah Cohen, interview by author, Palo Alto, CA, June 24, 2010.

28. Ibid.

29. Peter Baker, telephone interview by author, November 17, 2010.

30. Sarah Cohen, interview by author, Palo Alto, CA, June 24, 2010.

Chapter Four

1. These findings are produced by running an unparameterized time-series pooled cross-sectional model of the number of front-page stories issue i receives at time t (using a fixed-effects estimator). When run on the *Times* front-page dataset at the topic level by month, this model shows that 66% of the variance in attention is due to group-level (i.e., topic) variation in means while 34% of the variance is due to temporal variation in means. Calculated in Stata at the major topic level, the coefficient for sigma_u (topic) = 11.27 and the coefficient for sigma_e (time) = 8.01. Calculating ρ = sigma_u^2 / (sigma_u^2 + sigma_e^2), we see

that the fraction of the variance due to u_i is 0.66. The F test that all u_i = 0 is statistically significant (F (26, 3537) = 261.05; Prob > F = .000), meaning that we can reject the null that all issues are homogenous. When run at the subtopic level by month, group-level variation accounts for only 38% of the variance, while temporal variation accounts for 62%. At the subtopic level, the coefficient for sigma_u = 2.16 and sigma_e = 2.76, so ρ = 0.38. Again, the F-statistic for ρ is significant at the 0.000 level.

2. Most stories in the dataset are stories in the traditional sense, but stand-alone photographs with captions were treated as stories, too, since these photographs also send topic cues to readers. However, the "inside" blurbs at the bottom of the page (advertising stories inside the paper) were not included, since unlike front-page photographs these blurbs do not capture reader attention in the same way as full stories. Photographs, on the other hand, are a very different medium of communication. Although beyond the scope of this study, our understanding of the news-generation process would benefit from additional studies examining the differential news patterns (and media effects) exhibited by text-only stories as compared to stories using photographs and/or graphics, as well as features of news presentation such as page placement (e.g., above and below the fold), story length, even title font size. See chapter 8 for discussion of how newspapers tend to construct broadsheet vs. online titles.

3. See Althaus, Edy, and Phalen 2001, McCombs and Reynolds 2002, Soroka 2002, Van Belle 2003, and Winter and Eyal 1981. Also related is Druckman 2005. But for competing evidence see Woolley 2000, and for evidence of liberal bias see Fritz, Keefer, and Nyhan 2004 and Kuypers 2006.

4. The Policy Agendas Topics Codebook (http://www.policyagendas.org), designed initially for the coding of congressional budget and hearing data, is understandably imperfect in its application to news stories. The codes are easy enough to apply to articles at the major topic level, as the Policy Agendas Project did in collecting its sampled *NYT* dataset, but the task of assigning the more fine-grained subtopic codes to news stories requires forethought and judiciousness. See, for example, the "Admitting Defeat" section of Baumgartner, Jones and MacLeod's paper entitled "Lessons from the Trenches: Quality, Reliability, and Usability in a New Data Source" (1998). To address this challenge, I developed an annotated version of the Policy Agendas Codebook complete with explicit instructions on how to apply the codes to the specific demands of newspaper text analysis. This annotated codebook can be found on the webpage for this book.

5. In order to maximize reliability and consistency, coders underwent extensive training on sample articles and were required to demonstrate high intercoder reliability on this training dataset (a Krippendorf's alpha value of at least 0.90 at the topic level and 0.80 at the subtopic level) before being allowed to code raw data. Once coding commenced, I safeguarded against drift (across

coders and across time) in four ways. First, coders recorded all questions about ambiguous observations rather than making independent judgment calls. Second, coders met weekly as a group to discuss these questions, allowing me to reinforce coding protocols to ensure conformity. In a few rare instances, coding issues arose that affected data already collected; in these cases, all relevant observations were isolated and recoded. Third, unbeknownst to the coders, I embedded common observations in their assigned datasets at intervals throughout the coding process in order to keep track of intercoder reliability. Fourth and finally, after each article was assigned a code by an initial coder, the articles were compiled into one massive dataset, sorted by subtopic code and, within each subtopic, by date, and then cleaned by more experienced "expert" coders. In this way, every story in the dataset was assessed by at least two people.

6. For example, a sample of 311 stories coded by two coders (without the coders knowing these stories would be tracked for intercoder reliability) yielded the following representative intercoder reliability measures: At the topic level, percent agreement = 93.2%, Cohen's kappa = 0.925, Krippendorff's alpha = 0.925; at the subtopic level, percent agreement = 90.7%, Cohen's kappa = 0.897, Krippendorff's alpha = 0.898.

7. The original Policy Agendas Codebook, used to code congressional, presidential, and Supreme Court documents as well as the Gallup "most important problem" survey data, contains only the first nineteen topic categories in this list. Baumgartner and Jones added the remaining eight topics for the task of coding articles sampled from the full *NYT*. Unlike the original nineteen topics, these eight do not contain four-digit subtopic categories.

8. The following subtopics have zero observations in the *Times* front-page dataset: 110, 344, 898, 899, 1404, 1407, 1410, and 2199.

9. In general, from this point forward I use the term "topic" to refer to the 27 major topic categories and the term "issue" or "subtopic" to refer to the 225 subtopic categories, though in broad discussion of the news-generation process I employ the term "issue" generically.

10. Code 1619 is used to capture all stories about U.S. military actions in the war on terror, including military operations in Afghanistan beginning in 2001 and operations in Iraq beginning in 2003. Note that, because the 9/11 attacks occurred in the United States, stories about the attacks themselves are coded under Civil Defense (code 1615) rather than International Terrorism/Hijacking (code 1927).

11. Note that there are many issues we might normally think of as "government operations" that are not contained in the Government Operations topic category, like the administration of taxes, Social Security stipends, and Medicaid benefits. These stories are categorized according to the substantive nature of the problem they address—so taxes fall under Macroeconomics, Social Security falls under Social Welfare, and Medicaid falls under Health. The Government

Operations topic deals rather with the structural functions of national government, like elections, nominations, intergovernmental relations, impeachment, and other government scandal. As mentioned in chapter 1, many of the election stories in particular are light on the policy and heavy on political maneuvering. Stories about political maneuvering linked explicitly or implicitly to a policy issue are coded according to that policy issue. Stories that are truly about the horse race itself are coded under Elections. Thus, the resulting categorizations of stories by policy issue are to some extent a necessary contrivance, but one largely restricted to the single issue code of Elections (subtopic 2012). Note again that, while horse-race coverage and the separate but related prevalence of soft news are real phenomena throughout the media system, most nonfeature stories on the *Times* front page can be linked, at least implicitly, to clear policy issues.

12. The Churches and Religion topic (code 31) is treated as nonpolicy because it is used for stories about churches, churchgoing, and religiosity generically, while more policy-related stories about religious freedom and separation of church and state are coded in the topic of Civil Rights and Liberties (code 2). In order to be consistent with how other stories about child abuse are treated, stories about child sexual abuses by Catholic priests are coded under Law and Crime (code 12).

13. Considering that the 9/11 attacks only affected news coverage for the last three and a half months of 2001, with the first eight months of 2001 reflecting the same basic level of attention to Defense as in 2000, the surge in attention to Defense in 2001 is colossal.

14. See the book webpage for the graphs showing the full dataset at the monthly and weekly levels.

Chapter Five

1. In each case, we would need an empirical indicator capturing variance only across topics (on the assumption that the variable remains stable over time), variance only across time (on the assumption that the variable performs in the same way for all topics), or variance across both. We can imagine some creative solutions to this challenge. For example, in thinking about *institutional setup*, we could ask news editors to assign each topic an "incentive" value, indicating the degree of perceived institutional incentive (within their specific news outlet and/or the media market at large) to cover events in that topic area. Such measures are beyond the scope of this book but warrant future study—especially toward the aim of building models of media attention and media effects that account for different types of events and how these events can be framed in different ways.

2. See n. 9 below.

3. See book webpage for more detail on the selection of this modeling approach.

4. Using a dependent variable of front-page attention as the proportion of all front-page stories or as the count of all front-page stories produces substantively identical results to those presented in this chapter, with the exception that the *agenda congestion* variable ceases to be significant.

5. Additionally, by capturing the dependent variable in proportions rather than counts, I avoid problems that arise from using the count variable, which is far from normally distributed. As we saw in chapter 4 and will see again in chapter 7, the distribution of the front-page agenda across topics is highly skewed. This skew poses two problems for modeling front-page attention as a count variable. First, this count series is highly overdispersed—that is to say, the distribution of the variable has a much higher variance than a normal distribution. Second, the high frequency of zeroes in the series poses a particular challenge. These zeroes cannot be ignored; they are real zeroes, representing the multitude of months in which an arguably important policy topic received no front-page attention. Both these challenges suggest using the log odds approach I employ rather than measuring the dependent variable as raw counts (or proportions).

6. The Policy Agendas Project measures used in this book were originally collected by Frank R. Baumgartner and Bryan D. Jones, with the support of National Science Foundation grant number SBR 9320922, and were distributed through the Department of Government at the University of Texas at Austin and/or the Department of Political Science at the University of North Carolina, Chapel Hill. Neither NSF nor the original collectors of the data bear any responsibility for the analysis reported here.

7. E. Scott Adler and John Wilkerson, *Congressional Bills Project: 1996–2006*, NSF grant numbers 00880066 and 00880061. The views expressed here are those of the author and not the original collectors of the data or the National Science Foundation.

8. Measuring the public's concern for a given topic using the proportion of responses for that topic out of all responses in that survey can be problematic in some contexts, since doing so "artificially increases the evident interdependence among different categories" (Wlezien 2005, 561). However, since the modeling endeavor here involves treating each agenda as a zero-sum amount of attention, using the proportion of MIP responses is appropriate and consistent with using proportion measures of the other variables.

9. Consider, for example, the adjusted R^2 value as a very rough approximation of how good a job the model shown in table 5.4 does at explaining variance in front-page news. For the model run on all policy values, the adjusted R^2 value is 0.427 meaning—again, by very rough approximation—that the variables included in this model explain about 43% of the variance in front-page news. When run using a dependent variable measured either as the proportion or the count of front-page stories, this adjusted R^2 value increases to 0.732 and 0.729, respectively, suggesting that when unencumbered by the (methodologically ap-

propriate) log odds approach employed here, in fact the model explains something more like 73% of variance in front-page news. In any case, not bad, given that this model does not account for events (or for institutional setup or context)! But when *prior attention* is excluded from any of these models, the adjusted R^2 value decreases dramatically: from 0.427 to 0.320, and from 0.732 (0.729) to 0.269 (0.272). No other included variable comes close to this level of impact. Of course, many statistical caveats apply to interpreting these numbers, along with the strong possibility that prior attention is in fact tracking with unmeasured events. Still, in this model it is fair to say that prior attention accounts for somewhere between 10% and 35% of variance in front-page attention.

10. This calculation is performed by taking the inverse logit of the log odds proportional values and then multiplying each proportional effect by the mean number of front-page stories per month (235).

11. See online webpage for the specific values used.

Chapter Six

1. I use the term "war on terror" for simplicity, recognizing that the phrase is itself an example of framing (see Reese and Lewis 2009 for a discussion of how this label was coined by the Bush administration and adopted and internalized by the press and public; see also Snow, Rochford, Worden, and Benford 1986).

2. For example, see the Gallup Organization's time series showing public opinion on whether "the United States made a mistake in sending military forces [troops] to Afghanistan [Iraq]." For Afghanistan: http://www.gallup.com/poll/116233/Afghanistan.aspx. For Iraq: http://www.gallup.com/poll/1633/Iraq.aspx. The percentage of Gallup respondents who supported the war according to this measure (i.e., by saying they thought the United States had *not* made a mistake by sending troops) declined in the case of Afghanistan from 89% in November 2001 to 63% in August 2008 and in the case of Iraq from 75% in March 2003 to 39% in October 2008.

3. For example, see Gallup's time series showing public opinion in response to the question "Are you in favor of the death penalty for a person convicted of murder?": http://www.gallup.com/poll/1606/Death-Penalty.aspx. By this measure, public support for capital punishment rose from 42% in May 1966 to 80% in September 1994, before a relatively rapid decline to 64% by October 2003. Later surveys from Gallup (and other survey organizations) indicate that this lower level of support has since held relatively steady, with 2011 and 2012 surveys showing even lower levels (e.g., a 2011 Gallup poll registered support at 61%).

4. To identify relevant *Wall Street Journal* stories (which are only available in abstract form in the LexisNexis archives), we conducted a LexisNexis search using the following search string: <Iraq! OR Afghan! OR terror!>. The validity of

this keyword approach can be seen by examining those stories in the complete *Times* front-page database that would be retrieved by this same approach. Using the same keywords within the *Times* database shows that, of the 4,227 stories that were manually tagged as being relevant to the war on terror, all 4,227 were retrieved by the keywords. An additional 40 stories contained one of these keywords but were accurately identified by the coders as irrelevant, and these stories did not appear to be systematic in any way. These findings suggest that the keywords employed are highly accurate, retrieving all relevant stories as well as a small number of (randomly distributed) irrelevant stories estimated to comprise less than 10% of the stories retrieved.

5. Department of Defense, Military Casualty Information, http://siadapp .dmdc.osd.mil/personnel/CASUALTY/oef_date_of_death_list.pdf and http:// siadapp.dmdc.osd.mil/personnel/CASUALTY/oif_date_of_death_list.pdf (retrieved August 12, 2007).

6. The LexisNexis search employed here was not restricted to the summary of each case, meaning that the observations include cases tangentially related to capital punishment as well as those (rare) cases addressing the punishment directly. Even these tangential cases draw legal attention to capital punishment.

7. Calculated based on all repeated surveys across all survey houses, smoothed using Stimson's WCalc algorithm; see Baumgartner, De Boef, and Boydstun 2008.

8. For an excellent overview of framing theory, see Chong and Druckman 2007b.

9. See online webpage for more detail on the selection of this modeling approach.

Chapter Seven

1. Based on a LexisNexis search using a precise set of vetted keywords (formally: <Catholic w/15 priest w/15 sexual w/15 abuse>, indexed as being relevant to the United States).

2. ABC News Poll, February 2002, iPOLL Databank, Roper Center for Public Opinion Research, University of Connecticut, http://www.ropercenter.uconn .edu/data_access/ipoll/ipoll.html (retrieved October 25, 2011).

3. The inverse normalized Shannon's H is arguably a more appropriate measure of skew—or, in its standard form, diversity (Strömbäck and Kiousis 2010)—as it performs better at differentiating between extreme values (Boydstun, Bevan, and Thomas 2013). Still, in contrast to the l-kurtosis measure discussed below, it is difficult to establish a direct comparison between the skew of a given agenda and that of a normally distributed agenda, as the Shannon's H formula treats a normal distribution as falling very close to a uniform distribu-

tion, yielding a skew value close to zero. In this way though, any non-zero value represents true skew.

4. L-kurtosis, capturing the fourth moment of a distribution around its mean, is the established method of choice for policy agendas scholars in assessing the degree of explosiveness in an agenda's dynamics—that is, the degree of nonincremental, punctuated equilibrium change. L-kurtosis is considered a more stable measure than traditional kurtosis, which can be inflated by outlier observations (e.g., Boushey 2010; Breunig 2006; Hosking 1990; see Breunig and Jones 2011, for discussion of l-moments statistics as applied to policy agendas).

5. Jones, Larsen-Price and Wilkerson (2009) report the following l-kurtosis values (in parentheses) calculated at the yearly level: bill introductions (0.16); *New York Times* articles (sampled from the full paper, which we would expect to be less explosive than the front page) (0.24); State of the Union speeches (0.26); Solicitor General briefs (0.21); executive orders (0.25); laws (0.25); congressional roll-call votes (0.27); *Congressional Quarterly* coverage (0.29); congressional hearings (0.30); Supreme Court cases (0.31).

6. A full explanation of the simulation, along with the R code, is available on the book webpage. In brief, each of the simulation's parameters can be adjusted one at a time or in concert in order to gain a more nuanced understanding of the formal principles affecting the flow of information in and out of the news-generation process. Which issues capture each of the three stories on the artificial front page is determined, at each time point, by a simple formula whereby the "pressure" of each artificial policy issue "pushes" for attention, with the stories assigned randomly at time zero. The three front-page story slots are given to the three issues with the highest amounts of pressure, unless the second and/or third issues have pressure values of less than 50% of the next highest issue's pressure, in which case the higher issue receives the story slot for that issue. (This threshold of 50% can be adjusted in the simulation.) Thus, depending on the pressure values, an issue can receive one, two, or all three story slots in a given time point. The pressure value of each issue at each time point (which determines which issues receive front-page stories) is calculated as a function of one or more of the following four independent variables (each parameter can be varied in the simulation): (1) events, (2) random error, (3) negative feedback (in the form of an attention baseline), and (4) positive feedback. The three conditions investigated here capture three different combinations of these variables.

Chapter Eight

1. For an excellent comparative study of citizen engagement with digital media see Anduiza, Jensen, and Jorba 2012.

2. Bzdek interview.

3. Ibid.

4. Sarah Cohen, interview by author, Palo Alto, CA, June 24, 2010.

5. Sarah Cohen, interview by author, Washington, DC, September 3, 2010.

6. Bzdek interview.

7. Ibid.

8. Many thanks to Mel Atkinson, Frank Baumgartner, Tim Jurka, John Lovett, Jon Moody, and Trey Thomas for the collaborative effort to collect this data and for allowing me to present it here.

9. Unfortunately, the Google News Archive home page is no longer available in the form we used for this analysis, making future data collection efforts such as the one performed here more challenging. See: http://searchengineland.com/google-news-archive-search-page-gone-forever-or-temporary-bug-89768.

10. Note that the final category—online-only news—encapsulates both attention in the form of news coverage (e.g., stories by "official" online news sources) and attention *to* news coverage (e.g., blogs). While this distinction is an important one, I combine these sources toward the ultimate goal of testing the degree to which the cues sent to citizens from online-only sources (of any type) exhibit skew and explosiveness.

11. But for competing evidence, see d'Haenens, Jankowski, and Heuvelman 2004.

12. https://sites.google.com/site/chroniclesoftheinternet/educational/the-remarkable-history-of-the-internet-and-the-world-wide-web.

Chapter Nine

1. Vector autoregression is the traditional model of choice for examining mutual-influence between agendas, but this model cannot accommodate panel data. Thus, having tested the influence of policymaker attention and public concern on media attention in chapters 5 and 6, I simply test the effects in the other direction here.

2. Note that, unlike the figures in chapter 5, the lines in this figure are straight because each dependent variable is calculated as a proportion, rather than the log odds approach I took with media attention as the dependent variable.

3. Bzdek interview.

References

Ahlers, Douglas. 2006. "News Consumption and the New Electronic Media." *Harvard International Journal of Press/Politics* 11 (1): 29–52. doi:10.1177/1081180X05284317.

Ajdacic-Gross, Vladeta, Matthias Bopp, Roberto Sansossio, Christoph Lauber, Michal Gostynski, Dominique Eich, Felix Gutzwiller, and Wulf Rössler. 2005. "Diversity and Change in Suicide Seasonality over 125 Years." *Journal of Epidemiology and Community Health* 59 (11): 967–72. doi:10.1136/jech.2004.030981.

Althaus, Scott. 2003. "When News Norms Collide, Follow the Lead: New Evidence for Press Independence." *Political Communication* 20 (3): 381–414. doi:10.1080/10584600390244158.

Althaus, Scott L., Jill A. Edy, and Patricia F. Phalen. 2001. "Using Substitutes for Full-Text News Stories in Content Analysis: Which Text Is Best?" *American Journal of Political Science* 45 (3): 707–23. doi:10.1177/1940161209333089.

Althaus, Scott, and David Tewksbury. 2002. "Agenda Setting and the 'New' News: Patterns of Issue Importance among Readers of the Paper and Online Versions of the *New York Times*." *Communication Research* 29 (2): 180–207. doi:10.1177/0093650202029002004.

Alvarez, Lizette. 2012. "Justice Department Investigation Is Sought in Florida Teenager's Shooting Death." *New York Times*, March 16, 2012: A10. http://www.nytimes.com/2012/03/17/us/justice-department-investigation-is-sought-in-florida-teenagers-shooting-death.html.

Alvarez, R. Michael, and John Brehm. 2002. *Hard Choices, Easy Answers: Values, Information, and American Public Opinion*. Princeton, NJ: Princeton University Press.

Alzheimer's Association. 2012. 2012 Alzheimer's Disease Facts and Figures. Chicago: Alzheimer's Association.

Anduiza, Eva, Michael James Jensen, and Laia Jorba. 2012. *Digital Media and*

Political Engagement Worldwide: A Comparative Study. Communication, Society and Politics. New York: Cambridge University Press.

Armstrong, Elizabeth M., Daniel P. Carpenter, and Marie Hojnacki. 2006. "Whose Deaths Matter? Mortality, Advocacy, and Attention to Disease in the Mass Media." *Journal of Health Politics, Policy and Law* 31 (4): 729–72. doi:10.1215/03616878-2006-002.

Associated Press. 2005. "Mother of Fallen Soldier Protests at Bush Ranch." *Washington Post*, August 7. http://www.washingtonpost.com/wp-dyn/content/article/2005/08/06/AR2005080601337.html.

Athukorala, Prema-chandra, and Budy P. Resosudarmo. 2005. "The Indian Ocean Tsunami: Economic Impact, Disaster Management, and Lessons." *Asian Economic Papers* 4 (1): 1–39. doi:10.1162/asep.2005.4.1.1.

Auletta, Ken. 2010. "Non-Stop News." *New Yorker*, January 25, 2010, 38–47.

Bachrach, Peter, and Morton S. Baratz. 1962. "Two Faces of Power." *American Political Science Review* 56 (4): 947–52. doi:http://dx.doi.org/10.1017/S0003055406222561.

Bagdikian, Ben. 2004. *The New Media Monopoly.* Boston: Beacon Press.

Banerjee, Abhijit V. 1992. "A Simple Model of Herd Behavior." *Quarterly Journal of Economics* 107 (3): 797–817. doi:10.2307/2118364.

Barabasi, Albert-Laszlo. 2003. *Linked: How Everything Is Connected to Everything Else and What It Means.* New York: Plume.

Barstow, David. 2008. "Message Machine: Behind TV Analysts, Pentagon's Hidden Hand." *New York Times*, April 20, 2008: A1. http://www.nytimes.com/2008/04/20/us/20generals.html.

Bartels, Larry M. 1988. *Presidential Primaries and the Dynamics of Public Choice.* Princeton, NJ: Princeton University Press.

Baum, Matthew A. 2002. "Sex, Lies and War: How Soft News Brings Foreign Policy to the Inattentive Public." *American Political Science Review* 96 (1): 91–109. doi:http://dx.doi.org/10.1017/S0003055402004252.

———. 2003. *Soft News Goes to War: Public Opinion and American Foreign Policy in the New Media Age.* Princeton, NJ: Princeton University Press.

Baum, Matthew A., and Tim Groeling. 2008. "New Media and the Polarization of American Political Discourse." *Political Communication* 25 (4): 345–65. doi:10.1080/10584600802426965.

Baum, Matthew A., and Angela S. Jamison. 2006. "The *Oprah* Effect: How Soft News Helps Inattentive Citizens Vote Consistently." *Journal of Politics* 68 (4): 946–59. doi:10.1111/j.1468-2508.2006.00480.x.

Baum, Matthew A., and Philip B. K. Potter. 2008. "The Relationships between Mass Media, Public Opinion, and Foreign Policy: Toward a Theoretical Synthesis." *Annual Review of Political Science* 11 (1): 39–65. doi:10.1111/j.1468-2508.2006.00480.x.

Baumgartner, Frank R., Jeffrey M. Berry, Marie Hojnacki, David C. Kimball, and Beth L. Leech. 2009. *Lobbying and Policy Change: Who Wins, Who Loses, and Why.* Chicago: University of Chicago Press.

Baumgartner, Frank R., Christian Breunig, Christoffer Green-Pedersen, Bryan D. Jones, Peter B. Mortensen, Michiel Nuytemans, and Stefaan Walgrave. 2009. "Punctuated Equilibrium in Comparative Perspective." *American Journal of Political Science* 53 (3): 603–20. doi:10.1111/j.1540-5907.2009 .00389.x.

Baumgartner, Frank R., Suzanna L. De Boef, and Amber E. Boydstun. 2008. *The Decline of the Death Penalty and the Discovery of Innocence.* New York: Cambridge University Press.

Baumgartner, Frank R., and Bryan D. Jones. 2006. Policy Agendas Project Topic Codebook. Updated by E. Scott Adler and John Wilkerson. http://www .policyagendas.org/page/topic-codebook.

———. 2009. *Agendas and Instability in American Politics.* 2nd ed. Chicago: University of Chicago Press.

Baumgartner, Frank R., Bryan D. Jones, and Beth L. Leech. 1997. "Media Attention and Congressional Agendas." In *Do the Media Govern? Politicians, Voters and Reporters in America*, ed. Shanto Iyengar and Richard Reeves, 349–63. Thousand Oaks, CA: Sage.

Baumgartner, Frank R., Bryan D. Jones, and Michael C. MacLeod. 1998. "Lessons from the Trenches: Ensuring Quality, Reliability, and Usability in the Creation of a New Data Source." *Political Methodologist* 8 (2): 1–10.

Baumgartner, Frank R., Suzanna Linn, and Amber E. Boydstun. 2010. "The Decline of the Death Penalty: How Media Framing Changed Capital Punishment in America." In *Winning with Words: The Origins and Impact of Political Framing*, ed. Brian F. Schaffner and Patrick J. Sellers, 159–84. New York: Taylor and Francis.

Beaudoin, Christopher E., and Esther Thorson. 2002. "A Marketplace Theory of Media Use." *Mass Communication and Society* 5 (3): 241–62. doi:10.1207/ S15327825MCS0503_1.

Becker, Gary S. 1991. "A Note on Restaurant Pricing and Other Examples of Social Influences on Price." *Journal of Political Economy* 99 (5): 1109–16. doi:10.2307/2937660.

Behr, Roy L., and Shanto Iyengar. 1985. "Television News, Real-World Cues, and Changes in the Public Agenda." *Public Opinion Quarterly* 49 (1): 38–57. doi:10.1086/268900.

Bellafante, Ginia. 2005. "The Power of Images to Create a Cause." *New York Times*, March 27, 2012. http://www.nytimes.com/2005/03/27/weekinreview/ 27bella.html.

Bennett, W. Lance. 1990. "Toward a Theory of Press-State Relations in the United States." *Journal of Communication* 40 (2): 103–25. doi:10.1111/j.1460-2466.1990 .tb02265.x.

———. 2003. "The Burglar Alarm That Just Keeps Ringing: A Response to Zaller." *Political Communication* 20 (2): 131–38. doi:10.1080/10584600390211145.

Bennett, W. Lance, Regina G. Lawrence, and Steven Livingston. 2006. "None Dare Call It Torture: Indexing and the Limits of Press Independence in the Abu Ghraib Scandal." *Journal of Communication* 56 (3): 467–85. doi:10.1111/j.1460-2466.2006.00296.x.

———. 2007. *When the Press Fails: Political Power and the News Media from Iraq to Katrina*. Chicago: University of Chicago Press.

Berkowitz, Dan. 1990. "Redefining the Gatekeeping Metaphor for Local Television News." *Journal of Broadcasting and Electronic Media* 34 (1): 55–58. doi:10.1080/08838159009386725.

———. 1992. "Who Sets the Media Agenda? The Ability of Policymakers to Determine News Decisions." In *Public Opinion, the Press and Public Policy*, ed. David Kennamer, 81–103. Westport, CT: Praeger.

Bernstein, Carl, and Bob Woodward. 1994. *All the President's Men*. 2nd ed. New York: Simon and Schuster.

Bernstein, Nina. 2011. "On Campus, a Law Enforcement System to Itself." *New York Times*, November 12, 2011: A1. http://www.nytimes.com/2011/11/12/us/on-college-campuses-athletes-often-get-off-easy.html.

Bikhchandani, Sushil, David Hirshleifer, and Ivo Welch. 1992. "A Theory of Fads, Fashion, Custom, and Cultural Change as Informational Cascades." *Journal of Political Economy* 100 (5): 992–1026. doi:10.2307/2138632.

Bilham, Roger. 2010. "Lessons from the Haiti Earthquake." *Nature* 463 (18): 878–79. doi:10.1038/463878a.

Birkland, Thomas A. 1997. *After Disaster: Agenda Setting, Public Policy, and Focusing Events*. Washington, DC: Georgetown University Press.

———. 1998. "Focusing Events, Mobilization and Agenda Setting." *Journal of Public Policy* 18 (3): 53–74. doi:10.1017/S0143814X98000038.

Birkland, Thomas A., and Regina G. Lawrence. 2009. "Media Framing and Policy Change after Columbine." *American Behavioral Scientist* 52 (10): 1405–25. doi:10.1177/0002764209332555.

Blodget, Henry. 2010. "The Truth about Investigative Journalism (A Tweetifesto)." *Business Insider*. http://www.businessinsider.com/henry-blodget-the-truth-about-this-investigative-journalism-thing-a-tweetifesto-2010-3#-1.

Boczkowski, Pablo J. 2009. "Technology, Monitoring, and Imitation in Contemporary News Work." *Communication, Culture and Critique* 2 (1): 39–59. doi:10.1111/j.1753-9137.2008.01028.x.

Boushey, Graeme. 2010. *Policy Diffusion Dynamics in America*. New York: Cambridge University Press.

Boydstun, Amber E., Shaun Bevan, and Herschel F. Thomas. 2013. "The Importance of Attention Diversity and How to Measure It." Working manuscript.

Boydstun, Amber E., Anne Hardy, and Stefaan Walgrave. 2013. "Two Faces of Media Attention: Media Storm vs. Non Media Storm Coverage." Working manuscript.

Boydstun, Amber E., Jon Moody, and Herschel Thomas III. 2013. "Same Day, Different Agenda? A Comparison of News Coverage across Print, Television, and Online Media Outlets." Working manuscript.

Boydstun, Amber E., Rens Vliegenthart, Stefaan Walgrave, and Anne Hardy. 2013. "The Non-Linear Effects of Media Attention." Working manuscript.

Boyle, Thomas. 2001. "Intermedia Agenda-Setting in the 1996 Presidential Election." *Journalism and Mass Communication Quarterly* 78 (1): 26–44. doi:10.1177/107769900107800103.

Brader, Ted. 2006. *Campaigning for Hearts and Minds.* Chicago: University of Chicago Press.

Brandenburg, Heinz. 2005. "Journalists Embedded in Culture: War Stories as Political Strategy." In *Bring 'Em On: Media and Politics in the Iraq War*, ed. Lee Artz and Yahya R. Kamalipour, 225–38. Lanham, MD: Rowman and Littlefield.

Breunig, Christian. 2006. "The More Things Change, the More Things Stay the Same: A Comparative Analysis of Budget Punctuations." *Journal for European Public Policy* 13 (7): 1069–86. doi:10.1080/13501760600924167.

Breunig, Christian, and Bryan D. Jones. 2011. "Stochastic Process Methods with an Application to Budgetary Data." *Political Analysis* 19 (1): 103–17. doi:10.1093/pan/mpq038.

Browne, William P. 1990. "Organized Interests and Their Issue Niches: A Search for Pluralism in a Policy Domain." *Journal of Politics* 52 (2): 477–509. doi:http://dx.doi.org/10.2307/2131903.

Callaghan, Karen J., and Frauke K. Schnell. 2005. *Framing American Politics.* Pittsburgh, PA: University of Pittsburgh Press.

Carlson, Nicholas. 2010. "At Last—The Full Story of How Facebook Was Founded." *Business Insider*, March 5, 2010. http://www.businessinsider.com/how-facebook-was-founded-2010-3?op=1.

Carmines, Edward G., and James A. Stimson. 1989. *Issue Evolution: Race and the Transformation of American Politics.* Princeton, NJ: Princeton University Press.

Carrington, Paul D., and Roger C. Cramton. 2009. "Judicial Independence in Excess: Reviving the Judicial Duty of the Supreme Court." *94 Cornell Law Review* 587:627–28.

Casper, Jonathan D. 1976. "The Supreme Court and National Policy Making." *American Political Science Review* 70 (1): 50–63.

Cater, Douglass. 1959. *The Fourth Branch of Government.* Boston: Houghton Mifflin.

Cerf, Vinton. 2005. Letter to U.S. congressional hearing on "Net neutrality." http://voices.washingtonpost.com/posttech/Net%20Pioneers%20Letter%20 to%20Chairman%20Genachowski%20Oct09.pdf.

Chong, D., and J. N. Druckman. 2007a. "A Theory of Framing and Opinion Formation in Competitive Elite Environments." *Journal of Communication* 57 (1): 99–118. doi:10.1111/j.1460–2466.2006.00331.x.

———. 2007b. "Framing Theory." *Annual Review of Political Science* 10:103–26. doi:10.1146/annurev.polisci.10.072805.103054.

Cobb, Roger W., and Charles D. Elder. 1983. *Participation in American Politics: The Dynamics of Agenda-Building.* 2nd ed. Boston: Allyn and Bacon.

Cohen, Bernard. 1963. *The Press and Foreign Policy.* Princeton. NJ: Princeton University Press.

Cook, Timothy E. 1998. *Governing with the News: The News Media as a Political Institution.* Chicago: University of Chicago Press.

Crawford, Amanda J. 2012. "Killing Stalls Stand Your Ground Laws as NRA Lobbies in Alaska." *Bloomberg News,* March 29, 2012. http://www.bloomberg .com/news/2012-03-30/killing-stalls-stand-your-ground-laws-as-nra-lobbies -in-alaska.html.

Crouse, Timothy. 1972. *The Boys on the Bus.* New York: Random House.

d'Haenens, Leen, Nicholas Jankowski, and Ard Heuvelman. 2004. "News in Online and Print Newspapers: Differences in Reader Consumption and Recall." *New Media Society* 6 (3): 363–82. doi:10.1177/1461444804042520.

David, Paul A. 1985. "Clio and the Economics of QWERTY." *American Economic Review* 75 (2): 332–37.

De Souza, Raymond J. 2011. "The Coming Decade of Scandal and Shame." *National Post,* December 29, 2011. http://fullcomment.nationalpost.com/2011/12/ 29/father-raymond-j-de-souza-the-coming-decade-of-scandal-and-shame/.

de Waal, Ester, and Klaus Schönbach. 2008. "Presentation Style and Beyond: How Print Newspapers and Online News Expand Awareness of Public Affairs Issues." *Mass Communication and Society* 11 (2): 161–76. doi:10.1080/15205430701668113.

Dearing, James W., and Everett M. Rogers. 1996. *Agenda-Setting.* Thousand Oaks, CA: Sage Publications.

Delli Carpini, Michael X. 2004. "Mediating Democratic Engagement: The Impact of Communications on Citizens' Involvement in Political and Civic Life." In *Handbook of Political Communication Research,* ed. Linda L. Kaid, 395–434. New York: Lawrence Erlbaum Associates.

Delli Carpini, Michael X., and Scott Keeter. 2002. "The Internet and an Informed Citizenry." In *The Civic Web,* ed. David Anderson and Michael Cornfield, 129–53. Lanham, MD: Rowman and Littlefield.

Diamond, Edwin. 1993. *Behind the Times: Inside the New York Times.* New York: Villard Books.

Diermeier, Daniel, and Keith Krehbiel. 2003. "Institutionalism as a Methodology." *Journal of Theoretical Politics* 15 (2): 123–44. doi:10.1177/0951629803015002645.

Dimmick, John, Yan Chen, and Zhan Li. 2004. "Competition between the Internet and Traditional News Media: The Gratification-Opportunities Niche Dimension." *Journal of Media Economics* 17 (1): 19–33. doi:10.1207/s15327736me1701_2.

Domke, David, David P. Fan, Michael Fibison, Dhanvan V. Shah, Steven S. Smith, and Mark D. Watts. 1997. "News Media, Candidates and Issues, and Public Opinion in the 1996 Presidential Campaign." *Journalism and Mass Communication Quarterly* 74 (4): 718–37. doi:10.1177/107769909707400405.

Downs, Anthony. 1972. "Up and Down with Ecology: The 'Issue-Attention Cycle.'" *Public Interest* 28 (Summer): 38–50.

Druckman, James N. 2001. "On the Limits of Framing Effects: Who Can Frame?" *Journal of Politics* 63 (4): 1041–66. doi:http://dx.doi.org/10.1111/0022-3816.00100.

———. 2005. "Media Matter: How Newspapers and Television News Cover Campaigns and Influence Voters." *Political Communication* 22 (4): 463–81. doi:10.1080/10584600500311394.

Edwards, George C., III, Andrew Barrett, and Jeffrey Peake. 1997. "The Legislative Impact of Divided Government." *American Journal of Political Science* 41 (2): 545–63.

Edwards, George C., and B. Dan Wood. 1999. "Who Influences Whom? The President, Congress, and the Media." *American Political Science Review* 93 (2): 327–44.

Ehrlich, Matthew C. 2004. *Journalism in the Movies*. Champaign: University of Illinois Press.

Elmelund-Præstekær, Christian, and Charlotte Wien. 2008. "What's the Fuss About? The Interplay of Media Hypes and Politics." *International Journal of Press/Politics* 13 (3): 247–66. doi:10.1177/1940161208319292.

Entman, Robert M. 2003. "Cascading Activation: Contesting the White House's Frame after 9/11." *Political Communication* 20 (4): 415–32. doi:10.1080/10584600390244176.

Eshbaugh-Soha, Matthew, and Jeffrey S. Peake. 2004. "Presidential Influence over the Systemic Agenda." *Congress and the Presidency* 31 (2): 161–81.

ESPN. 2011. "Penn State to Pay AD's Legal Costs." *ESPN.com News Services*, November 6. http://espn.go.com/college-football/story/_/id/7199068/penn-state-nittany-lions-bar-accused-ex-coach-jerry-sandusky-campus.

Farrell, Henry, and Daniel W. Drezner. 2008. "The Power and Politics of Blogs." *Public Choice* 134 (1–2): 15–30. doi:10.1007/s11127-007-9198-1.

Fineout, Gary. 2012. "Trayvon Martin Case: Task Force Wants Changes in Stand Your Ground." *Christian Science Monitor*, April 30, 2012. http://www

.csmonitor.com/USA/Latest-News-Wires/2012/0430/Trayvon-Martin-case
-Task-force-wants-changes-in-Stand-Your-Ground.

Fisher, Louis. 2003. "Deciding on War against Iraq." *Perspectives on Politics* 32
(3): 135–40. doi:10.1080/10457090309604843.

Flemming, Roy B., and B. Dan Wood. 1999. "Attention to Issues in a System of
Separated Powers: The Macrodynamics of American Policy Agendas." *Journal of Politics* 61 (1): 76–108.

Forman, Tyrone A., and Amanda E. Lewis. 2006. "Racial Apathy and Hurricane
Katrina: The Social Anatomy of Prejudice in the Post–Civil Rights Era." *Du
Bois Review* 3 (1): 175–202. doi:10.1017/S1742058X06060127.

Franklin, Bob, and David Murphy. 1991. *What News? The Market, Politics and
the Local Press*. London: Routledge.

Franklin, Charles. 2007. "Three Elements of Iraq War Opinion." Pollster.com.
http://www.huffingtonpost.com/charles-franklin/three_elements_of_iraq
_war_opi_b_722901.html.

Freeh, Louis. 2012. "Report of the Special Investigative Counsel Regarding the Actions of The Pennsylvania State University Related to the Child Sexual Abuse
Committed by Gerald A. Sandusky." Freeh Sporking and Sullivan, LLP.

Fritz, Ben, Bryan Keefer, and Brendan Nyhan. 2004. *All the President's Spin:
George W. Bush, the Media, and the Truth*. New York: Simon and Schuster.

Galtung, Johan, and Mari Holmboe Ruge. 1965. "The Structure of Foreign News."
Journal of Peace Research 2 (1): 64–91. doi:10.1177/002234336500200104.

Gamson, William A., and Andre Modigliani. 1987. "The Changing Culture
of Affirmative Action." In *Research in Political Sociology*, ed. Richard G.
Braungart and Margaret M. Braungart, 137–77. Greenwich, CT: JAI Press.

———. 1989. "Media Discourse and Public Opinion on Nuclear Power: A Constructionist Approach." *American Journal of Sociology* 95 (1): 1–37. doi:10
.2307/2780405.

Gandy, Oscar H., Jr. 1982. *Beyond Agenda Setting: Information Subsidies and
Public Policy*. Norwood, NJ: Ablex Publishers.

Ganim, Sara. 2011. "Jerry Sandusky, Former Penn State Football Staffer, Subject of Grand Jury Investigation." *Harrisburg Patriot-News*, March 31, 2011.
http://www.pennlive.com/midstate/index.ssf/2011/03/jerry_sandusky_former
_penn_sta.html.

Gans, Herbert J. 2004. *Deciding What's News: A Study of CBS Evening News,
NBC Nightly News, Newsweek, and Time*. Evanston, IL: Northwestern University Press.

Gaventa, John. 1980. *Power and Powerlessness: Quiescence and Rebellion in an
Appalachian Valley*. Chicago: University of Chicago Press.

Gladwell, Malcolm. 2000. *The Tipping Point: How Little Things Can Make a
Big Difference*. Boston: Little, Brown.

Glazier, Rebecca A., and Amber E. Boydstun. 2012. "The President, the Press, and the War: A Tale of Two Framing Agendas." *Political Communication* 29 (4): 428–46. doi:10.1080/10584609.2012.721870.

Golan, Guy. 2006. "Intermedia Agenda Setting and Global News Coverage." *Journalism Studies* 7 (2): 323–33. doi:10.1080/14616700500533643.

Goodnough, Abby. 2003. "Governor of Florida Orders Woman Fed in Right-to-Die Case." *New York Times*, October 22, 2003.

Graber, Doris. 1971. "The Press as Public Opinion Resource during the 1968 Presidential Campaign." *Public Opinion Quarterly* 35 (2): 162–82. doi:10.1086/267888.

———. 2003a. "The Media and Democracy: Beyond Myths and Stereotypes." *Annual Review of Political Science* 6 (1): 139–60. doi:10.1146/annurev.polisci.6.121901.085707

———. 2003b. "The Rocky Road to New Paradigms: Modernizing News and Citizenship Standards." *Political Communication* 20 (2): 145–48. doi:10.1080/10584600390211163.

———. 2006. *Mass Media and American Politics.* 7th ed. Washington, DC: CQ Press.

———. 2007. *Media Power in Politics.* Washington, DC: CQ Press.

Graefe, Andreas, and J. Scott Armstrong. 2012. "Predicting Elections from the Most Important Issue: A Test of the Take-the-Best Heuristic." *Journal of Behavioral Decision Making* 25 (1): 41–48. doi:10.1002/bdm.710.

Granovetter, Mark. 1978. "Threshold Models of Collective Behavior." *American Journal of Sociology* 83 (6): 1420–43. doi:10.1086/226707.

———. 1985. "Economic Action and Social Structure: The Problem of Embeddedness." *American Journal of Sociology* 91 (3): 481.

Granovetter, Mark, and Roland Soong. 1988. "Threshold Models of Diversity: Chinese Restaurants, Residential Segregation, and the Spiral of Silence." *Sociological Methodology* 18: 69–104.

Green, Penelope. 2010. "The Audacity of Taupe." *New York Times*, September 2, 2010, D1.

Gross, Kimberly. 2008. "Framing Persuasive Appeals: Episodic and Thematic Framing, Emotional Response, and Policy Opinion." *Political Psychology* 29 (2): 169–92. doi:10.1111/j.1467-9221.2008.00622.x.

Grossman, Emiliano. 2011. "The Agenda-Setting Power of 'Le Monde': Issue Dynamics and Typology in France." Paper presented at Comparative Policy Agendas Conference, Catania, Italy, June 23–25.

Grusin, Elinor Kelley, and Sandra H. Utt. 2005. *Media in an American Crisis: Studies of September 11, 2001.* Lanham, MD: University Press of America.

Hallin, Daniel, and Paolo Mancini. 2004. *Comparing Media Systems. Three Models of Media and Politics.* New York: Cambridge University Press.

Hamilton, James T. 2004. *All the News That's Fit to Sell: How the Market Transforms Information into News.* Princeton, NJ: Princeton University Press.

Hänggli, Regula. 2013. "Flow of Messages: Framing and Opinion Formation in Direct-Democratic Campaigns." Working manuscript.

Heclo, Hugh. 1978. "Issue Networks and the Executive Branch." In *The New American Political System*, ed. Anthony King, 87–124. Washington, DC: American Enterprise Institute.

Henley, Jon. 2010. "How the *Boston Globe* Exposed the Abuse Scandal that Rocked the Catholic Church." *The Guardian*, April 21, 2010. http://www .guardian.co.uk/world/2010/apr/21/boston-globe-abuse-scandal-catholic.

Hindman, Matthew. 2009. *The Myth of Digital Democracy*. Princeton, NJ: Princeton University Press.

Hindman, Matthew, Kostas Tsioutsiouliklis, and Judy A. Johnson. 2003. "'Googlearchy': How a Few Heavily-Linked Sites Dominate Politics on the Web." Paper presented at the Annual Meeting of the Midwest Political Science Association. Chicago, IL. April 3–6.

———. 2004. "Measuring Media Diversity Online and Offline: Evidence from Political Websites." Presented at the 32nd Annual Telecommunications Policy Research Conference, George Mason University, September.

Hirsch, Joy. 2005. "Raising Consciousness." *Journal of Clinical Investigation* 115 (5): 1102–3. doi:10.1172/JCI25320.

Hosking, Jonathan R. M. 1990. "L-Moments: Analysis and Estimation of Distributions Using Linear Combinations of Order Statistics." *Journal of the Royal Statistical Society* 52 (1): 105–24. doi:10.1177/0002716296546001006.

Hoskins, Colin, Stuart McFayden, and Adam Finn. 2004. *Media Economics: Applying Economics to New and Traditional Media*. Thousand Oaks, CA: Sage Publications.

Iyengar, Shanto. 1991. *Is Anyone Responsible? How Television Frames Political Issues*. Chicago: University of Chicago Press.

———. 1996. "Framing Responsibility for Political Issues." *Annals of the American Academy of Political and Social Science* 546 (12): 59–70.

Iyengar, Shanto, and Donald R. Kinder. 1987. *News That Matters: Television and American Opinion*. Chicago: University of Chicago Press.

Iyengar, Shanto, and Jennifer A. McGrady. 2007. *Media Politics: A Citizen's Guide*. New York: W. W. Norton.

Iyengar, Shanto, Helmut Norpoth, and Kyu S. Hanh. 2004. "Consumer Demand for Election News: The Horserace Sells." *Journal of Politics* 66 (1): 157–75. doi:10.1046/j.1468-2508.2004.00146.x.

Jacobs, Andrew. 2004. "The Struggle for Iraq: The National Mood; Shock over Abuse Reports, but Support for the Troops." *New York Times*, May 8, 2004. http://www .nytimes.com/2004/05/08/world/struggle-for-iraq-national-mood-shock-over -abuse-reports-but-support-for-troops.html?pagewanted=2&src=pm.

Jacoby, Susan. 2012. "Taking Responsibility for Death." *New York Times*,

March 30, 2012: A19. http://www.nytimes.com/2012/03/31/opinion/taking -responsibility-for-death.html.

Jennings, Will, and Christopher Wlezien. 2011. "Distinguishing between Most Important Problems and Issues?" *Public Opinion Quarterly* 75 (3): 545–55. doi:10.1093/poq/nfr025.

Jensen, Klaus Bruhn. 1986. *Making Sense of the News: Towards a Theory and an Empirical Model of Reception for the Study of Mass Communication.* Aarhus, Denmark: Aarhus University Press.

Johnson, Clay A. 2012. *The Information Diet.* Sebastopol, CA: O'Reilly Media.

Jones, Bryan. 1994. *Reconceiving Decision-Making in Democratic Politics: Attention, Choice and Public Policy.* Chicago: University of Chicago Press.

———. 2001. *Politics and the Architecture of Choice.* Chicago: University of Chicago Press.

Jones, Bryan D., and Frank R. Baumgartner. 2005. *The Politics of Attention: How Government Prioritizes Problems.* Chicago: University of Chicago Press.

Jones, Bryan D., Heather Larsen-Price, and John Wilkerson. 2009. "Representation and American Governing Institutions." *Journal of Politics* 71 (1): 277–90. doi:http://dx.doi.org/10.1017/S002238160809018X.

Jones, Bryan D., Tracy Sulkin, and Heather A. Larsen. 2003. "Policy Punctuations in American Political Institutions." *American Political Science Review* 97 (1): 151–69. doi:http://dx.doi.org/10.1017/S0003055403000583.

Kahneman, Daniel. 2003. "Maps of Bounded Rationality: Psychology for Behavioral Economics." *American Economic Review* 93 (5): 1449–75. doi:10.2307/1914185.

Kahneman, Daniel, and Amos Tversky. 1979. "Prospect Theory: An Analysis of Decision under Risk." *Econometrica* 47: 263–91.

Kaye, Barbara K., and Thomas J. Johnson. 2002. "Online and in the Know: Uses and Gratifications of the Web for Political Information." *Journal of Broadcasting and Electronic Media* 46 (1): 54–71. doi:10.1207/s15506878jobem4601_4.

Keller, Bill. 2006. "Talk to the Newsroom." *New York Times* http://www.nytimes .com/2006/04/14/business/media/14asktheeditors.html?pagewanted=all.

———. 2007. "Not Dead Yet: The Newspaper in the Days of Digital Anarchy." Hugo Young Memorial Lecture delivered at Chatham House, London, England, November 29. http://www.guardian.co.uk/media/2007/nov/29/ pressandpublishing.digitalmedia1.

King, Oona. 2005. "An American Journey." *The Guardian*, October 17, 2005. http://www.guardian.co.uk/politics/2005/oct/18/usa.world.

Kingdon, John W. 1993. "How Do Issues Get on Public Policy Agendas?" In *Sociology and the Public Agenda*, ed. William Julius Wilson, 40–50. Newbury Park, CA: Sage.

———. 1995. *Agendas, Alternatives, and Public Policies.* New York: Harper Collins.

Kirkpatrick, David D. 2005. "TV Host Says U.S. Paid Him to Back Policy." *New York Times*, January 8, 2005. http://www.nytimes.com/2005/01/08/national/08education.html.

Kollman, Ken. 1998. *Outside Lobbying: Public Opinion and Interest Group Strategies.* Princeton, NJ: Princeton University Press.

Kovach, Bill, and Tom Rosenstiel. 2007. *The Elements of Journalism: What Newspeople Should Know and the Public Should Expect.* New York: Three Rivers Press.

Kuypers, Jim A. 2006. *Bush's War: Media Bias and Justifications for War in a Terrorist Age.* Lanham, MD: Rowman and Littlefield.

Lake, Celinda, and Jennifer Sosin. 1998. "Public Opinion Polling and the Future of Democracy." *National Civic Review* 87 (1): 65–70. doi:10.1002/ncr.87105.

Lasswell, Harold. 1936. *Who Gets What, When, and How?* New York: McGraw-Hill.

Lawrence, Regina G. 2000a. "Game-Framing the Issues: Tracking the Strategy Frame in Public Policy News." *Political Communication* 17 (2): 93–114. doi:10.1080/105846000198422.

———. 2000b. *The Politics of Force: Media and the Construction of Police Brutality.* Berkeley: University of California Press.

———. 2001. "Defining Events: Problem Definition in the Media Arena." In *Politics, Discourse, and American Society*, ed. Roderick P. Hart and Bartholomew H. Sparrow, 91–110. New York: Rowman and Littlefield.

Lawrence, Regina G., and Thomas A. Birkland. 2004. "Guns, Hollywood, and School Safety: Defining the School-Shooting Problem across Public Arenas." *Social Science Quarterly* 85 (5): 1193–1207. doi:10.1111/j.0038–4941.2004.00271.

Ledgerwood, Alison, and Amber E. Boydstun. 2013. "Sticky Prospects: Loss Frames are Cognitively Stickier than Gain Frames." *Journal of Experimental Psychology: General.*

Leskovec, Jure, Lars Backstrom, and Jon Klienberg. 2009. "Meme-tracking and the Dynamics of the News Cycle." Paper read at ACM SIGDKK International Conference on Knowledge Discovery and Data Mining, Paris, France, June 28–July 1.

Lewin, Kurt. 1947. "Frontiers in Group Dynamics II: Channels of Group Life; Social Planning and Action Research." *Human Relations* 1 (2): 143–53. doi:10.1177/001872674700100201.

———. 1951. *Field Theory in Social Science: Selected Theoretical Papers.* New York: Harper Bros.

Lichtblau, Eric. 2012. "Martin Death Spurs Group to Readjust Policy Focus." *New York Times*, April 17: A13. http://www.nytimes.com/2012/04/18/us/trayvon-martin-death-spurs-group-to-readjust-policy-focus.html.

Lippmann, Walter. 1922. *Public Opinion.* New York: Free Press.

Livingston, S. 1997. "Beyond the 'CNN-Effect': The Media-Foreign Policy Dynamic." In *Politics and the Press: The News Media and Their Influences*, ed. P. Norris, 291–314. Boulder, CO: Lynne Rienner.

Livingston, Steven, and W. Lance Bennett. 2003. "Gatekeeping, Indexing, and Live-Event News: Is Technology Altering the Construction of News?" *Political Communication* 20 (4): 363–80. doi:10.1080/10584600390244121.

Madden, Mark. 2011. "Sandusky a State Secret." *Timesonline*, April 4, 2011. http://www.timesonline.com/columnists/sports/mark_madden/madden-sandusky-a-state-secret/article_863d3c82-5e6f-11e0-9ae5-001a4bcf6878.html.

Mahoney, Christine. 2008. *Brussels versus the Beltway: Advocacy in the United States and the European Union.* Washington, DC: Georgetown University Press.

Mayhew, David R. 1974. *Congress: The Electoral Connection.* New Haven, CT: Yale University Press.

McCarthy, Rory, Duncan Campbell, and Richard Norton-Taylor. 2003. "Fear of $80bn Iraq Bill Moves Bush to Address Nation." *The Guardian*, September 7. http://www.guardian.co.uk/world/2003/sep/08/usa.iraq.

McCombs, Maxwell. 2004. *Setting the Agenda: The Mass Media and Public Opinion.* Cambridge: Polity Press.

McCombs, Maxwell, Edna Einsidel, and David Weaver. 1991. *Contemporary Public Opinion: Issues and the News.* Hillsdale, NJ: Erlbaum.

McCombs, Maxwell, Lance Holbert, Spiro Kiousis, and Wayne Wanta. 2011. *The News and Public Opinion: Media Effects on Civic Life.* Cambridge: Polity Press.

McCombs, Maxwell, and Amy Reynolds. 2002. "News Influence on Our Pictures in the World." In *Media Effects: Advances in Theory and Research*, ed. Jennings Bryant and Dolf Zillmann, 1–18. Mahwah, NJ: Erlbaum.

McCombs, Maxwell E., and Donald L. Shaw. 1972. "The Agenda-Setting Function of Mass Media." *Public Opinion Quarterly* 36 (2): 176–87. doi:10.1086/267990.

McCombs, Maxwell. E., Donald L. Shaw, and David Weaver. 1997. *Communication and Democracy. Exploring the Intellectual Frontiers in Agenda-Setting Theory.* Mahwah, NJ: Lawrence Erlbaum Associates.

McCubbins, Mathew D., and Thomas Schwartz. 1984. "Congressional Oversight Overlooked: Police Patrols versus Fire Alarms." *American Journal of Political Science* 28 (1): 165–79.

McDonald, Mark. 2009. "CNN Interview Sets Off Skeptics on Balloon Boy's Story." *New York Times*, October 17, 2009. http://www.nytimes.com/2009/10/17/us/17blitzer.html.

McManus, John. 1995. "A Market-Based Model of News Production." *Communication Theory* 5 (4): 301–38. doi:10.1111/j.1468–2885.1995.tb00113.x.

Min, Seong-Jae, and John C. Feaster. 2010. "Missing Children in National News Coverage: Racial and Gender Representations of Missing Children Cases." *Communication Research Reports* 27 (3): 207–16. doi:10.1080/0882409100 3776289.

Molotch, Harvey, and Marilyn Lester. 1974. "News as Purposive Behavior: On the Strategic Use of Routine Events, Accidents, and Scandals." *American Sociological Review* 39 (1): 101–12.

Mullainathan, Sendhil, and Andrei Shleifer. 2005. "The Market for News." *American Economic Review* 95 (4): 1031–53.

Nelson, Barbara J. 1984. *Making an Issue of Child Abuse: Political Agenda Setting for Social Problems*. Chicago: University of Chicago Press.

Nelson, Thomas E., Rosalee A. Clawson, and Zoe Oxley. 1997. "Media Framing of a Civil Liberties Controversy and its Effect on Tolerance." *American Political Science Review* 91 (3): 567–84.

Nelson, Thomas E., and Zoe M. Oxley. 1999. "Framing Effects on Belief Importance and Opinion." *Journal of Politics* 61 (4): 1040–67. doi:http://dx.doi .org/10.2307/2647553.

Newman, Maria. 2005. "Justices Set Back Florida's Right-to-Die Case." *New York Times*, January 24, 2005. http://www.nytimes.com/2005/01/24/national/ 24cnd-schia.html.

Norris, Pippa. 1996. "Does Television Erode Social Capital? A Reply to Putnam." *PS: Political Science and Politics* 29 (3): 474–80.

———. 2011. *Democratic Deficit: Critical Citizens Revisited*. New York: Cambridge University Press.

Nusca, Andrew. 2010. "The Truth about the Price of Investigative Journalism Online." *The Editorialiste*. http://editorialiste.blogspot.com/2010/03/truth -about-price-of-investigative.html.

Padgett, John F. 1980. "Bounded Rationality in Budgetary Research." *American Political Science Review* 74 (2): 354–72.

———. 1981. "Hierarchy and Ecological Control in Federal Budgetary Decision Making." *American Journal of Sociology* 87 (1): 75–129.

Page, Benjamin. 1996. "The Mass Media as Political Actors." *PS: Political Science and Politics* 29 (1): 20–24.

Page, Scott E. 2007. *The Difference: How the Power of Diversity Creates Better Groups, Firms, Schools, and Societies*. Princeton, NJ: Princeton University Press.

Pappano, Laura. 2012. "How Big-Time Sports Ate College Life." *New York Times*, January 22, 2012: ED22. http://www.nytimes.com/2012/01/22/education/edlife/ how-big-time-sports-ate-college-life.html.

Parenti, Michael. 1986. *Inventing Reality: The Politics of the Mass Media*. New York: St. Martin's Press.

Patterson, Thomas E. 1994. *Out of Order*. New York: Vintage Books.

———. 2000. "Doing Well and Doing Good: How Soft News and Critical Journalism Are Shrinking the New Audience and Weakening Democracy—And
What News Outlets Can Do about It." Research Report. Cambridge, MA:
Harvard University, Joan Shorenstein Center on the Press, Politics, and Public Policy.

———. 2003. "The Search for a Standard: Markets and Media." *Political Communication* 20 (2): 139–43. doi:10.1080/10584600390211154.

Peake, Jeffrey S., and Matthew Eshbaugh-Soha. 2008. "The Agenda-Setting Impact of Major Presidential TV Addresses." *Political Communication* 25 (2):
113–37. doi:10.1080/10584600701641490.

Penn, Mark J. (with E. Kinney Zalesne). 2007. *Microtrends: The Small Forces
behind Tomorrow's Big Changes.* New York: Twelve.

Perez-Peña, Richard. 2009. "New York Times Accepting Display Ads on Its Front
Page." *New York Times,* January 5. http://www.nytimes.com/2009/01/05/
technology/05iht-times.3.19093143.html.

Pfau, Michael, Elaine M. Wittenberg, Carolyn Jackson, Phil Mehringer, Rob
Lanier, Michael Hatfield, and Kristina Brockman. 2005. "Embedding Journalists in Military Combat Units: How Embedding Alters Television News
Stories." *Mass Communication and Society* 8 (3): 179–95. doi:10.1207/
s15327825mcs0803_1.

Pfetsch, Barbara. 2007. "Government News Management: Institutional Ap-
proaches and Strategies in Three Western Democracies." In *The Politics of
News: The News of Politics* ed. Doris Graber, Dennis McQuail and Pippa
Norris, 71–97. Washington, DC: Congressional Quarterly Press.

Plasser, Fritz. 2005. "From Hard to Soft News Standards?: How Political Journalists in Different Media Systems Evaluate Shifting Quality of News."
Harvard International Journal of Press/Politics 10 (2): 47–68. doi:10.1177/
1081180X05277746.

Popkin, Samuel L. 1991. *The Reasoning Voter: Communication and Persuasion
in Presidential Campaigns.* Chicago: University of Chicago Press.

Price, Vincent, and David Tewksbury. 1997. "News Values and Public Opin-
ion: A Theoretical Account of Media Priming and Framing." In *Progress in
Communication Sciences: Advances in Persuasion,* ed. George Barnett and
Frank J. Boster, 173–212. Greenwich, CT: Amblex Publishing.

Price, Vincent, David Tewksbury, and Elizabeth Powers. 1997. "Switching Trains
of Thought: The Impact of News Frames on Readers' Cognitive Responses."
Communication Research 24 (5): 481–506. doi:10.1177/009365097024005002.

Prior, Markus. 2003. "Any Good News in Soft News? The Impact of Soft News
Preference on Political Knowledge." *Political Communication* 20 (2): 149–71.
doi:10.1080/10584600390211172.

Rafail, Patrick S., Edward T. Walker, Winston B. Tripp, and John D. McCarthy.
2008. "Queuing the News that's Fit to Print: An Analysis of Page Placement

Patterns for Protest Events in the *New York Times*, 1960–1990." Paper presented at American Sociological Association Annual Meeting, Boston, MA. July 31.

Reese, Stephen D. 1991. "Setting the Media's Agenda: A Power Balance Perspective." *Communication Yearbook* 14:309–40.

Reese, Stephen D. and Seth C. Lewis. 2009. "Framing the War on Terror: The Internalization of Policy in the US Press." *Journalism* 10 (6): 777–797. doi:10.1177/1464884909344480.

Reese, Stephen D., and Lucig H. Danielian. 1989. "Intermedia Influence and the Drugs Issue: Converging on Cocaine." In *Communication Campaigns about Drugs: Government, Media, and the Public*, ed. Pamela Shoemaker, 29–45. Hillsdale NJ: Lawrence Erlbaum Associates.

Repetto, Robert C. 2006. *Punctuated Equilibrium and the Dynamics of U.S. Environmental Policy*. New Haven, CT: Yale University Press.

Rhodes, R.A.W. 2007. "Understanding Governance: Ten Years On." *Organization Studies* 28 (8): 1243–64. doi:10.1177/0170840607076586.

Riker, William H. 1986. *The Art of Political Manipulation*. New Haven, CT: Yale University Press.

Rochefort, David A., and Roger W. Cobb. 1994. *The Politics of Problem Definition: Shaping the Policy Agenda*. Lawrence: University Press of Kansas.

Schattschneider, E. E. 1960. *The Semisovereign People: A Realist's View of Democracy in America*. New York: Holt, Rinehart and Winston.

Schelling, Thomas C. 1972. "A Process of Residential Segregation: Neighborhood Tipping." In *Racial Discrimination in Economic Life*, ed. Anthony Pascal, 157–84. Lexington, MA: D. C. Heath.

Scheufele, Dietram A. 2000. "Agenda-Setting, Priming, and Framing Revisited: Another Look at Cognitive Effects of Political Communication." *Mass Communication and Society* 2 (3): 297–316. doi:10.1207/S15327825MCS0323_07.

Scheufele, Dietram A., and David Tewksbury. 2007. "Framing, Agenda Setting, and Priming: The Evolution of Three Media Effect Models." *Journal of Communication* 57 (1): 9–20. doi:10.1111/j.0021-9916.2007.00326.x.

Schmitt, Eric. 2004. "Troops' Queries Leave Rumsfeld on the Defensive." *New York Times*, December 9. http://www.nytimes.com/2004/12/09/international/middleeast/09rumsfeld.html.

Schmitz, Gregor Peter, and Thomas Schulz. 2010. "Interview with Washington Post Editor, part 2, "Newspapers Have Some Control over their Destiny." *Spiegel*, May 20, 2010. http://www.spiegel.de/international/business/spiegel-interview-with-washington-post-editor-we-should-not-let-nostalgia-for-newspapers-cloud-our-thinking-a-693985-2.html.

Schneider, Anne, and Helen Ingram. 1993. "Social Construction of Target Populations: Implications for Politics and Policy." *American Political Science Review* 87 (2): 334–47.

Schönbach, Klaus, Ester de Waal, and Edmund Lauf. 2005. "Online and Print Newspapers: Their Impact on the Extent of the Perceived Public Agenda." *European Journal of Communication* 20 (2): 245–58. doi:10.1177/0267323 105052300.

Schudson, M. 1997. "The Sociology of News Production." In *Social Meanings of News: A Text Reader*, ed. Daniel Allen Berkowitz, 7–22. Thousand Oaks, CA: Sage. doi:10.1177/016344389011003002.

———. 1998. *The Good Citizen: A History of American Public Life.* New York: Free Press.

———. 2002. "The News Media as Political Institutions." *Annual Review of Political Science* 5 (1): 249–69. doi:10.1146/annurev.polisci.5.111201.115816.

———. 2003. *The Sociology of News.* New York: W. W. Norton.

Seelye, Katharine Q. 2006a. "Times to Reduce Page Size and Close a Plant in 2008." *New York Times*, July 18. http://www.nytimes.com/2006/07/18/business/media/18web.html.

———. 2006b. "In Tough Times, a Redesigned Journal." *New York Times*, December 4. http://www.nytimes.com/2006/12/04/business/media/04journal.html.

Segal, Jeffrey A., and Harold J. Spaeth. 2002. *The Supreme Court and the Attitudinal Model Revisited.* New York: Cambridge University Press.

Sellers, Patrick. 2010. *Cycles of Spin: Strategic Communication in the US Congress.* Cambridge: Cambridge University Press.

Sellers, Patrick J., and Brian F. Schaffner. 2009. *Winning with Words: The Origins and Impact of Framing.* New York: Routledge Press.

Selnow, Gary W. 1998. *Electronic Whistle-Stops: The Impact of the Internet on American Politics.* Westport, CT: Praeger.

Sharkey, Patrick. 2007. "Survival and Death in New Orleans: An Empirical Look at the Human Impact of Katrina." *Journal of Black Studies* 37 (4): 482–501. doi:10.1177/0021934706296188.

Shaw, Donald L., and Maxwell McCombs. 1977. *The Emergence of American Political Issues: The Agenda-Setting Function of the Press.* St. Paul, MN: West Publishing.

Shepsle, Kenneth A. 1979. "Institutional Arrangements and Equilibrium in Multidimensional Voting Models." *American Journal of Political Science* 23 (1): 27–59. doi:10.2307/2110770.

Shepsle, Kenneth A., and Barry R. Weingast. 1981. "Structure-Induced Equilibrium and Legislative Choice." *Public Choices* 37 (3): 503–19. doi:10.1007/BF00133748.

———. 1987. "The Institutional Foundations of Committee Power." *American Political Science Review* 81 (1): 85–104.

Shiller, Robert J. 1995. "Conversation, Information, and Herd Behavior." *American Economic Review* 85 (2): 181–85.

———. 2000. *Irrational Exuberance.* Princeton, NJ: Princeton University Press.

Shoemaker, Pamela J. 1996. "Hardwired for News: Using Biological and Cultural Evolution to Explain the Surveillance Function." *Journal of Communication* 46 (3): 32–47. doi:10.1111/j.1460-2466.1996.tb01487.x

Shoemaker, Pamela J. and Tim P. Vos. 2008. "Media Gatekeeping." In *An Integrated Approach to Communication Theory and Research*, ed. Michael B. Salwen and Don W. Stacks, 75–89. New York: Routledge.

Shoemaker, Pamela J., and Tim P. Vos. 2009. *Gatekeeping Theory*. New York: Routledge.

Simon, Herbert A. 1957. *Models of Man, Social and Rational: Mathematical Essays on Rational Human Behavior in a Social Setting*. New York: John Wiley and Sons.

Skewes, Elizabeth A. 2007. *Message Control: How News Is Made on the Presidential Campaign Trail*. Lanham, MD: Rowman and Littlefield.

Smith, Conrad. 1992. *Media and Apocalypse: News Coverage of the Yellowstone Forest Fires, Exxon Valdez Oil Spill, and Loma Prieta Earthquake*. Westport, CT: Greenwood Press.

Smith, Valerie. 1990. "Split Affinities: The Case of Interracial Rape." In *Conflicts in Feminism*, ed. Marianne Hirsch and Evelyn Fox Keller, 271–87. New York: Routledge.

Snell, Tracy L. 2006. "Capital Punishment, 2005." NCJ-215083. *Bureau of Justice Statistics Bulletin*, December. http://bjs.ojp.usdoj.gov/content/pub/pdf/cp05.pdf .

Snow, David A., E. Burke Rochford Jr., Steven K. Worden, and Robert D. Benford. 1986. "Frame Alignment Processes, Micromobilization, and Movement Participation." *American Sociological Review* 51 (4): 464–81. doi:10.2307/2095581

Sornette, Didier. 2003. *Why Stock Markets Crash: Critical Events in Complex Financial Systems*. Princeton, NJ: Princeton University Press.

Soroka, Stuart N. 2002. *Agenda-Setting Dynamics in Canada*. Vancouver: UBC Press.

———. 2003. "Media, Public Opinion and Foreign Policy." *Harvard Journal of Press and Politics* 8 (1): 27–48. doi:10.1177/1081180X02238783.

———. 2006. "Good News and Bad News: Asymmetric Responses to Economic Information." *Journal of Politics* 68 (2): 372–85. doi:http://dx.doi.org/10.1111/j.1468-2508.2006.00413.x.

Sparrow, Bartholomew H. 1998. *Uncertain Guardians: The News Media as a Political Institution*. Chicago: University of Chicago Press.

———. 2006. "A Research Agenda for an Institutional Media." *Political Communication* 23 (2): 145–57. doi:10.1080/10584600600629695.

Spencer, Tom. 2002. "Truth and Public Affairs." *Journal of Public Affairs* 2 (3): 186–89. doi:10.1002/pa.109.

Stacy, Mitch. 2006. "Schiavo Case Prompts More Living Wills." Associated Press, March 30. http://www.uslivingwillregistry.com/Schiavo.shtm.

Strauss, Peter L. 1987. "One Hundred Fifty Cases per Year: Some Implications of the Supreme Court's Limited Resources for Judicial Review of Agency Action." *Columbia Law Review* 87 (6): 1093–1136.

Strömbäck, Jesper, and Spiro Kiousis. 2010. "A New Look at Agenda-Setting Effects—Comparing the Predictive Power of Overall Political News Consumption and Specific News Media Consumption across Different Media Channels and Media Types." *Journal of Communication* 60 (2): 271–92. doi: 10.1111/j.1460-2466.2010.01482.x.

Strupp, Joe. 2005. "Swapping Scoops: Every Night the NY Times and Wash Post Exchange Front Pages." *Editor and Publisher*, September 15, 2005. http://www.editorandpublisher.com/Archive/Swapping-Scoops-Every-Night -the-NY-Times-and-Wash-Post-Exchange-Front-Pages-for-the-Following -Day.

Sudore, Rebecca L., C. Seth Landefield, Steven Z. Pantilat, Kathryn M. Noyes, and Dean Schillinger. 2008. "Reach and Impact of a Mass Media Event among Vulnerable Patients: The Terri Schiavo Story." *Journal of General Internal Medicine* 23 (11): 1854–57. doi:10.1007/s11606-008-0733-7.

Surowiecki, James. 2005. *The Wisdom of Crowds: Why the Many Are Smarter Than the Few and How Collective Wisdom Shapes Business, Economies, Societies and Nations.* New York: Doubleday.

Terry, Karen J., Margaret Leland Smith, Katarina Schuth, James R. Kelly, Brenda Vollman, and Christina Massey. 2011. "The Causes and Context of Sexual Abuse of Minors by Catholic Priests in the United States, 1950–2010." Presented to the United States Conference of Catholic Bishops, John Jay College, Washington, DC.

Tewksbury, David, and Scott Althaus. 2000. "Differences in Knowledge Acquisition among Readers of the Paper and Online Versions of National Newspaper." *Journalism and Mass Communication Quarterly* 77 (3): 457–79. doi:10.1177/107769900007700301.

Tewksbury, David, and Jason Rittenberg. 2012. *News on the Internet: Information and Citizenship in the 21st Century.* Oxford: Oxford University Press.

Time. 1974. "Covering Watergate: Success and Backlash." July 8. http://www .time.com/time/magazine/article/0,9171,943934,00.html.

Timpane, John. 2012. "Did Media Fan Flames over Paterno?" *Philadelphia Inquirer*, January 25, 2012. http://articles.philly.com/2012-01-25/news/30663370 _1_sexual-abuse-media-coverage-paterno.

Tyler, Amanda L. 2010. "Setting the Supreme Court's Agenda: Is There a Place for Certification?" *George Washington Law Review* 78:101–18.

Van Belle, Douglas A. 2003. "Bureaucratic Responsiveness to the News Media: Comparing the Influence of the *New York Times* and Network Television News Coverage on US Foreign Aid Allocations." *Political Communication* 20 (3): 263–85. doi:10.1177/107769900007700301.

Varian, Hal. 1995. "The Information Economy." *Scientific American*, September, 200–201.

Vasterman, Peter L. M. 2005. "Media-Hype: Self-Reinforcing News Waves, Journalistic Standards and the Construction of Social Problems." *European Journal of Communication* 20 (4): 508–30. doi:10.1177/0267323105058254.

Viera, Mark. 2011. "Former Coach at Penn State Is Charged with Abuse." *New York Times*, November 5, 2011. http://www.nytimes.com/2011/11/06/sports/ncaafootball/former-coach-at-penn-state-is-charged-with-abuse.html.

Vliegenthart, Rens, and Stefaan Walgrave. 2008. "The Contingency of Intermedia Agenda-Setting. A Longitudinal Study in Belgium." *Journalism and Mass Communication Quarterly* 85 (4): 860–77. doi:10.1177/107769900808500409.

———. 2010. "When Media Matter for Politics. Partisan Moderators of Mass Media's Agenda-Setting Influence on Parliament in Belgium." *Party Politics* 17 (3): 321–42.

Walgrave, Stefaan, and Rens Vliegenthart. 2010. "Why Are Policy Agendas Punctuated? Friction and Cascading in Parliament and Mass Media in Belgium." *Journal for European Public Policy* 17 (8): 1145–68. doi:10.1080/1350 1763.2010.513562.

White, David Manning. 1950. "The Gatekeeper." *Journalism Quarterly* 27: 383–90.

Wien, Charlotte, and Elmelund-Præstekær. 2009. "An Anatomy of Media Hypes: Developing a Model for the Dynamics and Structure of Intense Media Coverage of Single Issues." *European Journal of Communication* 24 (2): 183–201. doi:10.1177/0267323108101831.

Williams, Bruce A., and Michael X. Delli Carpini. 2000. "Unchained Reaction: The Collapse of Media Gatekeeping and the Clinton-Lewinsky Scandal." *Journalism* 1 (1): 61–85. doi: 10.1177/146488490000100113.

Winter, James P., and Chaim H. Eyal. 1981. "Agenda Setting for the Civil Right Issue." *Public Opinion Quarterly* 45 (3): 376–83. doi:10.1086/268671.

Wlezien, Christopher. 2004. "Patterns of Representation: Dynamics of Public Preferences and Policy." *Journal of Politics* 66 (1): 1–24. doi:http://dx.doi.org/10.1046/j.1468-2508.2004.00139.x.

———. 2005. "On the Salience of Political Issues: The Problem with 'Most Important Problem.'" *Electoral Studies* 24 (4): 555–79. doi:10.1016/j.electstud.2005.01.009.

Wolfe, Michelle, Amber E. Boydstun, and Frank R. Baumgartner. 2009. "Comparing the Topics of Front-Page and Full-Paper Stories in the *New York Times*." Paper presented at the Annual Meeting of the Midwest Political Science Association. Chicago.

Wolfsfeld, Gadi. 1997. *Media and Political Conflict: News from the Middle East.* Cambridge: Cambridge University Press.

Wolfsfeld, Gadi, and Tamir Sheafer. 2006. "Competing Actors and the Construction of Political News: The Contest over Waves in Israel." *Political Communication* 23 (3): 333–54. doi:10.1080/10584600600808927.

Wood, B. Dan, and Jeffrey S. Peake. 1998. "The Dynamics of Foreign Policy Agenda Setting." *American Political Science Review* 92 (1): 173–84.

Woolley, John T. 2000. "Using Media-Based Data in Studies of Politics." *American Journal of Political Science* 44 (1): 156–73.

Workman, Samuel, Bryan D. Jones, and Ashley E. Jochim. 2009. "Information Processing and Policy Dynamics." *Policy Studies Journal* 37 (1): 75–92. doi:10.1111/j.1541-0072.2008.00296.x.

Xenos, Michael, and Patricia Moy. 2007. "Direct and Differential Effects of the Internet on Political and Civic Engagement." *Journal of Communication* 57 (4): 704–18. doi:10.1111/j.1460-2466.2007.00364.x.

Yagade, Aileen, and David M. Dozier. 1990. "The Media Agenda-Setting Effect of Concrete versus Abstract Issues." *Journalism Quarterly* 67 (1): 3–10. doi:10.1177/107769909006700102.

Yoon, Jiso, and Amber E. Boydstun. 2011. "Dominating the News: Government Officials in Front-Page Coverage of Public Affairs of the United States and Korea." Paper presented at the Midwest Political Science Association Annual Meeting, Chicago, March 31–April 3.

Zaller, John. 1998. "A Theory of Media Politics: How the Interests of Politicians, Journalists, and Citizens Shape the News." Working manuscript.

———. 2003. "A New Standard of News Quality: Burglar Alarms for the Monitorial Citizen." *Political Communication* 20 (2): 109–30. doi:10.1080/10584600390211136.

Zhu, Jian-Hua. 1992. "Issue Competition and Attention Distraction: A Zero-Sum Theory of Agenda-Setting." *Journalism Quarterly* 67 (4): 3–10. doi: 10.1177/107769909206900403.

Zinser, Lynn. 2011. "Penn State Scandal Foreseen by a Few." *New York Times*, November 9. http://thequad.blogs.nytimes.com/2011/11/09/penn-state-scandal-foreseen-by-a-few/.

Zucker, Harold. 1978. "The Variable Nature of News Media Influence." In *Communication Yearbook*, ed. B. D. Rubin, 225–45. New Brunswick NJ: Transaction Books.

Index

Page numbers in *italics* refer to tables and figures.